DEADLY FORCE, COLONIALISM, AND THE RULE OF LAW

Recent Titles in
Contributions in Comparative Colonial Studies

Imperialism and Colonialism: Essays on the History of European Expansion
H. L. Wesseling

The Racial Dimension of American Overseas Colonial Policy
Hazel M. McFerson

Meeting Technology's Advance: Social Change in China and Zimbabwe in the Railway Age
James Zheng Gao

U.S. Imperialism in Latin America: Bryan's Challenges and Contributions, 1900–1920
Edward S. Kaplan

The Kingdom of Swaziland: Studies in Political History
D. Hugh Gillis

The Bringing of Wonder: Trade and the Indians of the Southeast, 1700–1783
Michael P. Morris

Policing Islam: The British Occupation of Egypt and the Anglo–Egyptian Struggle over Control of the Police, 1882–1914
Harold Tollefson

India: The Seductive and Seduced "Other" of German Orientalism
Kamakshi P. Murti

The Betrothed of Death: The Spanish Foreign Legion During the Rif Rebellion, 1920–1927
José E. Álvarez

Britain's Sterling Colonial Policy and Decolonization, 1939–1958
Allister Hinds

Mixed Blessing: The Impact of the American Colonial Experience on Politics and Society in the Philippines
Hazel M. McFerson, editor

Law and Justice in Post-British Nigeria
Nọnso Okereafọezeke

DEADLY FORCE, COLONIALISM, AND THE RULE OF LAW

POLICE VIOLENCE IN GUYANA

JOAN R. MARS

CONTRIBUTIONS IN COMPARATIVE COLONIAL STUDIES, NUMBER 46

GREENWOOD PRESS
Westport, Connecticut • London

Library of Congress Cataloging-in-Publication Data

Mars, Joan R., 1954–
Deadly force, colonialism, and the rule of law : police violence in Guyana / Joan R. Mars.
p. cm.—(Contributions in comparative colonial studies ISSN 0163–3813 ; no. 46)
Includes bibliographical references and index.
ISBN 0–313–31104–8 (alk. paper)
1. Police brutality—Guyana—History. 2. Police—Guyana—History. I. Title. II. Series.
HV8189.3.A3 M37 2002
363.2'32—dc21 2002019547

British Library Cataloguing in Publication Data is available.

Library of Congress Catalog Card Number: 2002019547
ISBN: 0–313–31104–8
ISSN: 0163–3813

First published in 2002

Greenwood Press, 88 Post Road West, Westport, CT 06881
An imprint of Greenwood Publishing Group, Inc.
www.greenwood.com

Printed in the United States of America

The paper used in this book complies with the Permanent Paper Standard issued by the National Information Standards Organization (Z39.48–1984).

10 9 8 7 6 5 4 3 2 1

For my father, William Fitzgerald Ward

Contents

Figures and Tables

FIGURES

TABLES

Acknowledgments

Several individuals and institutions contributed directly to this study. The Guyana Police Force and the Ministry of Home Affairs provided valuable information on the police in Guyana. In this regard I wish to thank the former Commissioner of Police, Mr. Laurie Lewis, and Assistant Commissioner of Police, Mr. Henry Greene. I am indebted to Mr. Feroze Mohammed, former Minister of Home Affairs, and his former Permanent Secretary, Mr. Fraser, who were both gracious and generous in facilitating interviews and discussions on the police, as well as in providing me with personal copies of statistical reports on crime in Guyana. The current permanent Secretary in the Ministry of Home Affairs, Mr. Randolph Williams has also been very helpful in this regard, for which I am most grateful.

A large debt is owed to the Guyana Human Rights Association; its Directors, Mr. Mike McCormack and Mrs. Merle McCormack; and staff and volunteers, who have worked tirelessly for decades to gather and publish information on the police, and were steadfast in their support and encouragement for this project. In addition to providing me with unlimited access to their records and archival materials, and valuable advice, Mrs. Merle McCormack generously gave of her time in facilitating interviews and discussions on the police, for which I am especially grateful.

This study could not have been completed without the assistance of the former Hon. Chancellor of the Judiciary of Guyana, Mr. Justice Aubrey Bishop, who provided me with access to the library of the Court of Appeal, and took time out of his busy schedule to engage in discussions on the law relating to police powers. My gratitude is also extended to the Attorney General's Chambers and the Chambers of the Director of Public Prosecutions for granting me access to their extremely valuable library and archival records. In addition, Mr. Bernard De Santos, former Attorney General, provided me with technical support for which I am most grateful. My past colleagues, Mr. Fitz Peters, former Solicitor General; Mr. Johnny Fung-a-Fatt, Chief Parliamentary Counsel; and Mr. Ian Chang, former Director of Public Prosecutions, provided insightful discussion, advice, and assistance. My gratitude is extended to Ms. Lana Best, Librarian, Attorney General Chambers, for the many hours of work spent searching for archival records that she willingly undertook on my behalf. I am also grateful to the former Dean of the Faculty of Social Sciences, University of Guyana, Mr. Michael Parris, who provided me with office space and the use of the University's facilities. Ms. Karen Sills of the Georgetown Public Library also provided valuable assistance in unearthing historical material on the police.

Special thanks are extended to my reviewers for their helpful comments and suggestions. Professors David Britt, Leon Wilson, Monica Schuler, Marvin Zalman, and Jacqueline Huey, all of Wayne State University, provided guidance and insightful comments on earlier drafts of this work. My sincere appreciation is extended to Professor Mark Blumberg of Central Missouri State University for his unselfish support and encouragement, and for devoting valuable time to reading the original draft and providing critical comments. I am especially grateful to my husband, Perry, for providing valuable advice on the political aspects of this work, patiently reviewing various drafts, and ensuring that I stayed on task. This work could not have been completed without his support and encouragement. Finally, I want to express my most sincere thanks to my editor, Heather Ruland Staines of Greenwood Press for her patience and understanding, and for granting me the additional time required to complete this work.

Introduction

No other aspect of policing is more critical and controversial than the use of deadly force. Compared with the frequency of the use of the death penalty, the use of fatal force in police work is perhaps the most popular method by which the modern state takes the lives of its own citizens. In Guyana, although the law provides a mandatory death sentence for murder, no executions took place between 1970 and 1985, during which time sentences of death had always been commuted to life imprisonment by the President, upon the recommendation of the Advisory Council on the Prerogative of Mercy. However, for the period 1980 to 1985 alone, data that were collected from the Guyana Human Rights Association (GHRA) revealed that a conservative estimate of at least eighty-eight persons met their deaths at the hands of the police, an average of fourteen persons annually. This constitutes a very high figure for a country with a total population of only an estimated 834,000 persons.[1]

In July 1988 the GHRA submitted a *Brief on Police Violence* to the Guyana Bar Association, the Director of Public Prosecutions (DPP), the Guyana Medical Association, and the Commissioner of Police, in which it expressed grave concern: not only that it was receiving an increased number of reports of police violence from various parts of the country (including Georgetown, Parika, Leonora, Bartica, Sparendaam, Beterverwagting, and Fort Wellington), but the reports also seemed to indicate that "police methods have reached an unprecedented level of barbarity."[2] As a result of this publication, the executive offficers of the GHRA were sued jointly and severally for libel by members of the *Quick Reaction Group*, an undercover police swat team, accused of committing barbarous acts of violence against civilians, including women.[3] The libel suit was subsequently abandoned, and the police denied the existence of any *Quick Reaction Group* in interviews conducted with the researcher in Georgetown, Guyana, in August, 1995. However, the *Guyana Police Force Annual Report* (1987) reported the formation and "successful operation" of two *Quick Reaction Groups* under the auspices of the Criminal Investigation Department and operating mainly in "A" and "B" Divisions (city of Georgetown and county of Berbice).[4]

After the year 1992, official references to the *Quick Reaction Groups* in the *Guyana Police Force Annual Report* ceased, but the GHRA has continued to receive complaints of the excessive use of force by the police. During one week in 1994, the GHRA reported that it had received seventeen complaints of police brutality and shootings from around the country "more than in any other single week in its fifteen year history."[5] Between 1980 and 1999, the GHRA issued a total of seventeen reports and forty-five press releases on police conduct, many of which called for civilian oversight of police behavior, and for action to be taken to reduce the frequent use of deadly force by police.

Police violence in Guyana has also attracted the attention of the international human rights community. Amnesty International, in its yearly *Reports,* has consistently documented cases of police brutality and killings in Guyana, urging that those officers responsible be brought to justice.[6] The United States Department of State in its *Country Reports on Human Rights Practices* has repeatedly condemned deliberate police shootings and brutality, including beatings and torture during arrests and detention, often lamenting that members of the police force continue to "commit abuses with impunity."[7] To date, repeated calls for mechanisms to be put in place to require police accountability have consistently been ignored, resulting in poor police–community relations and widespread distrust of the police.[8]

THE IMPORTANCE OF CONTEXT

This study investigates the problem of police violence, and develops an explanation for the use of excessive and deadly force by police in the context of the historical, social, legal, and political arrangements in Guyana. We argue that the problem of police violence in Guyana cannot be adequately addressed without an understanding of the enduring legacy of colonialism and its role in the definition of the police function. We extend current approaches in the search for causal explanations of police-caused homicide beyond the focus on micro-level variables, to include the contextual framework for police operations across space and time. The sociohistorical process of inquiry adopted in this study covers both the colonial and the post-colonial periods, and investigates how macro-level structural factors combine with situations at the micro-level to influence police behavior. The role of the colonial and post-colonial authoritarian state, economic stagnation, racial and political conflict, and the rule of law in the production of police violence—as well as the relationship between community violence and police violence—are examined.

In order to arrive at an assessment of the proximate situation in which police violence occurs in Guyana, interpretive analysis was conducted on a convenience sample of 24 of the 150 cases of police-caused homicide that were verified as having occurred in Guyana during the period 1980 to 1994. The purpose of this analysis was to determine to what extent police-caused homicide in Guyana meets the requirements under the law of justifiable homicide, in which case the loss of life would be excused. The findings relating to the individual circumstances surrounding the use of force by police are then combined with the conclusions reached as a result of the procedures described above, in order to construct a causal explanation for police violence in Guyana. We argue that the propensity toward the excessive use of deadly force is a legacy of coercive colonial state rule and the historical legitimization of violence in police work. The prevailing levels of violence in the community fail to justify the continuing violence in police work, and there is urgent need for the return to professional, civilian policing and the implementation of measures to curb the use of excessive force by police.

Although this study is concerned with the Guyana Police Force, comparisons could be drawn with other countries in both the developed and developing worlds that share a similar history with Guyana as a dependency of the United Kingdom under some form of colonial rule. Similar models of policing were established in more than forty individual countries that were under British rule in the nineteenth century when formal police forces were established. Under this colonial, quasi-military model, distinct from traditional policing, violence is identified with the role and function of the police. It is hoped that the findings in this study will not only fill an existing gap in the literature on the Guyana Police, but also extend current explanations of police-caused homicide and add to the understanding of the causes of police violence throughout the developing world.

Chapter 1 of this study sets out the contextual and theoretical framework within which this examination of police violence is conducted. The period covered briefly includes early attempts at colonial policing, from seventeenth-century Dutch settlements to modern times. Following a review of the relevant literature, a schematic is constructed to describe factors thought to account for variation in the use of deadly force by police over time. These factors are derived from the conflict theoretical perspective, the community violence hypothesis, the legacy of colonialism, and the legal system. The specific research questions that will be addressed in this study are then outlined under three headings: the historical-colonial context, the socio-political and legal context, and the proximate/community context.

Chapter 2 outlines the research design and methodological procedures utilized in this work. Detailed explanations of the data collection and methodological procedures for analysis of the various sources of data are provided for the early period, covering the slavery and colonial era, and the later post-independence period. A matrix setting out the specific sources of data used for the investigation of the research questions is presented in Table 3.1. The chapter provides a discussion of the inadequacies of data sources for the early period of Guyana's police history, the difficulty in obtaining reliable and accurate counts of police-caused homicide, not only in Guyana but worldwide, and the limitations of the study.

Chapter 3 outlines the social and political history of Guyana during the colonial period and focuses on the early attempts at social and political control of vast numbers of ethnic and culturally diverse peoples transplanted from Africa and Asia to facilitate economic profiteering in the plantation colony. The significance of political developments under the Dutch and British administration of the colony, racial and social segmentation, and divide-and-rule colonial policies are discussed to provide the context for the development of formal policing, which is the subject of the next chapter.

Chapter 4 traces the evolution of policing in colonial Guyana and identifies various activities of the newly transplanted, culturally diverse population that threatened colonial rule and control of the colony and called forth a coercive official response. More specifically, this chapter discusses how social stratification, class, and ethnic differentiation were strategically used in the organization of police forces to ensure police loyalty to the rulers. The particular "type" of policing that developed in the Colony is examined in order to determine how the role and function of the police as defined in this early period continue to influence police practices today. Finally, incidences where the police used deadly force against civilians are discussed, and several distinctive characteristics of policing emerging from the available historical evidence are identified.

Chapter 5 takes the examination of policing into the immediate pre-independence period of colonial "self-rule" rule, and the post-independence period when concerted attempts were made to dismantle the colonial system. In particular, this chapter focuses on the political policing of public disorder and ethnic warfare between the two largest ethnic groups in the country, East Indians and Blacks, immediately preceding the independence period, and the policing of the threat of social conflict and social unrest during the immediate post-independence period. Attention is also given to the continuing consolidation of violence in police work after independence, as the quasi-military force was further prepared for internal surveillance, the repression of political opponents, and the fulfillment of nationalist goals. The chapter also discusses the increased militarization of the force and the inadequacies of existing legal controls on police use of deadly force.

Analyses of current crime and police homicide data covering the period 1980 to 1994 are conducted in Chapter 6 to describe the frequency of police-caused homicide during this period and to facilitate comparisons with other countries in both the developed and developing worlds. The relationship between police violence and community violence is also investigated to determine whether contemporary police violence may be a response to levels of violence in the community and the everyday dangers of police work. Interpretive analysis of a convenience sample of cases of police-caused homicide is also conducted using the "alternative credible version technique," to determine whether these killings could be excused under the existing law of justifiable homicide.

Chapter 7 discusses the results of the various ways in which police violence, in particular police use of deadly force in Guyana, was examined and brings together the major conclusions of the previous chapters. The importance of the contextual approach and the legacy of colonialism in understanding current police behavior and the relevance of our findings for other developing countries is discussed. Finally, this study calls for urgent attention to be given to police reform in Guyana and the implementation of measures to prevent the excessive use of deadly force by police.

NOTES

1. United Nations Department for Economic and Social Information and Policy Analysis. 1995. *World Statistics in Brief.* Series V, No. 16. New York: United Nations.

2. Guyana Human Rights Association. July 6, 1988. *Brief on Police Violence.* Georgetown, Guyana: Guyana Human Rights Association.

3. Ibid. See also Amnesty Internation, 1989 and 1990 (*Annual Report*, United Kingdom: Amesty International Publications), where the libel suit is mentioned in the chapter on Guyana.

4. Guyana Police Force. 1987. *Guyana Police Force Annual Report.* Georgetown, Guyana: Guyana Police Force, pp. 21–22.

5. See chapter on Guyana in *The United States Department of State's Country Report on Human Rights Practices, 1994.*

6. See *Amnesty International Report, 1985, 1986, 1987, 1988, 1989, 1990, 1991, 1992, 1993, 1994, 1995* for examples and letter dated 30 December, 1993, to the Minister of Home Affairs and the Attorney General and Minister of Legal Affairs for Guyana.

7. See chapter pertaining to Guyana in United States Department of State *Country Reports on Human Rights Practices, 1994.* Washington D.C.: United States Department of State. See also U.S. Department of State *Country Report on Human Rights Practices, 2000.*

8. In a recent public opinion survey conducted by the St. Augustine Research Associates (SARA), 75 percent of those interviewed expressed distrust of the police. See St. Augustine Research Associates. 2000. *Hopes and Aspirations: Political Attitudes and Party Choices in Contemporary Guyana.* St. Augustine, Trinidad: Institute of Social and Economic Research.

Abbreviations

AID	Agency for International Development
BJS	Bureau of Justice Statistics
CIA	Central Intelligence Agency
DPP	Director of Public Prosecutions
EIA	East Indian Association
FBI	Federal Bureau of Investigation
GHRA	Guyana Human Rights Association
GPF	Guyana Police Force
INPOLSE	International Police Services, Inc.
LCP	League of Colored People
NIJ	National Institute of Justice
OPS	Office of Public Safety
PNC	People's National Congress
PPP	People's Progressive Party
UCR	Uniform Crime Reports
UF	United Force
SARA	St. Augustine Research Association
WPA	Working People's Alliance

1

Contextual and Theoretical Framework

> History is not a person apart, using man for its own particular aims; history is nothing but the activity of man pursuing his aims.
>
> —Marx and Engels, *The Holy Family* (1844), p. 125.

THE COLONIAL CONDITION

The importance of historical antecedents in generating explanatory insights into current phenomena has been consistently argued by social commentators ranging from Marx and Engels in the early nineteenth century,[1] to Huntington[2] and Tilly.[3] With reference to developing countries in particular, the profound influence of the colonial past in the shaping of social and political institutions has received wide recognition among leading social science scholars.[4] However, researchers have tended to import and adapt Western theories on legal institutions, crime, and the justice system, to reflect the nature of underdeveloped economies, and the presumed consequences of rapid industrialization and urbanization. Modernization theorists, for example, posit that current crime problems in less developed countries are similar to those experienced by the developed world in the nineteenth century, during the industrial revolution.[5]

Similar conclusions based on deficiencies in "civilizing influences"—culture and values arising from the "primitive" or "backward" nature of developing societies—have also grounded explanations of criminality. In an early study, Wolfgang and Ferracuti opined that their subculture-of-violence theory would be particularly useful in explaining violence in developing countries partly because of the presence of "subcultural pockets . . . of island retainers of older value systems more adapted to primitive and underdeveloped conditions."[6] Under such value systems, the capacity for aggression is considered a virtue, and violence is highly rated as the appropriate way to resolve disputes. Howard Jones subsequently adopted this cultural approach to explain variations in crime rates among racial groups in Guyana.[7]

One recent study on police behavior adopted a similar explanation for police violence, thereby revealing a complete misreading of the colonial condition and the resulting complexities of social life in the region. In comparing police violence in the United States with that in Latin America and the Caribbean, Chevigny argued that the prevalence of police violence was directly related to the degree of "pacification" or "civilization" of the urban population. He described this process of "pacification" as follows:

> Both of the changes in police practices—the minimization of physical coercion in interrogations and the great drop in the use of deadly force—seem to me to be late products of the very long process of pacification and change in the consciousness of urban Americans, reflected in their institutions; unnecessary killings and tortures become offensive to the sensibilities of many.[8]

According to Chevigny, a key element of this civilizing process, which is yet to be fully attained in societies that "had colonial rule or slavery (commonly both)" is "the increasing revulsion against brutal and public punishment, accompanied by a growing desire for privacy, a desire to exclude even the awareness of violence from one's personal life."[9] What is needed therefore is more "pacification," more of the civilizing process that has occurred in the United States, more mechanisms for police accountability, and a strengthening of the rule of law.

The fallacies inherent in these theoretical approaches have been subject to some criticism,[10] and the case made for a more radical criminology, grounded in an understanding of the unique social reality of people living in post-colonial societies. Explanations for crime and violence in the Caribbean should take into account the social structure of the plantation system that was implemented in the conquered territories in the Caribbean, and the lasting effects of prolonged exposure to colonial culture and institutions.[11] During centuries of economic profiteering by metropolitan imperialists, violence was the primary means of communication. Indigenous populations were ruthlessly decimated and the colonies resettled by the violent transfer and exploitation of populations from Africa and Asia. A new social order came into being under which, like Goffman's total institution, the plantation maintained complete control over all aspects of the lives of the transplanted people. Under the colonial system, the inculcation of British values, education, modes of dress, behavior, discipline, and etiquette received the highest priority. Social, legal, and political institutions existing in the metropolitan "home" country were transplanted and adapted to conditions in the colonies, as a result of which, descendants of the transplanted populations became not only proud imitators of the European way of life but also in many instances, "more British than the British." If these countries, including Guyana are still deficient in "civilizing" influences, then it is certainly not because of a lack of adaptation to the culture and values of the developed world, but rather as a result of it.

This study investigates the use of deadly force by police in Guyana, and explores the significance of the colonial heritage in the shaping of police culture and behavior. The contextual framework consists of the historical, socio-political, and legal arrangements in Guyana, which shared a common legacy of British colonial rule with more than forty other dependencies of the United Kingdom.[12] The time period covered briefly by this study includes the entire colonial era, beginning with Dutch settlements in the early seventeenth century and ending with the post-colonial period, which extends from 1966 to the present time. As far as the available data would allow, colonial influences on the evolution of policing in general and the use of deadly force in particular, and the factors connected therewith, are investigated in this study.

THE CONFLICT PERSPECTIVE

Although there is no shortage of studies on police behavior, no substantive explanatory framework has been developed, either with respect to law enforcement generally or police use of deadly force in particular.[13] Instead, studies have focused on micro-level variables associated with various factors thought to influence police behavior, such as characteristics of the individual officers, the situations in which police encounter citizens, and the organizational setting of police departments.[14] The problems associated with this piecemeal, quantitative approach, such as methodological shortcomings and weak or inconsistent relationships both at the bivariate and multivariate levels, have rendered explanations of police behavior derived from these studies to be of limited theoretical significance.[15]

With regard to explanations of police use of force, specifically, however, although the trend in micro-level, piecemeal research has continued,[16] several empirical studies have focused on developing macro-level, social structural explanations of police violence based on conflict theory. According to the conflict model of society, originally developed by the German philosopher Karl Marx, "(t)he history of all hitherto existing society is the history of class struggles."[17] Conflict is an inevitable and pervasive feature of all social systems and most frequently occurs between two major classes into which society is divided—the rich and powerful (the "haves") and the poor and powerless (the "have nots"). The dividing factor between these two classes is ownership and control of economic resources and the mode of production, which form the real basis of society and out of which arise all social institutions, ideological forms, and consciousness.[18] The exploitation of the working class and the disadvantaged extends beyond the marketplace and is accomplished through exposure to an unjust and destructive social order that is maintained by coercion. Radical criminologists have interpreted this to mean that once segments of the population become aware of their condition, they will begin to question the legitimacy of the social system and those who control it, and the agents of social and crime control will use force to protect the interests and property of the dominant class.[19]

An interesting extension of the discussion of class conflict is to be found in the work of Ralf Dahrendorf, who identified the authority structure and authority relations as the principal explanatory variable for understanding conflict in the social structure. In his book *Class and Class Conflict in Industrial Society*, Dahrendorf juxtaposed what he called "the *coercion* theory of society," based on the conflict perspective, with "the integration theory of society," based on the work of Parsons and other structural-functionalists.[20] Whereas the integration theory proposes that social cohesion is achieved by consensus, the coercion theory insists that the social structure is maintained by restraint and domination. This "ugly face" of authority presented by the coercion theory is one where society consists of two opposed groups or classes who are differentiated from each other by their primary interests. The dominant group, which usually signifies the ruling class and the elites, are usually a numerical minority and the subjected class or group, are usually but not necessarily always, the numerical majority. The dominant group exercises its power and authority to the exclusion of the subjected group and "it is not voluntary cooperation or general consensus, but enforced constraint that makes social organizations (society) cohere."[21] Dahrendorf felt that the conflict that is generated by differential power and authority could never be eradicated from society since such contentions are self-generating.

The conflict perspective began to appear in the literature on deviance and crime control in the latter half of the 1960s. In 1966, in his historical study of the origins of the modern police force, Silver identified the creation of an institutionalized police force with the desire by economic elites and the propertied classes to protect themselves from the crime and violence of the disadvantaged classes.[22] One of the earliest works that clearly recognized the impact of class differences in society on police behavior, however, was Niederhoffer's study entitled *Behind the Shield: The Police in Urban Society*. In specifying the protection of the interests of the powerful groups in society as the primary function of law enforcement, Niederhoffer endorsed the opinion of Joseph Lohman, who was then the Dean of the School of Criminology of the University of California at Berkeley, that "the police function [is] to support and enforce the interests of the dominant political, social, and economic interests of the town, and only incidentally to enforce the law."[23] Parks echoed the same theme when he argued that the major purpose of the police establishment was to maintain the status quo, wherein great disparity exists between the economic power of the dominant and the subordinated classes.[24] Paul Takagi also posited a relationship between the unequal distribution of wealth and police behavior, to wit, the incidence of death by police intervention in the United States. After reviewing the findings of existing studies on police-caused homicide, he concluded that the taking of human life appeared to be justified on the basis of an equation of property rights with human rights whereby a human life could be legitimately taken to protect the property of another.[25]

In developing an explanation of racial discrimination based on the size of the minority population in relation to Whites in the United States, Blalock found empirical support for the proposition that competition for scarce economic resources (primarily jobs) and political power was the source of the conflict between southern Blacks and Whites and this led to racial discrimination in order to address the perceived threat posed by Blacks.[26] Since Blalock's work introducing the concept of "threat" (in his case "power threat"), this concept has been used to explain the process whereby indicators of social conflict, such as income inequality, percentage of non-Whites and poor, violent crime index, and protest activities such as riots, generate police crime control activities.[27]

Jacobs and Britt were probably the first to find strong empirical support for a hypothesis based on conflict theory to explain the use of deadly force by police.[28] Focusing on economic inequality as the basis for social conflicts between the dominant and subordinate classes, the authors argued that force or the *threat* of force will be the source of cohesion in unequal societies. Further, they expected that such force will assume deadly proportions more frequently in societies where economic inequality is the most pronounced. Using data from the *Vital Statistics of the United States*, previously subjected to empirical testing of the impact of measures of class conflict (riots) on the police homicide rate with negative results,[29] they found that economic inequality was a strong predictor of the use of deadly force by police.

In developing a causal model of the "threat hypothesis" of the conflict perspective, to explain how structural variables result in crime control measures,[30] Liska conceptualized *threat* as *social threat to the existing order that results from the presence of persons who are perceived by police to be threatening, or whose acts are perceived to be threatening.* This formulation seems to be consistent with Blalock's ideas of "power threat" experienced by Whites as a result of competition by Blacks for political, economic, and status benefits in racially divided societies.[31] According to Liska, the focus in the conflict perspective of crime control and deviance is on the use of the State's lawmaking and law enforcement functions to protect the interests of the powerful classes in society from attack by people who are perceived to be threatening.

Liska and Yu subsequently applied this threat hypothesis to explain the effect of race threat on police use of deadly force using a sample of forty-five cities in the United States.[32] In so doing they operationalized "threatening people" as percentage of non-Whites, degree of racial segregation, and income inequality. The variable "threatening acts" was operationalized to include violent index crime, index crime, homicide rates, and homicides of the police. Support was found for the hypothesis, and findings indicated a positive and linear relationship between the percentage of non-Whites and police homicide as well as a moderately positive relationship between general homicide rates and police homicide. Liska and Yu, however, restricted the structural significance of their findings by stating that "we have not emphasized threat to elites and have not viewed police activities as simply serving the interests of elites; rather, we have emphasized threats to the police themselves."[33]

An interesting attempt to provide a structural explanation for police use of deadly force within the conflict theoretical perspective is to be found in the work of Paul Chevigny, who posited a relationship between frustration, the *threat of social unrest*, and social control in the form of state repression in research conducted in developing countries.[34] Chevigny used a "perceived threat of unrest scale" to measure what he termed the "unmobilized conflict" that could explain high levels of police-caused homicides that were present in the societies he investigated (Jamaica, Argentina, and Brazil).[35] This scale measured the *likelihood* of social unrest and was arrived at by calculating a differential based on the social mobilization and social welfare ranking of the individual countries. Chevigny found significant negative differentials to support the need for repressive police action in two developing countries with a history of high police homicide rates, Argentina (–.44) and Jamaica (–.36).[36]

More than three decades ago, in his review of police research in the United States, Galliher lamented the absence of class analysis in attempts at theory building, and the resulting failure to develop a coherent explanatory framework for understanding police behavior.[37] Galliher's social structural framework requires that the significance of class conflict be explored along with other factors that may be relevant to understanding the complex relationship between the police and society.[38] In the case of highly stratified, post-colonial, ex-plantation societies, such as those that exist in Guyana and the English-speaking Caribbean, class analysis is of central importance in explaining the behavior of police forces that were introduced primarily to maintain class divisions and to protect the persons and property of the ruling elites.

THE COMMUNITY VIOLENCE HYPOTHESIS

The "community violence hypothesis" offers a competing explanation for police violence and will also be investigated in this study. Basically, the argument is that the police are merely responding to the level of violence in the community and resort to the use of deadly force in order to protect themselves when faced with life-threatening situations in the performance of their duties. Empirical support for the relationship between community violence and police use of deadly force was established by Kania and Mackey[39] in their analysis of mortality data from the *Vital Statistics of the United States*. Kania and Mackey found that the strongest relationship between community characteristics and police use of deadly force existed with regard to variables measuring the levels of violent crime in the community, such as the violent crime rate and the public homicide rate. The effect of community violence as an alternative causal factor in police-caused homicide was also considered by Jacobs and Britt, but they found that although the violent crime rate was a significant predictor of police homicide, economic inequality remained a predictor of police homicide even after controlling for violent crime.[40]

In other studies at the individual case level of analysis, support was also found for the community violence hypothesis. One of the earliest studies conducted in the field concluded that in each of the 32 cases examined during the 11-year period 1950 to 1960 in Philadelphia, the officers were acting within a life-threatening situation and the decedents were generally responsible for their own deaths.[41] Binder and Fridell found that in two-thirds to three-fourths of the incidents studied where civilians were killed, they precipitated their own deaths by the use or threatened use of weapons against the police.[42] Fyfe also reported, in a study of firearms discharges by the New York City Police in the twenty command zones in New York City, that total police shooting rates were strongly correlated with arrest rates for violent crime (felonies) as well as general homicide rates, thereby implying that the police were probably responding to life-threatening situations when deadly force was used.[43] In a related study based on the same data Fyfe concluded that, like Los Angeles, New York City consisted of certain geographic areas that can be called "free fire zones" where incidents of community violence as well as police shootings were frequent[44] Matulia also found a robust and positive correlation between variables operationalizing community dangerousness and police-caused homicide rates in data collected in the 57 largest U.S. cities.[45]

This explanation of police violence is, however, confounded by research conducted by Sherman and Cohen, which reported that changes to a more restrictive firearms policy in almost all police departments serving large communities have been followed by a sharp decline in the number of shootings by law enforcement officers.[46] The number of civilians killed had declined from 353 in 1971 to 172 in 1984, despite the fact that the level of dangerousness in the communities had remained the same. In later studies, Fyfe also acknowledged the effect of police administrative and disciplinary procedures in reducing the numbers of police-caused homicides.[47] Blumberg and Chevigny have also made similar observations.[48] Improved training, disciplinary procedures, and the proliferation of civil suits by relatives of victims have all played a role in the decline of police-caused homicide rates in the United States.[49]

To the extent that the community violence hypothesis posits that police killings may only be indicative of the urgent and immediate need for self-defense, it may be the antithesis of the conflict hypothesis that locates the causal explanation for police violence in the social structure. Yet, an apparent merging of the community violence hypothesis into the conflict perspective could be discerned in the study conducted by Liska and Yu that was discussed previously. In the conflict model of the threat hypothesis proposed by Liska, the variables that represent "threatening acts" are the same variables that are used to measure dangerousness or community violence, and it would seem that the causal model incorporates the "community violence" hypothesis to the extent that the empirical indicators of these concepts could be classified as "threatening acts." It would appear, therefore, that the inclusion of "threatening acts" in the causal model is contradictory and would introduce situational factors into what is intended to be a structural level of analysis. The effect of "threatening acts" may need to be considered separately rather than as part of the conflict perspective. It is noteworthy, also, that the community violence hypothesis has been considered as a separate explanation for police violence in earlier studies[50] as well as in subsequent empirical analysis.[51]

An attempt to reconcile the conflict and community violence perspectives was conducted by Sorenson et al. using data from the F.B.I. Supplementary Homicide Reports.[52] Empirical support was found for the conflict hypothesis that posits a positive relationship between economic inequality, a high percentage of minority residents, and the police homicide rate; but with regard to the community violence hypothesis, measures of perceived dangerousness and community violence such as the violent crime rate, police per capita, and population density either did not influence the rate of police homicide directly (as in the case of the latter measures), or tended to act as an intervening variable (as in the case of the violent index rate) between other social variables and the police homicide rate. The analysis of Sorenson et al. further emphasized the distinction between antecedent, structural causes of police homicide such as economic inequality and community characteristics such as the violent crime rate. Although there is ample empirical support for the proposition that violent crimes rates do exert some influence on police homicide rates,[53] such indicators of community violence would seem to be only partially connected causally with police violence.

Figure 1.1 outlines the major hypotheses based on the conflict perspective and the community violence hypothesis that have so far been subjected to empirical testing to explain police use of deadly force.

Based on the relationships hypothesized in the research discussed previously, a schematic was constructed to apply the conflict perspective to the explanation of the use of deadly force in Guyana. This schematic combines factors thought to account for variation in the use of deadly force by police over time in Guyana based on the following:

1. Factors derived from the conflict perspective and empirical studies based on this perspective
2. Factors derived from the community violence hypothesis and empirical studies based on this perspective
3. Factors related to the legacy of colonialism
4. Factors related to the legal system

Figure 1.1
Major Hypotheses of the Conflict Perspective and the Community Violence Hypothesis for Explaining Police Use of Deadly Force

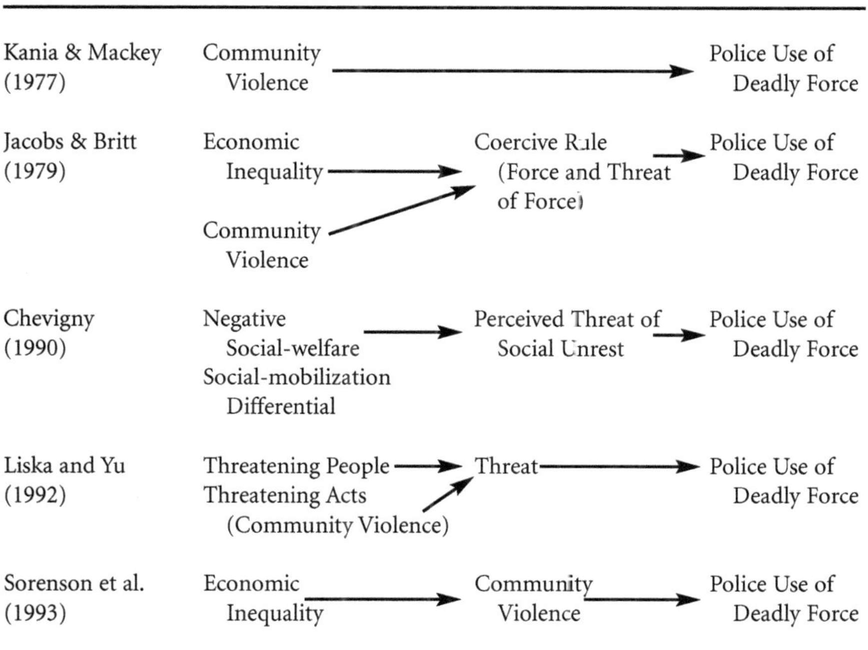

Factors Derived from the Conflict Perspective

Variables associated with the conflict perspective represented in the schematic (Fig. 1.2) include "Population Control," "Perceived Threat of Social/Political Unrest," and "Social Control." The exogenous variable "Authority Structure" is derived from the work of Dahrendorf as it extended the process by which the social structure could generate social conflict to include the authority structure. Dahrendorf's work is particularly relevant for guiding the development of an explanatory framework for police violence in Guyana as it developed in plantation society under British rule.

The "authority structure" influences police use of deadly force as social control either directly through coercive rule, which is achieved by force or the threat of force and which in turn results in the excessive use of lethal force (Jacobs and Britt) or, alternatively, the authority structure creates societal conditions that lead to either an actual threat of civil unrest (strikes, demonstrations, etc.) or consciousness of a perceived threat of political unrest (agitation for change by political opponents in the post-colonial period) in the estimation of the state authority. The authority feels the necessity to respond

Figure 1.2
Schematic of Factors Related to Police Use of Deadly Force in Guyana

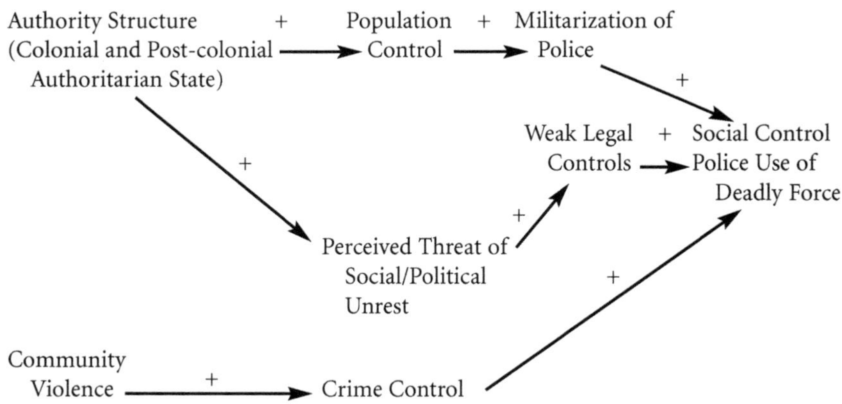

by the use of lethal means of social control—either to prevent the strikes or demonstrations from becoming a riot, or for the purposes of political repression to prevent the loss of political power to opposition political groups through legal or illegal means. The capacity of such action in creating further violence is moot.

Factors Derived from the Community Violence Hypothesis

"Community violence" and crime control are derived from empirical studies that found a relationship between these variables and police use of deadly force. Community violence is an exogenous variable that exerts a separate and distinct but positive influence on police homicide rates through efforts of the police to control crime in dangerous communities that have high levels of violent crime.

Factors Related to the Legacy of Colonialism

Interwoven into the authority structure of colonial and post-colonial Guyana is the nature of the state and policing and the unique psychological characteristics of the dominant classes who not only controlled state power, but also police power, and in so doing developed certain psychological characteristics that have been associated with police violence. Also of importance in this discussion of police violence is whether the legacy of colonialism has left a lasting influence on the nature of policing in those developing countries such as Guyana that were settled primarily by the British.

Police Violence and the Nature of the State— The Authoritarian State

According to Max Weber, a defining characteristic of the modern state is its monopoly on the legitimate use of force.[54] The nature of the state is important to an understanding of police practices because the state is responsible for regulating the behavior of citizens, and the police as agents of the state are charged with the responsibility of enforcing the law, apprehending criminals, and maintaining civil order. In so doing, the police are often called upon to make "split second" decisions in the exercise of the state's legitimate authority to use force, including deadly force. It is the state that creates the police and determines what function its police forces will serve in civil society. It is the state that determines the conditions under which the use of deadly force will be permitted and this study will argue that there is a direct relationship between the methods of rule that the state employed during both the colonial and post-colonial periods (which could be characterized as being authoritarian) and the frequency of the use of deadly force by the police.

Closely akin to the analysis of the authority structure by Dahrendorf, Carl Stone described the state system that emerged from colonialism as one that experiences severe "internal contradictions and internal class pressures."[55] Stone defined the Caribbean[56] state as being not only a collection of government institutions, but also a "system of power" that was derived from "the hegemony of the imperial power and related economic and military strength on which this colonial superstructure rested."[57] This "system of power" developed during the slavery and post-slavery periods in the colony, out of the need for the metropolitan power to delegate some of its authority to local forces to perform administrative functions and resolve conflicts between the separate and opposing groups (these groups consisted of slaves, their planter-masters, the "free" White settlers, the "free" Colored people, merchants, traders and, later, thousands of indentured servants transplanted mainly from the Indian subcontinent and Asia).

The problem of social control in a society settled for the sole purpose of exploitation was a daunting one for the metropolitan power throughout the colonial period. In the early period of colonial rule, the slave system dictated that measures be put in place to prevent rebellions and desertions, and *coercion* was the only viable means of communication between master and slave. It was only much later, well into the decolonization process, that the question of whether society was held together by consensus or conflict,[58] the distribution of resources and power in society, and the method of rule dictated thereby became pertinent to the discussion of the police use of force.

Coercion was used by the local state as the primary means of social control, subject to the ultimate authority of the metropolitan power. Resistance to the will of the rulers attracted a show of force including deadly force from the civil police and the military, depending on the perceived seriousness of the threat to the 'lawful' authority of the state. According to Thomas, "the colonial state from its beginning embodied both a system of (class) oppression and a system of national oppression, neither of which is independent of the other."[59] In his work *Rise of the Authoritarian State*, Thomas characterized the post-colonial state as essentially *authoritarian*. Focusing on the coercive methods of rule employed by such states, Thomas identified the expansion of the military apparatus, "the use of torture, assassination and other forms of physical violence against opponents, or would-be opponents," the deprofessionalization of the security services, and the use of the police to aid and abet "covert repression" in the form of death squads, as the means by which social control and political control were maintained.[60] Although the state was now occupied by local personnel rather than representatives of the metropolitan power, the violence and repression that characterized the colonial period continued.

Hamza Alavi related the problem of repression and official violence in other countries that experienced the legacy of colonialism, such as Pakistan, to the historical development of their political arrangements during and after colonial rule. Alavi argued that with the imposition of British colonial rule came the creation of a state apparatus to exercise dominion over all the indigenous social classes. The colonial state relied on a well-equipped, bureaucratic–military apparatus to subordinate the native classes, and this over-developed state apparatus was inherited by the post-colonial state and used to continue rule by repression and domination. As a result, the state in post-colonial society "is not the instrument of a single class."[61] The state maintains its links with the metropolitan structure until independence and thereafter; those at the top of the bureaucratic–military apparatus of the state continue to dominate by force and coercion. The state remains separate and independent, as well as in conflict with the native social classes, throughout this process.

Gittens adopted a somewhat different perspective in his attempts to justify the need, by the post-colonial state, for repressive methods of authoritarian rule. In so doing he characterized the nature of the post-colonial state as being one of "over efficiency" rather than over development. He described the post-colonial state as adopting a position of centrality to the economic process, which dictates an expansion of its coercive apparatus to suppress class conflicts that may threaten the process of developing capitalist production and the exploitation of labor.[62] In this way, the post-colonial state, though occupied by local personnel, maintains its independence from the subordinate classes in society and by necessity must adopt a highly powerful and repressive posture.

This characterization of the post-colonial state is in keeping with the predictions of Frederick Engels, whose classical works on the origin and development of the state reveals valuable insights for the purposes of this study. In describing the development of independence of the state, Engels had this to say:

> Because the State arose from the need to hold antagonism in check, but because it arose at the same time, in the midst of the conflict of these classes, it is as a rule, the state of the most powerful, economically dominant class, whereby, through the medium of the state, becomes also the politically dominant class. . . . *By way of exception, however, periods occur*

in which the warring classes balance each other so nearly that the state power as ostensible mediator, acquires for the moment, a certain degree of independence. (Italics mine).[63]

This "movement" of the state from being an instrument of the economically powerful planter class under colonialism toward a position of autonomy and independence during the post-colonial period is also emphasized by Stone in his insightful characterization of the nature of the post-colonial state. Stone also pointed out that the post-colonial Caribbean state does not reflect the contentions between capital and labor that were prominent during the colonial era. Due to the expansion and diversification of the economy, the planter-merchant, capitalist class that dictated state policies during the colonial era had slowly been reduced during the process of decolonization to "simply one class within a wider group of elite interests competing to influence the state," and state power "reflects contentions for political ascendancy by factions of the middle class against whose regimes organized labor and the local bourgeoisie (propertied class) develop natural opposition tendencies but on different issues."[64] Stone claims that the local, post-colonial state, having taken control of the economy and the destiny of its peoples from the foreign, metropolitan power, still finds itself in severe conflict with various classes and groups in society. He speaks of the "weaknesses" of the newly elected governments in the region, and the "excess social demand" built into the political system, whereby the expectations of the population are far beyond the resource capability of the society. Poverty, economic decline, high unemployment levels, and consumption demands patterned on North American influences result in widespread alienation and frustration that translates into political instability and the reliance on intimidation and repression in order to achieve social control.

Stone characterized the conflict between the state and the subjugated classes that gave rise to the need for coercive rule as being one that is not necessarily dictated by competition for scarce economic resources. Rather, Stone suggested that during the decolonization process the state comes under the control not of the propertied class, but local middle-class elites who fiercely compete for *political power* in the midst of economic decline and mass alienation. The post-colonial state, therefore, came to be identified with authoritarian and repressive methods of rule, through which the police were used *against* the population. The official violence, reminiscent of the colonial era, continued, though it was based on different considerations. This literature justifies the inclusion of state formation in Guyana in the schematic developed to explain police violence.

The "colonial and post-colonial state" is the sine qua non of police violence as represented in the schematic prepared for this study. It influences the police homicide rate through the resort to coercive rule, which is assisted by the militarization of police and the imposition of weak legal controls on police behavior. It also positively affects police use of deadly force through its response to the actual civil unrest, or the perceived threat of civil or political unrest. It prepares the police to use lethal force by the process of militarization.

Police Violence and the Nature of Policing— The Militarization of the Police

The history of policing in Guyana, and in many other countries that were dependencies of the United Kingdom, clearly illustrates that the police forces created by the official representatives of the metropolitan power were vastly different from the model used for police forces in Britain. Whereas the police forces of Britain were fashioned after the model designed by Sir Robert Peel, which emphasized the service function and the prevention and detection of crime, police forces in the colonies were designed primarily to maintain population control. This view has been espoused by some contemporary authors,[65] but a very convincing source is provided by Sir Charles Jeffries, K.C.M.G., O.B.E., Deputy Under-Secretary of State of the Colonies, who published his treatise *The Colonial Police* while he was still active in the Colonial Service.[66]

In his analyses of the colonial police forces of the territories mentioned, Sir Charles Jeffries stressed the fact that the "really effective influence upon the development of Colonial police forces during the nineteenth century was not that of the police of Great Britain, but that of the Royal Irish Constabulary."[67] The author also stated that the Royal Irish Constabulary was a "(C)onstant source of recruitment for officers of many Colonial police forces, and its training depot was regularly used as a center for courses of instruction for Colonial police officers."[68]

The importance of this fact is that the Royal Irish Constabulary was purposefully established as an armed paramilitary organization. It was a centralized force designed not to engage in the traditional police functions of crime prevention, but to "maintain the existing socio-political order on which British state authority rested."[69] Sir Charles Jeffries himself left no room for doubt as to the intended function of the colonial police when he had this to say:

> It is clear enough that from the point of view of the Colonies there was much attraction in an arrangement which provided what we should now call a "para-military" organization or gendarmerie, armed, and trained to operate as an agent of the central government in a country where the population was predominantly rural, communications were poor, social conditions were largely primitive, and the recourse to violence by members of the public who were "against the government" was not infrequent. It was natural that such a force, rather than one organized on the lines of the purely civilian and localised forces of Great Britain, should have been taken as a suitable model for adaptation to Colonial conditions.[70]

When policing is cast within a military role, there is a concurrent effort to provide military training, to secure military-type hardware, and to maintain social distance between police and citizens.[71] Vast sums of money are channeled into the acquisition of military-type weapons and other supplies, and "overseas" studies and training for police in metropolitan military institutions or police institutions fashioned along military lines.[72] The evidence in the case of Guyana is quite compelling.

Social distancing of police from the community was achieved during colonialism by the recruitment of expatriates even among the lower ranks in the early stages of colonial rule, and by stationing local police away from their neighborhoods.[73] The population was already divided into socially distinct groups under a colonial divide-and-rule policy based more on color and class differences than on true cultural distinctions associated with ethnic polarization, and these divisions were reflected in the colonial police force. After independence the policy of divide-and-rule was perpetuated by maintaining ethnic imbalances in the police force, which translated into political support for the dictatorship in political office. The militarization of the police also is characterized by large increases in the size of the force, heavy reliance on the use of force, and scant regard for civil rights and the rule of law. It is positively correlated with police homicide rates. The militarization of the police was not only continued after independence but was developed to a high level of perfection during almost three decades of dictatorial rule. It is an important factor in the explanation of Guyana's police homicide rates.

Police Violence and the Psychological Characteristics of the Middle Class—The Authoritarian Personality

Since independence, the post-colonial state, and the officer corps of the Guyana police force, have been dominated by members of the local middle class. The representation of this elite class in the officer corps of the Guyana Police Force is a direct result of the high esteem in which such positions have always been held under the colonial system,[74] so much so that the chain of command often passed from father to son.[75] Under the "cadet" system, which is another legacy from the organization of the force along military lines, educated members of the middle class were offered entry into the police force at the high level of "officer" after a short period of training abroad in the United States or the United Kingdom. The members of the officer corps of the police force are distinctive from the other members of the force by the different uniforms that they wear and the tremendous privileges they enjoyed under the colonial police system and still enjoy today. This section of the force was always identified with high status, as it was reserved exclusively for White colonial officials who were later joined by Mulattoes and Coloreds. Although today mostly Blacks, and to a lesser extent East Indians, make up the officer corps of the Guyana Police Force, the distinctions have been maintained.

With regard to the West Indian middle class it has been persuasively argued that the development of an authoritarian personality is among the numerous psychological scars of prolonged exposure to the colonial condition. Archie Singham referred to the psychological condition of the West Indian (Caribbean) middle class who replaced the colonial rulers in the region as follows:

> Despite their espousal of egalitarian and democratic ideas the elites in colonial societies tend to have basically authoritarian personalities. Authoritarianism is embedded in the entire social structure and the colonial personality structure; even those who rebel against the repression of colonialism retain their authoritarianism when they achieve power and

try to introduce change. Personalities of this type are both aggressive and submissive. When faced with authority, which they find difficult to challenge openly, they tend to become submissive. On the other hand, once they attain a position of authority they usually exercise that authority aggressively. One corollary of this deeply embedded authoritarianism is that it also characterized the elite-mass relationship in these societies.[76]

Lloyd Braithwaite developed the same theme when he divided the West Indian "Colored middle class" into two basic psychological types, one of which he identified as in keeping with the authoritarian character described by Maslow.[77] He attributes the causes of the development of this type of personality to the nature of colonial society, which was not only stratified on the basis of skin color but also practiced discrimination against darker-skinned groups, who were considered inferior and were prevented from enjoying upward mobility. This state of affairs resulted in much anxiety and resentment and resolved itself in the development of unique psychological coping mechanisms. Braithwaite emphasized the "tendency to hierarchy" displayed by the West Indian middle class as being one of the characteristics of authoritarian individuals whereby "(p)eople are regard(ed) . . . as challenging rivals who are either superior (and therefore to be feared, resented, bootlicked and admired) or inferior (and therefore to be scorned, humiliated and dominated)." In keeping with Maslow's observations, Braithwaite concludes that whatever power is possessed by the West Indian middle-class authoritarian type is likely to be used in the characteristic way "primarily to assuage his own psychological needs . . . in a selfish way, and . . . especially when challenged, . . . in a hard, cruel or even sadistic fashion."[78]

The most scathing criticism of post-colonial middle-class elites, however, is to be found in the work of Frantz Fanon. Describing them as voracious, self-indulgent, and "afflicted with precocious senility,"[79] Fanon made specific reference to the agents of social control in these societies as follows:

In these poor, under-developed countries, where the rule is that the greatest wealth is surrounded by the greatest poverty, the army and the police constitute the pillars of the regime; an army and a police force (another rule which must not be forgotten) which are advised by foreign experts. The strength of the police force and the power of the army are proportionate to the stagnation in which the rest of the nation is sunk. By dint of yearly loans, concessions are snatched up by foreigners; scandals are numerous, ministers grow rich, their wives doll themselves up, the members of parliament feather their nests and there is not a soul down to the simple policeman or the customs officer who does not join in the great procession of corruption.[80]

Specific support for the relevance of psychological characteristics identified with what has been termed the "authoritarian personality" to the propensity of police officers to engage in violence against civilians is found in the work of Arthur Niederhoffer, who identifies authoritarianism with a variety of personality traits, including the capacity for aggression and submission.[81] Niederhoffer suggests that the nature of the police role leads to the development of the authoritarian personality, but it is far from clear whether it is the police role that leads to the development of authoritarianism or whether the police force attracts people with the personality characteristics associated with authoritarianism. However, it is generally accepted that persons possessing authoritarian characteristics exhibit aggression and cynicism and tend to use power and authority in very cruel and selfish ways, and that these qualities are associated with police violence.

McNamara tested police recruits for authoritarianism by using the F scale that measures personality characteristics, before and after their period of training and again after one- and two-year periods of experience in doing police work.[82] He found cumulative increases in authoritarianism after each successive measure, thereby suggesting that the police role increases the personal qualities associated with authoritarian behavior in police officers. Although Bayley subsequently found that the police are no more authoritarian than other citizens, but rather less so,[83] the evidence points to authoritarianism as a factor that, along with other structural factors, could generate police violence.

The authoritarian personality characteristic is included in the schematic for this study as comprising an integral part of the authority structure represented by the middle-class elites in control of the post-colonial state and its coercive arm, the police force. Although the presence of authoritarianism among police officers was not submitted to empirical testing, the authoritarian personality is of contextual significance as one of the legacies of colonialism and is included for its descriptive, rather than explanatory, value.[84]

Factors Related to the Legal System

The variable "weak legal controls" is thought to influence police use of deadly force as an intervening variable that facilitates the functioning of the coercive mechanisms of the state. Without a conducive legal climate, police violence cannot flourish, and weak legal controls make it possible for the state authority to maintain a facade of the rule of law while covertly undermining it. The role of the law as a weapon in the hands of the ruling class is an integral part of criminological analysis based on the conflict perspective.[85] The effect of this variable illustrates how the legal system could be used by authoritarian state authorities to legitimate actions that violate fundamental principles of justice and equity. In practice, with regard to police use of deadly force, the construct "weak legal controls" means that despite the presence of a formal legal system, the system works to encourage, aid, and abet the use of lethal methods of social control in the form of police violence in the following ways:

(a) The passing of laws to expand the powers of the police
(b) Failure of police authorities to punish officers who kill without justification
(c) Failure of the state authority to impose effective restraints on police power to use deadly force

DEFINITIONS

For the purposes of this study, it is important to define what is meant by "police use of deadly force" and "police violence" and under what circumstances the use of deadly force amounts to violence, that is, becomes an illegitimate exercise of police power to take the lives of citizens. With regard to "deadly force" this study has adopted the definition provided by the International Association of Chiefs of Police as follows: "Any force which is intended to cause death or serious injury or which creates some specified degree of risk of death or serious injury." As such, the analysis refers to death and serious injury inflicted on civilians by the police, regardless of whether or not firearms were used.

With reference to the term "police violence" as used in the context of this study, no generally accepted definition is provided in the technical literature. The nature of violence in general and police violence in particular is not easy to define. After exploring the utility of several definitions of the concept of violence, Charles Tilly concluded that "in the present state of knowledge and theory concerning violence *any* definition will be arbitrary in some regards and debatable in many others."[86] In the context of police work, violence usually includes a trespass upon the person of another, and Tilly's definition of violence is thought-provoking: "*any observable interaction in the course of which persons or objects are seized or physically damaged over resistance.*"[87] In regular police work, force generally includes threats as well as trespasses against the person of another—seizure and/or physical damage—and it is generally applied to coerce compliance or to attain some objective "over resistance" of the victim. However, it is only when the use of force is excessive that it becomes "violence." Therefore, in keeping with Tilly's conceptualization, police violence may be defined to mean the use of excessive force against civilians by the police.

The next question that arises in the discussion of police violence concerns the issue of legality. The police are generally authorized to use force under certain circumstances, defined in the case of Guyana as where it is "reasonably justifiable"[88] or "necessary."[89] The existing literature on the subject suggest that the question of legitimacy can be approached in two ways. First, the issue is raised as to whether the use of force was authorized by existing law. For example, the police are the only agents of the state who may unilaterally exercise the power that the state possesses to take the life of its own citizens. When this power is legitimately exercised, that is, in accordance with existing law, the damage done is justifiable, and if death results it is excused under the law of justifiable homicide.[90] The protection of the right to life, which is enshrined in the *Constitution of the Cooperative Republic of Guyana*[91] is removed when death follows the use of force under the circumstances prescribed therein, but as Hadley Arkes points out, the ultimate question that is still left unanswered is whether the infringement of the right in each particular case, was *morally justified.*[92] But that is a separate question.

In the second instance, where the issue of legitimacy arises, the question is raised as to whether the use of force, though authorized by existing law, was more than required to contain the situation. In this regard, the legitimate use of force becomes transformed into illegitimate (criminal) violence, if, though authorized under existing law, it is excessive or "too much in the purely quantitative sense."[93] Excessive force is always illegitimate and always amounts to police violence, whether the use of force was initially authorized or not. It is the legal system, however, that determines what would amount to excessive force by the passing of laws to define it, and by judicial interpretation of common law rules relating to police use of force, such as the "fleeing felon rule" and the principles that apply to the law of justifiable homicide. The legal system plays an important role in the production of police homicide. When controls are weak, police homicide rates are likely to be high. Several studies have concluded that in at least one-third of all use-of-force incidents in the United States, excessive force was used by the police.[94] Analyses of current constitutional provisions, legislation, and case law will be included in this research.

Questions of police violence are also raised when the police abuse their authority and engage in criminal conduct completely outside of the circumstances in which the use of force is permitted. It is submitted that such cases would fall completely outside the pale of legality, as for example where a suspect is tortured to obtain a confession after the suspect has *already been taken into custody by the police.* Questions of legitimacy need not be considered when, as here, it would be a clear-cut case of criminal misconduct whereby the police are acting beyond the law. Fyfe's discussion of extralegal violence puts the situation clearly:

> Discussions of police violence are often blurred by the failure to distinguish between violence that is clearly extralegal and abusive and violence that is simply the necessary result of police incompetence. This distinction is important because the causes of these two types of violence, and the motivations of the officers involved, vary greatly. Extralegal violence involves the wilful and wrongful use of force by officers who knowingly exceed the bounds of their office.[95]

Although it is doubtful in the context of Guyana whether the use of excessive force under color of authority could be relegated to mere "police incompetence," Fyfe's characterization of extralegal violence hits the mark. Another example of extralegal violence would be the operation of death squads, where persons are targeted for execution and then sought out for that express purpose. These circumstances cannot be equated with routine police–citizen encounters out of which fatal or nonfatal force results.

THE RESEARCH QUESTIONS

Based on the theoretical perspectives discussed previously, and the relationships hypothesized in Figure 1.2, the following research questions will be investigated in this study:

1. **The Historical-Colonial Context:** What is the historical-colonial context within which police use of deadly force has occurred in Guyana?
   (a) What factors led to the development of policing in colonial Guyana?
   (b) What factors led to the resistance movement by slaves and the use of deadly force against slaves during the slavery period in British Guiana?
   (c) What factors led to the resistance movement by emancipated slaves and indentured immigrants and the use of deadly force against them during the post-slavery, colonial period?
   (d) What factors characterized policing in the colonial period?
2. **The Socio-Political and Legal Context:** What is the socio-political and legal environment within which police use of deadly force has occurred during the post-independence period in Guyana?
   (a) What was the nature of social conflict and social threat in the post-independence period?
   (b) What factors led to the use of deadly force during the post-independence period?
   (c) How broadly defined is the legal use of deadly force relative to constitutional law, statutory law, and the English common law?
   (d) How effective has the judiciary been in curbing police use of deadly force across time?
   (e) What factors characterized policing in the post-independence period?
3. **The Proximate/Community Context:** How has community violence been associated with police use of deadly force across time and to what extent is police-caused homicide justifiable?
   (a) To what extent has the use of deadly force by police in Guyana been excessive, across time?
   (b) How are levels of police use of deadly force associated across time with incidents of police being killed by civilians?
   (c) What is the ratio of fatal to nonfatal shootings by police over time?
   (d) How are levels of police use of deadly force associated across time with rates of crime in the community (including offenses involving violence and the use of firearms)?
   (e) To what extent are the homicides committed by police justifiable under existing law?

During both the colonial and post-colonial periods in Guyana, a clear relationship emerges between the modus operandi of the police and the political will of the executive power. As shown in the schematic, the demands of the authoritarian state for population control, the repression of perceived threats to the social order, and crime control, all resulted in the use of deadly force. The militarization of the police and the absence of adequate legal controls facilitated the abuse of police power and led to the emergence of the police as a formidable force for internal security.

NOTES

1. Karl Marx and Frederich Engels. 1968. *Selected Works.* Cited at p. 30 in *Dynamics of Social Change: A Reader in Marxist Social Science,* 1970, edited by Howard Selsam, David Goldway, and Harry Marel. New York: International Publishers; see also generally pp. 25–42.

2. Samuel P. Huntington. 1977. "Remarks on the Meanings of Stability in the Modern Era." In *Radicalism in the Contemporary Age, Vol. 3: Strategies and Impact of Contemporary Radicalism,* edited by Seweryn Bialer and Sophia Sluzar. Boulder, Colo.: Westview Press, pp. 269–82.

3. See Charles Tilly. 1975. "Revolutions and Collective Violence," *Handbook of Political Science,* Vol. III. Reading, Mass.: Addison-Wesley, Inc., p. 500.

4. J. S. Furnival. 1948. *Colonial Policy and Practice: A Comparative Study of Burma and Netherlands India.* London: Cambridge University Press; M. G. Smith. 1960. "Social and Cultural Pluralism." In *Social and Cultural Pluralism in the Caribbean, Annals of The New York Academy of Science,* Vol. 83 (1960), edited by Vera Rubin. New York: Annals of the New York Academy of Science, pp. 763–85; Lloyd Braithwaite. 1960. "Social Stratification and Cultural Pluralism." In *Social and Cultural Pluralism in the Caribbean, Annals of The New York Academy of Science,* Vol. 83 (1960), edited by Vera Rubin, pp. 816–36; Hamsa Alavi. 1979. "The State in Post-Colonial Societies: Pakistan and Bangladesh." In *Politics and State in the Third World,* edited by Harry Goulbourne. London: Macmillan, pp. 38–69; George Beckford. 1972. *Persistent Poverty.* London: Oxford University Press; Perry Mars. 1995. "State Intervention and Ethnic Conflict Resolution: Guyana and the Caribbean Experience," *Comparative Politics,* January, 1995.

5. M. B. Clinard and D. J. Abbott. 1973. *Crime in Developing Countries.* New York: John Wiley & Sons.

6. M. Wolfgang and F. Ferracuti. 1967. *The Subculture of Violence: Towards an Integrated Theory of Criminology.* New York: Tavistock Publications Ltd., p. 270.

7. Howard Jones. 1981. *Crime, Race, and Culture.* New York: John Wiley & Sons.

8. Paul Chevigny. 1995. *Edge of the Knife: Police Violence in the Americas.* New York: The New Press, p. 136.

9. Ibid., p. 257.

10. See Cynthia Mahabir. 1980. "Crime and Nation-Building: The Emergency Powers Act 1970, Trinidad and Tobago," *International Journal of the Sociology of Law,* 1980, 8, 129–48; C. Sumner. 1982. "Crime Justice and Underdevelopment: Beyond Modernization Theory." In *Crime, Justice and Underdevelopment,* edited by C. Sumner. London: Heineman Educational Books, Ltd., pp. 1–39; William Caslathes. 1990. "Jamaican Firearm Legislation: Crime Control, Politicization, and Social Control in a Developing Nation." *International Journal of the Sociology of Law,* 1990, 18, pp. 259–85; Ken Pryce. 1976. "Towards a Caribbean Criminology," *Caribbean Issues,* 11:2, pp. 78–92; Maureen Cain. 1996. "Crime and Criminology in the Caribbean: An Introduction," *Caribbean Quarterly,* Vol. 42, Nos. 2–3, 1996, pp. i–xvii.

11. Archie Singham. 1968. *The Hero and the Crowd.* New Haven: Yale University Press.

12. Some of the other countries that formed a part of the British Commonwealth include Pakistan, India, and Ceylon; countries of the Caribbean such as British Honduras, Jamaica, Trinidad, and Tobago; the Windward and Leeward Islands; countries of the Far East such as Malaya, Singapore, and Hong Kong; and countries in West, East, and Central Africa. See generally, Sir Charles Jeffries, K.C.M.G., O.B.E. 1952. *The Colonial Police.* London: Max Parrish & Co.

13. See John F. Galliher. 1985. "Explanations of Police Behavior: A Critical Review and Analysis." In *The Ambivalent Force: Perspectives on the Police,* 3rd ed., edited by Abraham S. Blumberg and Elaine Niederhoffer. New York: Holt, Rinehart, and Winston, Inc., pp. 56–63; Lawrence S. Sherman. 1980. "Causes of Police Behavior: The Current State of Quantitative Research." *Journal of Research in Crime and Delinquency* 17(1): pp. 69–100; Robert J. Friedrich. 1980. "Police Use of Force: Individuals, Situations and Organizations." *Annals of the American Academy of Political and Social Science* 452: 92–97; Jeffrey Ian Ross. 1994. "The Future of Municipal Police Violence in Advanced Industrialized Democracies: Towards a Structural Causal Model." *Police Studies* XVII:2:1–26; Luis Gerardo Gabaldon. 1993. "Police Violence and Uncertainty in Latin America: Linking the Macro- and Micro Levels of Analysis." *International Criminal Justice Review* 3:44–59 (p. 49).

14. See sources cited in note 13.

15. See Robert J. Friedrich. 1980. "Police Use of Force: Individuals, Situations and Organizations." *Annals of the American Academy of Political and Social Science* 452:82–97; Galliher, "Explanations of Police Behavior: A Critical Review and Analysis," and Sherman, "Causes of Police Behavior: The Current State of Quantitative Research."

16. For a detailed analysis of the various approaches used to examine police use of deadly force see Mark Blumberg. 1985. "Research on Police Use of Deadly Force: The State of the Art." In *The Ambivalent Force: Perspectives on the Police,* 3rd. ed., edited by Abraham S. Blumberg and Elaine Niederhoffer. New York: Holt, Rinehart, and Winston Inc. pp. 34–50; and more recently, Mark Blumberg. 1994. "Police Use of Deadly Force: Exploring Some Key Issues." In *Police Deviance,* 3rd ed., edited by Thomas Barker and David L. Carter. Cincinnati, Ohio: Anderson Publishing Co., pp. 201–15

17. Marx and Engels, *The Communist Manifesto* (1848), p. 35 in *Dynamics of Social Change: A Reader in Marxist Social Science*, edited by Howard Selsem, David Goldway, and Harry Martel. New York: International Publishers Co., Inc., pp. 43–51.

18. Marx, "Preface," *A Contribution to the Critique of Political Economy (1859), Selected Works*, pp. 182f in *Dynamics of Social Change: A Reader in Marxist Social Science*, edited by Howard Selsem, David Goldway, and Harry Martel. New York: International Publishers Co., Inc., pp. 52–53.

19. Richard Quinney. 1977. *Class, State and Crime.* New York: Mckay; Austin Turk. 1969. *Criminology and the Legal Order.* Chicago: Rand McNally; William J. Chambliss and Robert B. Seidman. 1971. *Law, Order and Power.* Reading, Mass.: Addison-Wesley, especially pp. 358–59.

20. Ralf Dahrendorf. 1968. *Class and Class Conflict in Industrial Society.* Stanford, Calif.: Stanford University Press, pp. 206–40.

21. Ibid., p. 165.

22. Allan Silver. 1966. "The Demand for Order in Civil Society. A Review of Some Themes in the History of Urban Crime, Police and Riot," in *The Police: Six Sociological Essays*, edited by David Bordua. New York: John Wiley.

23. Arthur Niederhoffer. 1969. *Behind the Shield: The Police in Urban Society.* New York: Doubleday & Co., pp. 12, 13.

24. Evelyn Parks. 1970. "From Constabulary to Police Society." *Catalyst* 5:76–97.

25. Paul Takagi. 1979. "Death by Police Intervention," in *A Community Concern: Police Use of Deadly Force*, edited by Robert N. Brenner and Marjorie Kravits. Washington, D.C.: U.S. Dept. of Justice, January 1979, pp. 31–38.

26. Hubert M. Blalock. 1967. *Toward a Theory of Minority-Group Relations.* New York: John Wiley.

27. David Jacobs. 1979. "Inequality and Police Strength: Conflict Theory and Coercive Control in Metropolitan Areas," *American Sociological Review.* Vol. 44, pp. 913–25; Allen E. Liska, Joseph J. Lawrence, and Michael Benson. 1981. "Perspectives on the Legal Order: The Capacity for Social Control. *American Journal of Sociology.* Vol. 87, pp. 412–26; Pamela I. Jackson. 1989. *Minority Group Threat, Crime, and Policing: Social Context and Social Control.* New York: Praeger; Stewart E. Tolnay and E. M. Beck. 1992. "Toward a Threat Model of Southern Black Lynchings," pp. 33–52 in Allen E. Liska (ed.), 1992. *Social Threat and Social Control.* Albany, N.Y.: State University of New York Press.

28. David Jacobs and David Britt. 1979. "Inequality and Police Use of Deadly Force: An Empirical Assessment of a Conflict Hypothesis," *Social Problems* 26:403–12.

29. Richard R. E. Kania and Wade C. Mackey. 1977. "Police Violence as a Function of Community Characteristics," *Criminology.* Vol. 15. No. 1, May 1977, pp. 27–48.

30. Allen E. Liska, ed. 1992. *Social Threat and Social Control.* Albany, N.Y.: State University of New York Press, pp. 17–21.

31. See Blalock, *Toward a Theory of Minority-Group Relations.*

32. Allen E. Liska and Jiang Yu. 1992. "Specifying and Testing the Threat Hypothesis: Police Use of Deadly Force." In *Social Threat and Social Control,* edited by Allen E. Liska. Albany, N.Y.: State University of New York Press, pp. 53–68.

33. Ibid., p. 68.

34. Paul Chevigny. 1990. "Police Deadly Force as Social Control: Jamaica, Argentina and Brazil." *Criminal Law Forum* 1:389–426.

35. Ibid., p. 404.

36. Ibid., pp. 400, 402.

37. Galliher, "Explanations of Police Behavior: A Critical Review and Analysis," pp. 56–63.

38. Ibid.

39. Kania and Mackey, "Police Violence as a Function of Community Characteristics," pp. 37–39.

40. David Jacobs and David Britt, "Inequality and Police Use of Deadly Force," pp. 409–10.

41. Gerald D. Robin. 1963. "Justifiable Homicide by Police Officers." *Journal of Criminal Law, Criminology and Police Science* 54:225–31.

42. A. Binder and L. A. Fridell. 1984. "Lethal Force as a Police Response," *Criminal Justice Abstracts* 16:250–80.

43. James J. Fyfe. 1978. *Shots Fired: An Examination of New York City Police Firearm Discharges.* Unpublished Ph.D. Dissertation. State University of New York at Albany.

44. James J. Fyfe. 1980. "Geographic Correlates of Police Shootings: A Microanalysis." *Journal of Research in Crime and Delinquency* 17:101–13.

45. Kenneth J. Matulia. 1985. *A Balance of Forces. Model Deadly Force Policies and Procedure.* 2d ed. Gaithersburg, Md.: International Association of Chiefs of Police.

46. Lawrence N. Sherman and E. Cohen with P. Garten, E. Hamilton, and D. Rogan. 1986. *Citizens Killed by Big City Police—1970–84.* Washington, D.C.: Crime Control Institute.

47. James J. Fyfe. 1988. "Police Use of Deadly Force: Research and Reform." *Justice Quarterly* 5:165–205.

48. Blumberg, "Police Use of Deadly Force," and Chevigny, "Police Deadly Force as Social Control."

49. See Victor E. Kappeler, Mark Blumberg, and Gary Potter. 1993. *The Mythology of Crime and Criminal Justice.* 2d ed. Prospect Heights, Ill.: Waveland Press, pp. 213–17.

50. Kania and Mackey, "Police Violence as a Function of Community Characteristics"; Jacobs and Britt, "Inequality and Police Use of Deadly Force."

51. Jonathan R. Sorenson, James W. Marquart, and Deon E. Brock. 1993. "Factors Related to Killings of Felons by Police Officers: A Test of the Community Violence and Conflict Hypotheses." *Justice Quarterly* 10:417–39.

52. Sorenson et al., "Factors Related to Killings of Felons by Police Officers."

53. With regard to empirical support, Kania and Mackey (1977) and Jacobs and Britt (1979) have also found a statistically significant relationship between rates of community violence and police homicide.

54. Max Weber. 1947. *The Theory of Social and Economic Organization.* Translated by A. M. Henderson and Talcott Parsons. New York: Oxford University Press, pp. 154, 156.

55. Carl Stone. 1978. *Decolonization and the Caribbean State System—The Case of Jamaica.* Paper presented to Conference on the Caribbean sponsored by the Center for Inter-American Relations, New York, March 31–April 1, p. 5.

56. "Caribbean" means the same as "West Indian." Both words refer to the same geographic region.

57. Carl Stone, *Decolonization and the Caribbean State System*, p. 6.

58. Ralf Dahrendorf. 1968; Ralf Dahrendorf. 1958. "Out of Utopia: Toward a Reorientation of Sociological Analysis." *American Journal of Sociology* 64:115–27; and Lewis Coser. 1966. "Prospects for the New Nations: Totalitarianism, Authoritarianism or Democracy?" in *Political Sociology*, edited by Lewis Coser. New York: Harper and Row.

59. Clive T. Thomas. 1984. *The Rise of the Authoritarian State.* New York: Monthly Review Press, p. 17.

60. Ibid., pp. 88–91.

61. Hamza Alavi. 1979. "The State in Post-Colonial Societies: Pakistan and Bangladesh." In *Politics and State in the Third World* edited by Harry Goulbourne. London: Macmillan, pp. 43–44.

62. Thomas Gittens. 1982. "The Post-Colonial State, Class Formation and Social Transformation: A Return to Theory." *Transition* 5:21–41.

63. Frederick Engels. 1977. *Marx and Engels: Selected Works.* New York: International Publishers, pp. 587–88.

64. Carl Stone, *Decolonization and the Caribbean State System,* pp. 7, 8.

65. Cynthia H. Enloe. 1980. *Police, Military and Ethnicity: Foundations of State Power.* New Brunswick, N.J.: Transaction, Inc., pp. 94–116 and passim, especially p. 110; David M. Anderson and David Killingray, eds. 1991. *Policing the Empire, Government, Authority and Control, 1830–1940.* Manchester, U.K.: Manchester University Press; and David M. Anderson and David Killingray, eds. 1992. *Policing and Decolonisation, Politics, Nationalism and the Police, 1917–1965.* Manchester, U.K.: Manchester University Press.

66. Sir Charles Jeffries, K.C.M.G., O.B.E. 1952. *The Colonial Police.* London: Max Parrish & Co.

67. Ibid., p. 30.

68. Ibid., p. 31.

69. Enloe, *Police, Military and Ethnicity,* p. 111.

70. Jeffries, *The Colonial Police*, p. 31.

71. Enloe, *Police, Military and Ethnicity.*

72. Jeffries, *The Colonial Police*; Michael T. Klare and Cynthia Arson. 1981. *Supplying Repression: U.S. Support for Authoritarian Regimes Abroad.* Washington, D.C.: Institute for Policy Studies; Jenny Pearce. 1981. *Under the Eagle.* Boston, Mass.: South End Press; Ivelaw Griffith. 1990. *The Quest for Security in the Caribbean.* Unpublished Ph.D. Thesis, City University of New York; Ivelaw Griffith. 1991. "The Military and the Politics of Change in Guyana." *Journal of Interamerican Studies and World Affairs* 33:141–73.

73. Howard Johnson. 1986. "Social Control and the Colonial State: The Reorganization of the Police Force in the Bahamas 1888–1893." *Slavery and Abolition* 7:46–58; Cynthia Enloe. 1980. pp. 5–29 and passim.

74. Enloe. *Police, Military and Ethnicity*, p. 136.

75. Jeffries, *The Colonial Police*, p. 64.

76. Archie Singham. 1968. *The Hero and the Crowd.* New Haven: Yale University Press, p. 10.

77. See Lloyd Braithwaite. 1953. "Social Stratification in Trinidad." *Social and Economic Studies* 22:111–20.

78. Ibid.

79. Frantz Fanon. 1974. *The Wretched of the Earth.* England: Penguin Books Ltd., p. 139.

80. Fanon. *The Wretched of the Earth*. p. 138.

81. Niederhoffer. *Behind the Shield*, pp. 109–60.

82. John H. McNamara. 1967. "Uncertainties in Police Work: The Relevance of Police Recruits' Backgrounds and Training." In *The Police,* edited by David J. Bordua. New York: John Wiley & Sons, pp. 163–252.

83. David H. Bayley and Harold Mendelsohn. 1969. *Minorities and the Police.* New York: The Free Press.

84. See Kania and Mackey, "Police Violence as a Function of Community Characteristics," p. 32.

85. See William J. Chambliss and Robert B. Seidman 1971, pp. 56–74 and passim; Austin Turk. 1969; Richard Quinney. 1979. *Criminology.* Boston, Mass.: Little, Brown and Co., pp. 78–112.

86. Charles Tilly. 1975. "Revolutions and Collective Violence." In *Handbook of Political Science*, Vol. III. Reading, Mass.: Addison-Wesley, Inc., p. 513.

87. Ibid.

88. Article 138(2), 1980. *Constitution of the Cooperative Republic of Guyana.* Georgetown, Guyana: Guyana National Lithographic Co. Ltd.

89. *Guyana Police Special Order,* April 23, 1963, No. 7/63. Georgetown, Guyana: Guyana Police Force.

90. Justification for an act in criminal law means that a normally actionable wrong has been committed, but the usual rules are suspended because of the supremacy of another policy. See Jerome Hall. 1961. *General Principles of Criminal Law.* Charlottesville, Va.: Michie.

91. *Constitution of the Cooperative Republic of Guyana,* Part 2, Title 1, Article 138, p. 48.

92. Hadley Arkes. 1990. *Beyond the Constitution.* Princeton, N.J.: Princeton University Press, pp. 66–67.

93. Candace McCoy. 1986. "The Cop's World: Modern Policing and the Difficulty of Legitimizing the Use of Force." *Human Rights Quarterly* 8:270–93.

94. Geoffrey P. Alpert and William C. Smith. 1994. "How Reasonable Is the Reasonable Man?: Police and Excessive Force." *The Journal of Criminal Law & Criminology* 85:481–501, p. 482.

95. James Fyfe. 1989. "The Split-Second Syndrome and Other Determinants of Police Violence." In *Critical Issues in Policing: Contemporary Readings,* edited by Roger G. Dunham and Geoffrey P. Alpert. Prospect Heights, Ill.: Waveland Press, p. 493.

2

Research Design and Methods

NATURE OF THE STUDY

This case study of police use of deadly force in Guyana utilizes a research method that has not so far been applied to the understanding or explanation of the persistent problem of police violence and the use of excessive force worldwide. Based on the methodology originally developed by two sociologists, Barney Glaser and Anselm Strauss, known as "the grounded theory approach,"[1] this study applies systematic qualitative research techniques to analyze data collected in the field with a view to developing a theoretical formulation of the realities of police violence in a post-colonial state. This study also combines this approach with that advocated by Burawoy in his development of the extended case method,[2] to the extent that interpretive analysis of the societal or structural context in which the phenomenon occurs will be utilized in order to pursue principles of general theoretical significance in the explanation of police violence. The intent is to develop a conceptual scheme that incorporates both macro- and micro-level variables that previous research has linked to police violence, while at the same time taking into account unique historical and contextual definitions of the situation. Where quantification is necessary to measure the frequency and degree of police violence and to enhance the validity of qualitative analysis, the data will also be subjected to quantitative procedures.

Beginning with the development of policing in colonial society, this study traces the evolution of a particular type of policing that manifests the most pervasive and entrenched legacies of prolonged exposure to colonial domination: authoritarianism, repression, and contempt for the rule of law. Currently, this police force not only enjoys an uncharacteristic degree of autonomy in the use of force, but appears to be fast becoming a law unto itself, substituting its own legitimation of violence for that prescribed by existing law.

The use of excessive and/or deadly force by the police is analyzed with reference to the structural and societal conditions in which it is embedded during two broad historical periods: the Slavery/Colonial Era (1613–1966), and the Post-Independence Period (1966–1994). The analysis is focused on variations that occurred in response to changing social and political arrangements as well as how structural colonial conditions continue to influence the current propensity of the police to abuse their power to use deadly force. The analysis of the factors that are causally connected to police violence involves a discussion not only of the evolving nature of events that are related to police use of deadly force, but also of how the larger historical and structural context and the interaction of conditions over time combine to produce their own definition of the situation and the current context within which police violence occurs.

DATA AND PROCEDURES

The Early Period—Slavery and the Colonial Era

The data for this study were collected in Guyana during field research over a two-month period in the summer of 1995. The discussion of the colonial condition and the social and political history of Guyana during the colonial period is based on documentary evidence consisting mainly of historical writings, parliamentary (Court of Policy) debates and speeches, newspaper reports, and annual official reports with appropriate illustrations by statistical tables gleaned from a variety of authoritative sources wherever appropriate. The matrix presented in Table 2.1 sets out the sources of data that will be relied on for investigation of the research questions that were outlined at the end of the last chapter. The primary objective of the analyses of this period is not only to answer the specific questions that are being investigated but also to illuminate significant patterns and trends in the nature of police use of deadly force in Guyana and to examine the social and political context in which policing evolved from the first settlement of the colony by the Dutch in 1613 up to the end of colonial rule with the attainment of independence from Britain in 1966.

Table 2.1
Sources of Data for Research Questions

RQ	PSI/ POL	PAR	Cases	GHRA REP/ Material	DS	Press Reps	Laws	Tapes
1a					X	X	X	
1b					X	X	X	
1c			X		X	X		
1d			X		X	X		
2a				X	X	X		
2b	X		X	X	X	X	X	X
2c			X				X	X
2d			X	X			X	X
2e	X	X	X	X	X	X	X	X
3a	X		X	X	X	X		
3b	X	X		X	X	X		
3c			X	X				
3d		X	X	X	X	X		
3e	X		X	X	X	X	X	X

Notes: RQ: Research questions.
PSI & POL: Police Survey Instrument and other information provided by the police.
PAR: *Police Annual Reports*, 1980–94.
Cases: Court records of criminal and civil proceedings resulting from police use of deadly force and reports of other cases of police-caused homicide.
GHRA REP: *Guyana Human Rights Reports*, 1981–1994; case files containing statements, medical reports, etc.
DS: Documentary sources include books, Commission Reports, etc.
Laws: Includes the constitutional law, statutory law, and case law.
Tapes: Taped interviews.

Inadequacy of Data Sources for the Early Period of Guyana's History

The sources relied on for data and information on Guyana's early history are mainly secondary, although a significant proportion is based on primary and official records of the period. This raises the problem of descriptive validity, which relates to the factual accuracy of the accounts that are presented and is not only peculiar to the Guyana situation. Rodway's three-volume work on the *History of British Guiana* is considered to be among the most important historical source for the country. Not only did Rodway rely on the actual records of Dutch planters (which he was capable of translating into English), but he was also the most self-conscious among the authors of the early periods about the accuracy of the statistical information that he obtained.[3] In addition, Rodway was the most comprehensive of the authors, and consequently reported more statistics and information on civil unrest that called forth intervention from the military and police forces during the earlier periods than any other source or combination of sources that the researcher was able to obtain.

However, because heavy reliance is placed on secondary sources in this part of the study (mainly Chapters 3 and 4), the risk of errors resulting from particular biases of the authors becomes more likely. One noticeable bias of these early historians is the tendency to be elitist in their orientation and their interpretation of history. Rodway, for example, seemed to be more concerned for the terrible plight of the White masters during a rebellion than for the cause of the oppressed population struggling for freedom and other human values.[4] Because of this elitist bias it is quite probable that matters affecting the masses of the population were slighted or even ignored by these authors, and this would result in low interpretive validity. In addition, the probability that the governing authorities at the time often suppressed reports of movements and events that were critical of such authorities would tend to aggravate this particular problem. Thus the combination of a peculiar historical bias away from small-scale instances of civil unrest with a conscious policy of suppressing information could lead to the underestimation of the volume and frequency of these events and the coercive measures adopted to control them, including the use of force by the civil peace-keeping authorities. The discussion of the frequency and extent of police violence during this period, therefore, needs to be understood in this context.

Another issue of concern relating to the use of secondary historical sources is that apart from Orrett's study on the police, none of these early authors was primarily concerned with tracing the history and development of policing in the colony of British Guiana. Information relating to policing in the colony had to be pieced together from material found in a variety of sources that related to the police and their various functions during the slavery and post-slavery periods. Since the authors were primarily concerned with providing information on other themes, it is possible that material that focuses on the police and that would be relevant to this study would have been omitted. For example, no record was found of the use of deadly force during the early period in the course of the regular law enforcement function of apprehending persons suspected of committing criminal offenses. The study of such activities of the police was not of concern to the authors, but this does not mean that such events never took place. The conclusions made in this study regarding the circumstances under which deadly force was used in the early years are therefore limited. Similarly, it is impossible to provide even an approximate estimation of the total number of persons killed by the police during this period.

The more adequate records directly relevant to the study of policing in Guyana during the early periods are located outside of Guyana, mainly in the Public Records Office in London and the Official Record Archives in Holland. Among the relevant sources obtainable in these overseas institutions are diaries, letters and other personal records of the early planters, the official criminal records of the colony, and also the multitude of regular *Despatches* by the colonial governors to the home authorities. These *Despatches* are essentially reports of incidents that are regarded as being of an urgent or problematic nature in the colonies and should shed light on matters pertaining to crime, civil unrest, or other events that would require coercive measures. Although it was not possible for the researcher to have access to these documents, this shortcoming should not seriously affect the analyses attempted in this study. There is sufficient data available, from the secondary sources utilized, to establish patterns and practices of the colonial authority in achieving social control of the population, and to define and explain the nature of policing and the use of deadly force. The study does not seek to provide an accurate count of police-caused homicide during this early period, or to explain *all* the circumstances under which deadly force was used. There is sufficient material available from which the modus operandi of the governing authority could be deduced and for conclusions to be drawn about the role and function of policing in the colony.

Yet, apart from providing valuable information concerning the use of deadly force by the civil policing authorities and an approximate count of the rate of police killings during these years, it is not unlikely that these documents would fail to provide significant improvement on the work of the secondary authors with regard to the problem of reliability and bias. First, these primary records would also tend to be elitist in their orientation since it is expected that planters and governors of the period would report with an interest in preserving the established political and economic order and the general status quo. Second, as Rodway himself observed, even these primary records are very often inaccurate in their statistical accounts.[5] Third, these early primary records usually contain many and significant gaps and omissions so that the researcher who wishes to be accurate is still left with the problem of making shrewd guesses where significant data are missing.

As a result of the matters stated, therefore, it must be emphasized that the chapters relating to the social and political history and the evolution of policing in colonial Guyana must be read subject to the deficiencies in descriptive validity just outlined. Material relating to the use of deadly force should not be taken as indicating an exhaustive account of all the instances in which deadly or excessive force was used by police against civilians in the colony, but only the instances that were recorded in the historical sources utilized. Yet, these data were considered adequate to provide valuable insights into the way in which policing developed in the colony and circumstances under which deadly force was used. More importantly, empirical data were collected in the field for the post-independence period, with which the remainder of the study is concerned.

The Later Period—Post-Independence

The data for this period were derived from the following: a descriptive, 71-item, multi-part question survey instrument, the *Guyana Police Force Annual Reports*, the annual reports of the Guyana Human Rights Association and the Police

Complaints Authority, submissions to the Government, press releases and other documentary material published by the Guyana Human Rights Association, newspaper reports, official documents, laws and legal documents, international human rights documents, records of court cases relating to the use of deadly force by the police (consisting of both criminal prosecutions brought by the state against individual police officers and civil actions brought by the relatives of civilians who had been killed by the police), and taped (oral) interviews. These materials were collected in the field during the summer of 1995. Table 2.1 (p. 29) shows how these sources of data interact with the research questions being pursued.

Letters of introduction from the chairperson of the sociology department, Wayne State University, which described the purpose and intent of the study, were distributed by the researcher to both the executive and judicial branches of government seeking their support for the research project. The functionaries that were personally contacted were the Minister of Home Affairs, who exercises executive authority over and has administrative responsibility for the Guyana Police Force; the Chancellor of the Judiciary, who is President of the Court of Appeal and Head of the Judiciary in Guyana; the Director of Public Prosecutions, who is in charge of all public prosecutions on behalf of the State; the Attorney General, who is the principal legal advisor to the Government of Guyana and is responsible for all civil proceedings by or on behalf of the Government; the Director of the Guyana Human Rights Association, who monitors human rights abuses in Guyana, including police brutality and the use of deadly force against civilians; the Commissioner of Police, who is the head of the Guyana Police Force; and the Police Complaints Authority, who is a person appointed by the President of Guyana to receive and investigate complaints of misconduct committed by members of the Guyana Police Force. Before meeting with the Commissioner of Police, letters of support directed to him were obtained from the Minister of Home Affairs, the Attorney General, and the Chancellor of the Judiciary, respectively.

The survey instrument was designed to collect data regarding yearly totals of the number of "use of deadly force" deaths by members of the Guyana Police Force from 1980 to the present time and the organizational factors concerning the officers involved; yearly totals concerning incidents in which police firearms were discharged in confrontations with civilians for the same period; the official procedure that should be followed after a firearm is discharged in such an incident; data relative to how personnel practices, training, policy procedure, equipment, and other organizational considerations, such as the use of SWAT units, might impact on the use of deadly force; and demographic characteristics of the force and the average age and educational attainment of police officers. Additionally, the Guyana Police were requested to furnish a copy of all current departmental orders, policies, procedures, and/or rules that relate to the use of deadly force. Copies of *Police Standing Orders No. 73* relating to the use of the baton, the *Commissioner's Circular No. 225* relating to the use of firearms, and *Special Order No. 7/63* relating to the use of force, including extreme force, were furnished by the police.

One of the objectives in administering the survey instrument and in requesting the supplementary materials was to gather general background information of a descriptive nature on the composition and operations of the Guyana Police. More importantly, however, reliable information was needed regarding the frequency of the use of deadly force, the circumstances surrounding the use of deadly force, training, departmental rules and regulations concerning the use of force, and the police perspective on the use of deadly force. The usefulness of the instrument was limited to some extent because the police were unable to provide responses to several of the items. In many instances, the reason stated was that the information was not readily available and more time was needed to obtain it. Efforts to get the police authorities to specify the amount of time required proved fruitless, and the researcher was given vague answers such as "maybe several months" or "we don't know for sure." The police had already taken approximately seven weeks working on the survey instrument, and the researcher was forced to leave the country at the end of a two-month period without the missing data being supplied. With regard to the police homicide counts that were specifically requested, information was only provided for the period 1991 to 1994.

Copies of the *Guyana Police Force Annual Report*, the only official source of crime data in the country, were generously provided by the Permanent Secretary, Ministry of Home Affairs,[6] for the years 1980 to 1992. At that time, the 1992 *Report* was the most recent one that was available for distribution to the public. The *Annual Report* is prepared and published yearly by the Guyana Police Force. It provides a comprehensive account of the composition, organization, and administration of the Guyana Police Force. Additionally, it provides information on the recruitment and training of officers and the activities of the various departments and branches of the Force (which includes the Criminal Investigation Department, Traffic Department, Research Planning and Publications Department, and the various branches such as the Mounted Branch, the Marine Section, the Communications Branch, the Tactical Services Unit, the Transport Branch, and the Special Constabulary). Information is also provided on all duties performed by the police, such as handling immigration, the issuing of passports, other travel documents, and certificates of identity. Crime statistics are provided under the sections dealing with the activities of the Criminal Investigation Department, and the Traffic Department, and statistical tables are presented in the Appendices, which provide data on crime for the year under review as well as comparisons with the two years preceding the year under review. The information is obtained from police internal records and court records. The *Annual Report* is presented in Parliament each year for approval before it is released to the public. Although the *Guyana Police Force Annual Report* does not contain any information on police-caused homicide or justifiable homicide, it is the only official source of crime data on Guyana and it is subject to the similar problems of validity as, for example, the FBI's (Federal Bureau of Investigation's) *Uniform Crime Reports.*[7] Apart from ordinary statistical errors and mistakes, some of the problems that affect validity, such as the underreporting of crimes to the police, are exacerbated by the fact that Guyana is a relatively small society and victims may be subject to a variety of influences that result in the failure or refusal to report criminal acts to the police. In some cases, the victim's address or place of work could be easily obtained and the fear of reprisals if the crime is reported is well founded. As in the United States, there is also significant underreporting of crimes such as rape or sexual assault as well as economic crimes such as robbery and larceny. In many instances of the latter, people feel that the police will be unable to solve the crime or that the loss is too trivial.

The recording practices of the police can also affect the validity of their data, and it is more than likely that the *Guyana Police Force Annual Report* suffers from the same deficiencies as the *Uniform Crime Reports* in this regard. Political pressure to reduce the crime rate leading to deliberate falsification of records, misclassification of crimes, and human error can result in inaccurate crime statistics.[8] Further, as Albert Meehan points out, police record-keeping practices inevitably reflect sensitivity to their own personal achievements as well as the organizational concerns of their department.[9] Conflict between organizational demands and public expectations, as well as personal career goals can result in the shaping of records in a way that may seriously affect reliability and validity. Wherever possible in this research, attempts have been made to utilize other sources of information to test the reliability of official police records.

However, the *Guyana Police Force Annual Report* was relied upon for the preparation of statistical tables and to conduct analyses for the purpose of validating relationships among the categories that emerge from selective coding of all the data. Figures showing trends in the incidence of police-caused homicide and various types and categories of crimes over time, and the relationship between police-caused homicide and civilian homicide, were prepared from this source. The statistical data were also used to calculate public homicide rates for the purpose of comparison with other countries as well as to conduct limited testing of the community violence hypothesis, which will be discussed later. Hence, as Table 2.1 (p. 29) shows, these reports are important in the examination of several research questions. They cannot stand alone, however; problems associated with descriptive and interpretive validity need to be taken into account.

The *Guyana Human Rights Report* is the main source of information concerning police use of excessive/deadly force in Guyana. The Guyana Human Rights Association (GHRA) was incorporated in 1979 to monitor human rights abuses in Guyana and in pursuance of this objective publishes its yearly *Report* on human rights observances in Guyana. Copies of all the reports published to date by the GHRA (1980–1994) were obtained. These reports provide tallies for the period 1980 to 1986 of the total numbers of fatal and nonfatal shootings of civilians by police, deaths of civilians in police custody, and victims of beatings and other forms of torture by the police that come to its attention each year. Summaries of the facts of each case are provided. The GHRA collects detailed statements from surviving victims, relatives of deceased victims, and/or eyewitnesses. Supporting documents such as death certificates, medical reports, and the reports of coroner's inquests are included for some of the cases reported. For the remaining years (1987–1994) the reports are much smaller in size and lack the specificity and detail that characterized earlier reports. As a result, the data for this period could not be relied upon for the purpose of the estimation of the yearly incidence of police-caused homicide. Uncertainty about the actual count for the year 1980 resulted in a similar decision not to use the data for that year for the purpose of estimation. With regard to all the information provided, the GHRA has warned that the list is partial and for the most part limited to Georgetown and that the actual figures of police-caused homicide may be much higher.[10]

The *Guyana Human Rights Report* is the main source of data utilized in this study for arriving at police homicide counts for Guyana. As Table 2.1 (p. 29) shows, the information obtained was verified by the use of several different sources of corroboration such as documentary sources, press reports, police reports, and actual cases. The only data that were provided from official sources were obtained from information supplied by the Guyana Police Force in response to an item on the survey instrument that requested the total yearly number of "deadly force" deaths caused by members of the Police Force during the period 1980 to 1995. In response, the police provided counts for the years 1991 to 1994 only, their reason being that they would need an extended and unknown period of time to access the records of police-caused homicide for the earlier years. In this regard, it must be noted that police department counts of police-caused homicide sometimes tend to be lower than figures obtained from other sources.[11] However, police figures had to be relied upon in the absence of any other acceptable source of estimation of the yearly incidence of police killings for the period 1991 to 1994. The GHRA was relied upon for an estimation the incidence of police-caused homicide during the early part of the period (1981–1986) for which statistical data were obtained. Because of the absence of a reliable source of information for the intervening years (1987–1990), police-caused homicide counts for those years were treated as missing data and assigned the mean value for the entire period (1980–1994). The mean value was also assigned to the year 1980, as it could not be verified with a sufficient degree of certainty whether some of the deaths had actually occurred in that year. Wherever possible, other sources of the same information, such as newspaper reports, were utilized to arrive at the most accurate count of police-caused homicide that the data would support.

Of central concern in this study is the fact that the GHRA reports are compiled from information brought to its attention on a purely voluntary basis. Interviews are routinely granted to members of the public who walk into their offices to make a complaint relating to human rights abuses by government. Documentary sources are also utilized by the GHRA. These include all the local newspapers, official documents, statements and other releases from the government; publications and releases from political parties; publications by trade unions and other civic organizations; and correspondence from citizens in various parts of the country. In matters relating to police violence, the GHRA is careful to point out that police homicide counts and tallies of cases of police brutality are for the most part limited to Georgetown, the capital city, where the GHRA has its headquarters. The GHRA also notes in its reports that since 1983 the state-owned press had significantly reduced its coverage of police shootings and that the actual number of deaths is probably much larger than the figures published in its reports. In any event, newspaper stories are not usually considered to be an adequate source for an accurate count of police homicides. In studies conducted in the United States it was found that variations in editorial policies substantially affected tallies nationwide, resulting in much lower counts than those derived from other sources, such as mortality statistics.[12]

The problem of arriving at reliable and accurate counts of police-caused homicide is by no means limited to Guyana. In the United States, for example, apart from police department records and newspaper accounts, death certificates constitute a valuable source of data on police-caused homicide because of their very nature and function. Yet, Sherman and Langworthy[13] have exhaustively detailed various flaws inherent in the U.S. system of death registration that, although adopting the category defined by the International Classification of Diseases (ICD) as "deaths by legal intervention—police" to be incorporated into the national mortality data published annually in the *Vital Statistics of the United States*, has failed to put in place measures that will ensure that death certificates are accurately and completely filled out. There is also no mechanism in place for ensuring that there is internal consistency in the coding practices of the National Center for Health Statistics, which is the agency that reduces the information on the death certificates into the ICD categories for entry into the national mortality data (*Vital Statistics*). These flaws routinely result in substantial underreporting of the number of police killings, and the better strategy for arriving at an accurate count involves the utilization of a variety of data sources.[14] Yet the *Vital Statistics of the United States* is relied upon heavily by researchers as the most accurate source of data on police-caused homicides in the United States. As far as is known, Guyana has not yet implemented a similar health statistics system for the recording of mortality data which employs the ICD categories for causes of death that have been agreed upon by the Geneva Conventions that establish them.[15]

However, scrutiny of death certificates issued by the General Register Office (Georgetown, Guyana) in cases of police-caused homicide reveal many of the flaws identified by Sherman and Langworthy that would no doubt make the accurate recording of mortality information all but impossible. In the case of a police homicide, a post-mortem examination is usually ordered; this is performed by a bacteriologist and/or pathologist from the Department of Forensic Medicine, Central Medical Laboratory, who is usually a registered medical practitioner. The bacteriologist and/or pathologist determines the cause of death and fills out and signs the death certificate, but invariably does not provide answers to items on the death certificate that relate to nonmedical particulars of the death. Items on the death certificate such as No. 2.10, which states "External Causes (How Injury Occurred)" are usually left unanswered. The close relationship between the police and this department may be related to this problem. Also important is the fact that autopsies are usually performed shortly after the incident and the pathologist may not be sufficiently certain of some of the information he is required to supply on the death certificate, and prefers to leave it blank. Whatever the reason, the result is that in Guyana, death records are not a useful source of information concerning police-caused homicide mainly because of missing information from which police involvement in the homicide can be ascertained.

In the United States, the Supplementary Homicide Reports, in which law enforcement agencies provide additional details about homicides that were reported in their jurisdictions as part of the Uniform Crime Reporting system, are a source for police-caused homicides that has only recently begun to gain popularity with researchers. The Supplementary Homicide Reports (SHR) is a part of the Uniform Crime Reporting Program whereby crime statistics for the United States are prepared and published annually by the FBI as *Crime in the United States.* Law enforcement agencies who participate in the Uniform Crime Reporting Program are asked by the FBI to provide additional information about homicides that were reported in their jurisdictions. The Uniform Crime Report form on which data for the Supplementary Homicide Report is collected is incidents-oriented and is submitted by agencies for each month in which homicides were reported to the police.[16] Each record includes details on the agency reporting the homicide, the incident, the victim, and since 1976, the offender/perpetrator of the homicide if known.[17] According to Tennenbaum,[18] the Supplementary Homicide Report also provides information about the incident that includes the "circumstances" (e.g., related to a felony) under which the homicide took place. The FBI, in processing the data for entry into machine-readable form has employed a coding scheme that includes 33 possible values for the variable "circumstances," one of which is "Justifiable—police," the total description being "Felon killed by police." Despite the reservations expressed by the FBI as to the quality of this data,[19] it is available to researchers through the Inter-University Consortium for Political and Social Research (ICPSR) or directly from the FBI master tape files. Researchers routinely list the reasons why the data may be biased and lacking in validity[20] and ask that the findings be qualified accordingly. Recently, the lack of reliable data about the use of excessive force by police in the United States was addressed by the United States Congress with the enactment of the Violent Crime Control and Law Enforcement Act of 1994. This act requires the Attorney General to acquire and publish an annual summary of data on the use of excessive force by law enforcement officers. As a result, the Bureau of Justice Statistics (BJS) and the National Institute of Justice have sponsored the creation of a National Police Use of Force Database, administered by the International Association of Chiefs of Police. Data collection on police use of force is currently ongoing. Guyana has no comparable data collection system, and the data on police-caused homicide must be assessed in light of the shortcomings outlined herein, but must still be used by researchers until an acceptable system is put in place.

Another source of data for this study consisted of *taped interviews.* The responses of judicial, legal, government, and police personnel to open-ended questions on the subject of the use of deadly force by the Guyana Police were utilized to enhance theoretical sensitivity and to capture process, to test the accuracy of explanations as to why action was being taken or not being taken, and to help corroborate links that have been established between conditions, actions and consequences. The relevant, unstructured, *taped interviews* that were used in this study were those conducted with the Minister of Home Affairs (who has administrative responsibility for the Guyana Police Force), the Chancellor of the Judiciary (who is the Head of the Judiciary in Guyana and the President of the Court of Appeal), the Attorney General and Minister of Legal Affairs, the Director of Public Prosecutions, the Program Manager of the Guyana Human Rights Association, and the Commissioner of Police. The Commissioner of Police always surrounded himself with about eight members of his officer corps during the interview sessions the researcher had with him, and they freely participated in the answering of questions. The result is that many unidentifiable responses appear on the tapes, for which it can only be stated that they were made by members of the officer corps.

Procedures for Testing the Community Violence Hypothesis

Data collected from the *Guyana Police Force Annual Reports* and the *Guyana Human Rights Reports* (in conjunction with the other sources of data on police-caused homicide already mentioned) were subjected to correlation analysis by the calculation of Pearson's *r* coefficients, and time sequence analysis. Correlation analysis was intended to measure the relationship between the crimes comprising the concept of community violence and police-caused homicide during the study period, and reliability analysis was used to chart variations across time.

With regard to correlation analysis, firstly, a choice had to be made of crimes that would adequately measure the underlying concept of community violence. This choice was guided by the selection of crimes used for this purpose in the technical literature on the community violence hypothesis. Current studies[21] (which have all been discussed in the previous chapter) have relied on the FBI's list of violent index crimes reported to the police, which includes such crimes as murder, rape, robbery, and a variety of other violent crimes. Public homicide rates and property crime rates have also been used.[22] In Guyana crimes are classified differently, being grouped in clusters such as "Homicide," which consists of murder, attempted murder, manslaughter, infanticide, and causing death by dangerous driving; "Violence Against the Person," which consists of assault causing and inflicting actual or grievous bodily harm, felonious wounding or wounding with intent, common assault, assault peace officer, throwing corrosive fluid, and other trespasses against the person; "Against Property with Violence," which consists of burglary, housebreaking and larceny, shop and store breaking and entering with intent, breaking and entering dwelling house with intent, and other trespasses on private property; "Sex," which consists of rape, attempted rape, carnal knowledge of girl between 12 and 13 years, buggery, abduction, incest, and attempted incest, and other sexual assaults; "Damage to Property," which includes arson and attempted arson, malicious damage to property, and other crimes involving the destruction of property; and "Robbery and Extortion," which includes robbery, assault with intent to rob, robbery with aggravation, robbery with violence, and robbery under arms etc.[23] Other headings include "White Collar," "Larceny," and "Others." As can be readily seen, there is an overlapping of violent crimes across categories, and violent crimes include crimes against property only.

In the final analysis the selection of crimes had to be guided by the underlying concept that was being measured in the context of the social construction of crime in Guyana. Of empirical importance also were the crimes that would permit the use of deadly force in the apprehension of suspects by the police under the laws of Guyana. As will be explained later, police in Guyana may only use deadly force to apprehend persons suspected of committing property crimes. There is also no limitation on the use of force with reference to the seriousness of the offense involved.[24] Some crimes though not appearing to be intentionally violent, may, because of the finality of their consequences (such as "causing death by dangerous driving") or their inherent egregiousness, such as the abduction of a child, may trigger an overzealous response from the police to apprehend suspects and result in violence.

To adequately represent the presence of violence in the community that can call forth a deadly response from the police in the prevention of crime or the apprehension of suspects, the selection of crimes was made based on the technical literature, the personal knowledge of the researcher of the content of the offenses, and the law regarding police power to use deadly force in the apprehension of suspects.

The crimes were grouped into categories represented by composite variables, and each category was correlated with police-homicide to determine if a relationship existed between the two. The first category, *civilian homicide,* includes the offenses of murder, infanticide, manslaughter, and causing death by dangerous driving. The second category, *violent crime*, includes attempted murder, rape, attempted rape, robbery with violence, robbery with aggravation, robbery and assault with intent to rob, larceny from the person, throwing corrosive fluid, felonious wounding and wounding with intent, assault causing and inflicting grievous bodily harm, assault causing and inflicting actual bodily harm, carnal knowledge of girl between 12 and 13, indecent assault, buggery, abduction, incest, and common assault. The third category, *property crime*, includes burglary, house breaking and larceny, shop and store breaking and entering with intent, break and enter dwelling house with intent, possession of house-breaking implements, attempt to break and enter dwelling house with intent, arson, attempted arson, and malicious damage to property. The fourth category of crime to measure community violence is *crimes involving the use of firearms*, which includes robbery under arms, discharging loaded firearm with intent, and unlawful possession of arms and ammunition. The final category, for which only one offense was found, was *crimes against the police*, which consists of assault peace officer.

The categories of *civilian homicide*, *violent crime* and *property crime* are based on classifications used in the technical literature cited previously. The other categories were added to adequately represent the state of community violence in Guyana. It was considered useful to classify *crimes involving the use of firearms* as a separate group because gun density has been positively correlated with police homicide in the technical literature,[25] and although there is no empirical data upon which an assessment of gun density in Guyana could be made, it was hoped that the separate analysis of crimes involving the use of guns would add valuable insights to arriving at an understanding of the subject. The category of *crimes against the police* was felt to be a very important one because police violence usually occurs when citizens engage in confrontations with the police.

Correlation analysis was also done between police-caused homicide and a variable representing the size of the police force. There is ample support in the technical literature for a causal relationship between the two,[26] the reasoning being that an increase in the latter results in a corresponding increase in the risk of interaction between the police and the public that may have violent consequences.

Because of the small size of the data set that was assembled with only between 13 and 15 cases, a combination of correlation and time sequence analyses were considered to be appropriate. First, *z* scores were calculated for each of the five categories of crime measuring the underlying concept of community violence. Then they were treated as items comprising a scale, and reliability analysis was conducted to determine the consistency with which the scale will measure the concept of community violence across time and across random samples.[27] The item-total correlations indicated how well the individual *z* scores calculated for each item during the 13-year period (1980–1992) measure the underlying concept of community violence.

Correlation analysis was done between the measures of community violence and police-caused homicide for the period under review for which data on both community violence and police-caused homicide are available (1980–1992). Correlation analysis is used to measure the relationship between two variables. The correlation coefficient indicates the strength of the relationship. The coefficient lies between +1.00 and –1.00. A positive 1.00 indicates a perfect positive association, which means that if there is an increase or decrease in one variable there will be a corresponding increase or decrease in the other variable. A –1.00 indicates a perfect negative relationship, which means that if there is an increase in one there is a corresponding decrease in the other and vice versa. A coefficient of zero would indicate that there is no relationship between the variables. Pearson's *r* correlation coefficients were calculated for the study period.

Line graphs were also prepared to evaluate the relationship that exists between the indicators of community violence, separately and together, with police-caused homicide. Because police-caused homicide is such a relatively rare event, comparison was made possible by standardizing the variables to a mean of zero and a standard deviation of one, by the computation of z scores. Time sequence line graphs were then prepared to chart the variation in the variables separately and together over time.

Procedures for Investigating Justifiable Homicide

The determination of the extent to which the homicide committed by police can be classified as justifiable homicide is one of the objectives of this study as stated in the research questions. Before this could be done, however, *constitutional provisions*, *statutory law* and *case law* are utilized to present the legal and human rights context of the use of excessive/deadly force in Guyana. This issue is pivotal to the discussion of police violence as the latter only results when force is used illegitimately and excessively. The Guyana Court of Appeal, the court of last resort in Guyana, in a recent, celebrated case reviewed all the existing authorities on the meaning of excessive force and laid down the law with respect thereto.[28] The actions of the police can only be evaluated meaningfully within this context, which raises the issue of justifiable homicide, or the circumstances under which the killing of civilians by police is authorized by or excused under the law.

After determining the circumstances under which police homicide in Guyana would be justified under the law, a convenience sample of twenty cases was analyzed to arrive at some idea of just how much justifiable police homicide was actually taking place and the circumstances surrounding such incidents in Guyana. Table 2.1 (p. 29) shows the sources of the data that were relied upon in the conduct of this analysis. Police violence rates are expected to be inversely related to the rates of justifiable police homicide, but it is often impossible to determine what actually occurred at the scene of a police shooting. Most shootings occur at times and under circumstances where independent witnesses are rarely present. The police tend to consider all killings as justifiable, and police cover-ups are considered to be part of their occupational subculture, which fosters a "cult of secrecy."[29] Researchers have documented instances in which officers falsely reported the actions of their fellow officers in order to make shootings appear justifiable.[30] Also, in the U.S. case of *Webster v City of Houston* (1982)[31] the court found that Houston police officers had been systematically trained by their department to carry a second gun, called a "drop gun" to lay next to their civilian victims who were initially unarmed, so as to create the scenario of a justifiable homicide.[32] The well-documented resourcefulness of the police in falsifying evidence makes it all but impossible to estimate how much criminal homicide is taking place and being reported as justifiable homicide. In Guyana, during the period 1980 to 1994 the Director of Public Prosecutions filed criminal charges against the police in only a handful of cases of the conservative estimate of at least 150 killings of civilians by police. Subject to these observations, the question of the extent to which police killings tend to amount to criminal homicide is addressed in this study.

Toward this end, complete records of *court cases* and *reported incidents* involving the use of excessive and/or deadly force have been subjected to an innovative analytical technique found in the technical literature on police killings. Along with this material, details of deadly force encounters reported in the *Guyana Human Rights Reports,* medical reports, autopsy reports, statements of independent witnesses, and other verifying documents obtained by this organization were also used to identify the sample of cases referred to previously. The sampling technique employed was dictated by the nature of the research problem and the availability of data on police killings. As recommended by Strauss and Corbin,[33] sampling was done on the basis of factors that appear to be relevant to the evolving explanation of police homicide, a process called "theoretical sampling." Limitations placed on the representativeness of the results of this analysis by the sampling procedure are of some concern, but for the purpose of this research a convenience sample based on cases that are available and would lend themselves to the analysis was considered to be more appropriate.[34]

The selection of cases was strategically designed to generate as many categories and properties of categories as possible and included a wide range of circumstances in which deadly force has been used in order to delimit explanations of the conditions and situations under which the killings occurred. Also utilized was the testimony of witnesses and surviving victims, some of which was recorded in the *taped interviews,* and the findings of the court in the instances where complete court proceedings were obtained. These cases are more fully described in the Appendix C. The procedure adopted to arrive at an approximate determination of how many of these killings more than likely involved criminal conduct by police officers was adopted from the technique employed by Richard W. Harding and Richard P. Fahey in their analysis of 85 killings by the Chicago police during the period 1969 to 1970.[35] Using the method they called the "alternative credible version technique," the authors found that there was prima facie evidence of murder or manslaughter in thirteen of the fatal shootings that were analyzed, and only in two of the thirteen cases had the police officers been charged.[36] In the other eleven cases, the police had failed to take into account the existence of an alternative credible version of the incident. This conclusion was based on the fact that some of the alternative credible versions supplied by independent witnesses tended to satisfy the requirement for probable cause to sustain the charging of the police officer involved with some degree of criminal homicide.

The authors defined an alternative credible version as one originating from one or more of the following sources:

1. The description of the incident as reported by the police themselves
2. The reports of the Coroner's pathologist, based on an autopsy
3. Credible witness testimony (i.e., sworn testimony given by a single witness who was clearly independent or by several witnesses who told the same story)[37]

The version of the incident derived from the alternative source (other than the police) becomes more credible in direct proportion as the police version becomes less believable. If the police version lacks corroboration, then the alternative version increases in credibility. The alternative credible version also increases in credibility if the police knew of the existence of an alternative credible account of the circumstances of the homicide but chose to ignore it in their investigations.

The authors then used this technique to assess the facts of each case to determine whether the police-caused homicide was justifiable or unjustifiable under the most credible version of the circumstances under which it occurred. Justifiable homicide was determined by prima facie evidence of factors that would make the homicide justifiable according to law. The types of situations that would result in the homicide being justifiable according to law were classified under the headings of (1) fleeing forcible felon, and (2) confrontation. Under "fleeing forcible felon" the authors included situations where the decedent was fleeing and armed with a firearm, knife, or other weapon or unarmed but fleeing (this was before the outlawing of the use of deadly force against unarmed nondangerous fleeing suspects by the U.S. Supreme Court in the case of *Tennessee v Garner*[38]). Under the heading "confrontation" the authors included situations where the victim was armed with a firearm, armed with a knife, or armed with another weapon and threatened the officer. Homicide that was considered not justifiable occurred where, although there was a confrontation, the victim was unarmed.

This model was adapted to reflect the laws of Guyana regarding the circumstances under which police-caused homicide is justifiable, and the alternative credible version technique was used to make an assessment as to whether the police-caused homicide was justified and therefore a legitimate use of deadly force. The laws under which police-homicide is justified are included in the categorization, and the weapons that are regularly used by criminals in Guyana, in addition to the firearm, such as sticks, galvanized pipe, and knives are included. For example, if it is established by several other credible accounts of the circumstances under which the homicide occurred that the victim was unarmed when shot, the case would be classified as unjustifiable if the shooting resulted from a confrontation with police where defense-of-life rules apply. Under the law, police are required, when faced with a confrontational situation to use only that amount of force that is proportionate to the force being repelled. To use a deadly weapon against an unarmed suspect who is resisting arrest is clearly outside the pale of legality. In the case of a fleeing felon however, the rules change and the law as it exists in Guyana allows deadly force to be used against a fleeing felon even if he/she is unarmed. Although it is never possible to ascertain what *really* happened in particular encounters between police and citizens, this procedure approximates that standard of relative truth that is the foundation of the adversarial system of a formal court hearing.

LIMITATIONS OF THE STUDY

Inherent in the case study method is the problem of objectivity, defined by Kirk and Miller as "the simultaneous realization of as much reliability and validity as possible."[39] The complex issues raised by the various sources of the data utilized in this study and the difficulty of obtaining accurate information regarding the frequency of police-caused homicide have already been outlined. The absence of reliable information from which a determination could be made as to whether the use of fatal force was justifiable was also a limitation in many cases. The police in Guyana have consistently displayed an inordinate sensitivity to requests for information concerning the use of deadly force. As a result, several sources of information were utilized to arrive at yearly totals that are as accurate as possible under the circumstances. The issue of missing data, though problematic, is not uncommon in studies of this nature in view of the paucity of official data on police-caused homicide worldwide. Wherever possible, internal validity was enhanced by a process of triangulation where multiple sources of the same information have been analyzed in order to obtain as much structural corroboration as possible.

Case studies, by their very nature, always raise the question of whether findings could be generalized beyond the specific case under investigation. Although this study is concerned with the Guyana Police, close observation of the various British West Indian territories, and the social and political arrangements in other developing countries previously colonized by the British, reveal similar problems with the use of deadly force by the police. The findings of this study should be useful for facilitating comparative research, as well as for making generalizations from the very specific case of Guyana to other countries that were settled as a result of European colonial expansion around the world.

NOTES

1. Barney Glaser and Anselm Strauss. 1967. *The Discovery of Grounded Theory.* Chicago: Aldine.

2. Michael Burawoy. 1991. "The Extended Case Method." In *Ethnography Unbound, Power and Resistance in the Modern Metropolis,* edited by Michael Burawoy et al. Berkeley, Calif.: University of California Press, pp. 271–87.

3. James A. Rodway. 1891. *A History of British Guiana from the Year 1668 to the Present Time.* Vol. I. Georgetown: J. Thompson, p. 173.

4. Ibid. Vol. I, p. 225 and James A. Rodway. 1891. *A History of British Guiana from the Year 1668 to the Present Time.* Vol. III. Georgetown: J. Thompson, p. 113.

5. Ibid. Vol. I, p. 173.

6. The Ministry of Home Affairs is the branch of Government that has direct responsibility for the Guyana Police.

7. Lawrence Sherman and Barry Glick. 1984. "The Quality of Arrest Statistics." *Police Foundation Reports* 2:1–8.

8. An interesting discussion of the subject can be found in John E. Conklin, *Criminology* (5th ed.). Boston, Mass.: Allyn & Bacon, pp. 44–48.

9. Albert J. Meehan. 1986. "Record-Keeping Practices in the Policing of Juveniles." *Urban Life* 15:70–102.

10. See Guyana Human Rights Association *Annual Reports.*

11. James Fyfe. 1978. *Shots Fired: An Examination of New York City Police Firearms Discharges.* Unpublished Ph.D. Dissertation, State University of New York at Albany.

12. Lawrence W. Sherman and Robert H. Langworthy. 1979. "Measuring Homicide by Police Officers." *The Journal of Criminal Law & Criminology* 70:546–60 (p. 551).

13. Ibid., pp. 547–50.

14. Victor E. Kappeler, Mark Blumberg, and Gary W. Potter. 1993. *The Mythology of Crime and Criminal Justice* (2d ed.). Prospect Heights, Ill.: Waveland Press, p. 129.

15. Membership in the worldwide system and use of the ICD categories is voluntary.

16. U.S. Department of Justice Federal Bureau of Investigation. 1984. *Uniform Crime Report Handbook.* Washington, D.C.

17. M. Reidel. 1990. "Nationwide Homicide Data Sets: An Evaluation of the Uniform Crime Reports and the National Center for Health Statistics Data." In *Measuring Crime: Large Scale, Long-Range Efforts* edited by D. Mackenzie Layton, P. J. Baunach and R. R. Roberg. Albany: State University of New York Press, pp. 175–205 (p. 178).

18. Abraham N. Tennenbaum. 1993. "The Supplemental Homicide Report: A Neglected But Valuable Source for Homicide Research." In *Questions and Answers in Lethal and Non-Lethal Violence: Proceedings of the Second Annual Workshop of the Homicide Research Working Group,* edited by Carolyn Rebecca Block and Richard L. Block. Washington, D.C.: National Institute of Justice, pp. 77–78 (p. 81).

19. Sherman and Langworthy, "Measuring Homicide by Police Officers," p. 54.

20. The usual reasons that are given are as follows: (a) Not all homicides in a particular jurisdiction are brought to the attention of the local police agency. (b) The possibility exists that not all data concerning homicides reach the FBI. Some agencies do not participate in the Uniform Crime Reporting Program, other agencies do not always send in their monthly reports, and in still other cases the data disappears somewhere between the local agency and the FBI headquarters. (c) Sometimes details of homicides are reported incorrectly either because of human mistake or because the information is not available at the time of investigation or the information changes substantially after the initial report is made.

21. See R. E. Kania and Wade Mackey. 1977. "Police Violence as a Function of Community Characteristics." *Criminology* 26(1):27–56; David Jacobs and David Britt. 1979. "Inequality and Police Use of Deadly Force: An Empirical Assessment of a Conflict Hypothesis." *Social Problems* 26:403–12; Jonathan R. Sorenson, James W. Marquart, and Deon E. Brock. 1993. "Factors Related to Killing of Felons by Police Officers: A Test of the Community Violence and Conflict Hypotheses." *Justice Quarterly* 10:417–40.

22. See especially, Kania and Mackey, "Police Violence as a Function of Community Characteristics."

23. See *Guyana Police Force Annual Reports* under the heading of "Cases of True Crimes and Offences Reported to the Police."

24. Article 138 of the *Constitution of Guyana.* 1980. Georgetown, Guyana. The circumstances under which the police may lawfully use deadly force against civilians are discussed in Chapter 6.

25. Sherman and Langworthy, "Measuring Homicide by Police Officers"; and Kenneth J. Matulia. 1985. *A Balance of Forces. Model Deadly Force Policies and Procedure.* (2d ed.). Gaithersburg, Md.: International Association of Chiefs of Police.

26. See Jacobs and Britt, "Inequality and Police Use of Deadly Force"; Kenneth Matulia, "Police Violence as a Function of Communty Characteristics"; and Sorenson et al., "Factors Related to the Killing of Felons by Police Officers," to name a few.

27. See Anthony Walsh. 1990. *Statistics for the Social Sciences.* New York.: Harper & Row, pp. 7, 336–37; Mordecai Ezekiel and Karl A. Fox. 1963. *Methods of Correlation and Regression Analysis.* New York: John Wiley & Sons, Inc., pp. 293–95.

28. *The State v Evelyn Dick and Alwyn Dodson Evelyn,* Criminal Appeals Nos. 42 and 43 (1983).

29. This "cult of secrecy" or "code of silence" was first identified by William A. Westley in a study of the police department in Gary, Indiana. Westley found, as a result of his research, that a subculture existed among police officers that was based on feelings of distrust of the general society and stressed support and loyalty to each other, secrecy, or an unwritten code of silence that endorses and condones illegal acts, including the use of violence. See William A. Westley. 1951. *The Police: A Sociological Study of Law, Custom and Morality.* Unpublished Ph.D. Dissertation, University of Chicago, Department of Sociology.

30. Arthur L. Kobler. 1975. "Police Homicide in a Democracy." *Journal of Social Issues* 31(1):163–84.

31. *Webster v City of Houston* 689 F2d 1220 (5th Cir 1982).

32. The court concluded in the *Webster* case, p. 1227 that: "The use of a throw down weapon was well nigh universal throughout the police department. From their earlier days in the police academy, recruits surreptitiously learn to 'protect themselves' by employing a throw down . . . (It was) a living part of official policy at HPD."

33. Anselm Strauss and Juliet Corbin. 1990. *Basics of Qualitative Research: Grounded Theory Procedures and Techniques.* Newbury Park, Calif.: Sage Publications, pp. 176–93.

34. Martyn Hammersley and Paul Atkinson. 1991. *Ethnography: Principles in Practice.* London: Tavistock Publications, p. 44.

35. Richard W. Harding and Richard P. Fahey. 1973. "Killings by Chicago Police, 1969–70: An Empirical Study." *Southern California Law Review* 46:284–315.

36. Ibid., pp. 292–94.

37. Ibid., p. 290.

38. *Tennessee v Garner* 471 US 1, 105 S.Ct 1694, 85 L.Ed.2d 1 (1985).

39. Jerome Kirk and Marc L. Miller. 1986. *Reliability and Validity in Qualitative Research.* Beverly Hills, Calif.: Sage Publications, Inc., p. 20.

3

The Social and Political History of Guyana

THE COUNTRY AND ITS PEOPLES

Guyana is situated on the northern coast of South America. It is bounded on the north by the Atlantic Ocean, on the east by Suriname, on the south by Brazil, and on the west by Venezuela. Guyana comprises an area of 83,000 square miles, and the approximately 834,000 persons[1] who inhabit this area are a product of its colonial history. A map of Guyana showing its geographic location is presented in Appendix A. The origins of the various ethnic groups that make up the population are disparate. The native Amerindians are the only indigenous people. All the other groups resulted from European colonial expansion in the West Indies. The ethnic composition of the population of Guyana as reported in the last two population censuses is presented in Table 3.1.

The transatlantic slave trade to the Caribbean dates back to the early sixteenth century. In the case of Guyana, Africans were imported as a cheap source of slave labor for the hundreds of plantations established first by Dutch and then by British profiteers cultivating sugar, cotton, and coffee.[2] After the abolition of the

Table 3.1
Guyana Population by Ethnic/Racial Group, 1970 and 1980

	1970		**1980**
Ethnic/Racial Group	*Number*	*Percent*	*Number**
East Indian	377,256	51.0	389,760
Black	227,091	30.7	231,330
White	4,056	1.9	770
Mixed	84,077	11.4	83,763
Portuguese	9,668	1.3	—
Chinese	4,678	0.4	1,842
Amerindian	32,794	4.4	39,867
Other	576	0.1	3,266
Total	740,196	100.0	750,598

*This number does not include the category "Not Stated" (821) or the Portuguese.

Source:
Population Census of the Commonwealth Caribbean, 1970.
Population Census of the Commonwealth Caribbean, 1980–81, Guyana, Vol. 3, Table D10.

British slave trade in 1807, the abolition of slavery in 1834, and the eventual emancipation of the slaves in 1838, the supply of cheap labor for the plantations became problematic, as the ex-slaves tended to migrate from the plantations, purchase their own land, set up communal villages, and cultivate their own crops.[3] Brian Moore estimates that between 1838 and 1850, the newly freed slaves had spent $1,012,194 on the purchase of land and an additional $1.5 million on the construction of houses, the preparation of land for cultivation, and the acquisition of farming necessities.[4] To alleviate the resulting labor shortage, the British government, through the instigation of local planters, implemented a policy of encouraging immigration of peoples from China, India, Madeira, and also Africa and the West Indies to work on the plantations.

These immigrants were contracted to work and live on the plantations under a system of indenture where conditions of service closely resembled those under chattel slavery. In return for meager wages, they were required to work for periods of between 5 and 10 years, after which they could return home, in theory at least. While the other ethnic groups tended to migrate from the plantations after their period of indenture, the East Indians were induced to stay by government grants of land and other privileges[5] and hence comprise the numerical majority group in the population today. Table 3.2 gives an indication of the numbers and the approximate dates of arrival of the various ethnic groups in the colony. Indian immigration was the last to end, and indentured servants continued arriving in regular "waves" until 1917, when the practice was abolished by the government of India.[6]

Table 3.2
Number of Contract Immigrants Arriving in British Guiana

Place of Origin	Number	Dates of Main Immigration
India	238,960	1838–1917
Madiera, Azores, and Cape Verde	31,628	1835–1882
Malta	208	1839
West Indies	42,562	1835–1928
Africa	13,255	1838–1865
China	14,189	1853–1912
United States of America	70	1840
Total	340,872	

Source: R. T. Smith. 1962. *British Guiana*. London: Oxford University Press, p. 44.

Racial and Social Segmentation in Colonial Guyana

Because of the disparate background of its various peoples, Guyana has been described as a plural society[7] in the sense that it consists of many ethnic and cultural groups, each occupying the main different geographic regions, and each to a large extent holding to its own separate ways, institutional patterns, and occupational specialization. In the plantation colony, established primarily for the production of sugar, cotton, and coffee for export to the metropolis as a profit-making enterprise, race and color were defining characteristics of social organization. The distinct, hierarchical, race-specific class structure, with the Europeans at the apex, a characteristic feature of colonial society, was also very evident in Guyana.

This minority but powerfully dominant European group consisted of the administrators of the colonial government and commercial houses, military personnel, traders, professionals (especially attorneys who serviced both metropolitan commercial and planter interests), and missionaries who clustered in Georgetown, the capital city. Also included were the plantation owners and managers who lived in luxury in segregated compounds on the estates. Their "big houses" stood in sharp contrast to the "logies" occupied by the laborers in the field, who lived under conditions of extreme squalor and deprivation. This European group was a transient population for whom "home" remained the land of their birth, mainly Britain and to a lesser extent Ireland and Holland. According to Moore, they "formed a kind of aristocracy with a quasi-monopoly of political and social power. . . . The colony was practically their fiefdom, and everyone paid them homage and obeisance."[8]

Having come to the colony as indentured laborers, the Portuguese, though White, were relegated to a lower status than the Europeans in the class hierarchy. They were very susceptible to tropical diseases, and many died while working on the plantations. They abandoned the plantations at the first opportunity and migrated to the city, becoming mainly peddlers, pawnbrokers, and shopkeepers. Aided by the preferential treatment they received from the Europeans (in the receipt of credit, loans, and licenses), by the 1880s they controlled the retail trade in the colony and owned most of the licensed businesses both in Georgetown and in the rural areas.[9]

The Chinese, who had also come to the colony as indentured servants, ranked next in line in the class structure. They also failed to adapt to plantation life and took a path similar to that taken by the Portuguese. They migrated from the estates as soon as their contracts ended, and opted for business and commerce.

The Colored or Mixed population, a sizeable group of mainly Mulattoes (about 11% of the population) came into existence "mainly by moral default."[10] They were not only the result of forcible rape committed by White masters on the female African slaves in the plantation setting, but they also resulted from the informal practice of individual planters throughout the West Indies granting manumissions (termination of bondage) to slaves on the basis of sexual and blood ties.[11] Although under the brutality of the slave system unwilling sexual partners were whipped and/or tortured into submission, the historical evidence suggests that some slave masters wanted more than a rape relationship, and adopted a paternalistic attitude toward their light-skinned offspring.[12] The female slaves desperately wanted freedom for themselves and their children, and by the end of the eighteenth century, the practice of European males cohabiting with female African slaves, and free Colored women was fairly common.[13] Arthur Stinchcombe, in describing the nature of slave–master agency in the Caribbean resulting from sexual ties between White male lovers and their African mistresses cited part of a letter written by one island authority to another and quoted by Peytraud (1897) as follows:

> If we did not take care to stop the manumission of slaves, there would be four times as many as there are, for here there is such great familiarity and liberty between masters and negresses, who are well formed, which results in a great quantity of mulattos, and the most usual recompense for their obliging compliance to the wishes of the masters is the promise of liberty which is so gratifying that, together with their sensuousness, the negresses determine to do everything their masters wish.[14]

Mulattoes, most of them born free and considered by their White fathers to be unsuited to the heavy field work on the plantations, were the first non-White inhabitants of the colony of British Guiana to achieve practical and legal equality with Whites. In a society where everything was determined by racial affiliation to the dominant White minority, they spared no pains in trying to enhance their civil status and life chances, using every means at their disposal to overcome their inevitable classification as an inferior caste. This led to deliberate social distancing from their African and, for the Mulattoes, even their own Colored, male counterparts. Speaking of the free people of Color in the West Indies and particularly in the Leeward Islands, Elsa Gouveia had this to say:

> (W)hile their sole prospect of social advancement lay in increasing their degree of whiteness, they had come to regard interbreeding and association with whites as the paramount objectives which they must strive to attain. As a result, their women looked upon legal marriage with men of their own rank as an unacceptable alternative to the benefits which might be derived from the customary practice of concubinage between women of color and white men.... Men of the free colored class, therefore, had to seek mates among the women slaves.[15]

In British Guiana, legal gains were also made by the free Coloreds. In 1816, a Demerara Ordinance provided as follows: "those free colored persons employed on any estate or land in this colony, who (on a representation made by their employer) shall be approved by His Excellency the Governor, shall, with respect to the provision of the present Ordinance, be considered in the same light as whites."[16] Discriminatory practices against non-Whites, hitherto authorized by legislation, were removed in the case of the free Coloreds, who were able to succeed to supervisory, clerical, and other appointments on the estates and within the colonial administration in the towns that were usually reserved for Whites, take up commissions in the White militia, and be buried in the same portion of the burial ground reserved for Whites.[17] The ban prohibiting marriage between Whites and free Colored persons was lifted in 1812. The Governor in 1822 issued a proclamation removing all disabilities and ordering that "the free colored inhabitants be placed upon a footing with their white brethren, and be taken and considered for all the purposes of the aforesaid Ordinance, as coming within the full scope, intent and meaning thereof," and by 1830 according to Shahabuddeen, laws that discriminated against them had apparently disappeared.[18] Many White men married their free Colored mistresses, and by the end of the nineteenth century interracial marriages between these two groups were quite common.[19]

Eager to maintain their favored occupations, and the higher social status accorded to them based on their "Whiteness," the Colored population adopted European culture and values with great fervor, while despising the servile masses on the plantations. Through the utilization of opportunities for education during the latter half of the nineteenth century they were able to succeed to high positions in the professions and colonial civil service. From the upper-class European point of view, they were considered, along with the Chinese and Portuguese, to be middle class and were very effective in the military and police forces of the colonial state after emancipation of the slaves in 1834.

Other than the Amerindians, who had always resided in the hinterland and were mostly self-sufficient farmers and hunters who did not participate in the social and political organization of the colonial society, the bottom rung of the social ladder was occupied by the Africans and the East Indians. Conditions under the system of indentured labor through which the East Indians had come were very similar to those under African slavery. East Indian laborers were bonded by contract for a fixed period and received wages (though meager), whereas the African slaves were chattel, forced to give their labor for free until death. The plantation was a place of brutal exploitation for these two groups, where subordination and subservience to the minority European class was enforced by the myth of White superiority as well as by force and coercion.

Partly because of poor wages and conditions of work, after emancipation the African slaves migrated from the plantations, forming their own communal villages. Allan Young describes some of the rules and regulations of estate labor that precipitated the first general strike in 1842 and drove the ex-slaves to consolidate the village movement that had already gotten underway since emancipation. In addition to the reduction of wages to the pre-emancipation level,[20] regulations provided for the following:

> (T)he customary allowances of food and medicine were to be discontinued; work performed after a certain hour in the morning was to go unpaid; a fine was to be imposed for failure to work on the estate; hogs in pens were to be destroyed; labourers quitting the estate were not to reap the provisions they had planted; and, most important of all, nonconformity with the regulations was punishable with summary ejection from the estate.[21]

Soon after becoming subsistence farmers for themselves, many ex-slaves experienced severe hardship due to economic pressure being brought to bear on them by the planter class to return to estate labor for survival. Loans for infrastructural land development to prevent flooding (an endemic problem in the colony) were denied them, and their crops were often ruined as a result of inadequate conditions of sea defense and drainage. Heavy rates and taxes imposed by the colonial government often resulted in the confiscation of their property.[22] As a result, many ex-slaves who had migrated into the villages soon became destitute and went into the gold and balata fields in the interior to find work. Others drifted into the towns and became mainly service employees (domestic servants, artisans, dockworkers and the like).[23] Along with the East Indians, this group became the frequent victims of deadly violence from colonial police in their struggle for equality and justice well into the twentieth century.

The East Indians, as stated previously, filled the gap created by the migration of the ex-slaves from the plantations and were given incentives to remain in the colony at the end of their period of indenture, which usually lasted for five years.[24] They established themselves in the agricultural sector, and were given a bounty of fifty dollars if they entered into new contracts of service.[25] Their conditions of indenture were laid down by the Consolidated Immigration Ordinance[26] and were just as onerous as those under which the ex-slaves had worked. Like the African slaves, the East Indians (called "coolies" by the masters) were relegated to the lowest status in colonial society. Though supposedly protected by the law, East Indians were cruelly exploited by the estate managers who, as Justices of the Peace, held "court" at regular intervals; this "court" was presided over by the manager himself, assisted by his employees. In this way, the very oppressor dispensed his own brand of "kadi justice," in Weberian terms.[27] In the regular magistrate's courts of the colony, managers could bring criminal prosecutions against immigrants for labor offenses and frequently did so, especially since immigrants were not allowed to testify in court until 1845, after which they still were not allowed to testify in matters where they were the defendant.[28] East Indians who were unable to find redress for their grievances resorted to frequent strikes and work stoppages on the sugar estates. By the turn of the eighteenth century, industrial conflict and state repression resulted in many instances of public disorder and the frequent use of deadly force to quell civil strife.

POLITICAL DEVELOPMENTS DURING THE COLONIAL ERA

The colonial years in Guyana began with the establishment of settlements by the Dutch in the early seventeenth century,[29] and continued (despite many changes of ownership during the Napoleonic wars) when the territory was captured by the British in 1803 and formally ceded to the British by the Treaty of Paris of May 30, 1814.[30] This period finally came to an end when the country became a sovereign, democratic state by virtue of the Guyana Independence Act, 1966.[31] European interest in this part of the "New World" had been stimulated by the famous voyages of Sir Walter Raleigh in search of that illusory city of gold (El Dorado). Raleigh's extravagant claims of great wealth to be found in the territory between the Amazon and Orinoco Rivers on the continent of South America excited competition between Holland, Britain, and France for the plunder and control of the area.[32] It was the Dutch, however, who first tackled the daunting task of reclaiming swampland from the sea in this "land of many waters" and established permanent settlements for the exploitation of its natural resources. The elaborate and enduring system of sea defense, drainage, and irrigation constructed by the Dutch, as Rodney points out, is a lasting reminder not only of their contribution to Guyanese coastal agriculture, but also of the contribution of the African slaves who provided the free labor that made it possible.[33]

The system of law and government established by the Dutch reflected not only their sole preoccupation with maximum exploitation of the colony's resources for profit, but also their barbaric ideas of justice. The essence of this system was preserved by the Articles of Capitulation under which the British assumed final ownership and control of the three separate colonies of Demerara, Essequibo, and Berbice (united in 1831), which became British Guiana.[34] The Articles formed the basis of the constitutional rule of the Colony until the British Parliament abolished the old structure of government and created a new Crown Colony Constitution in 1928.

The first system of government established by the Dutch in the Colony was authorized by an Order of Government issued by the States-General of Holland in 1629 whereby the Dutch West India Company (a slave-trading and privateering company charged with protecting Dutch commercial interests and establishing settlements in the "New World") was to set up as "a definite system of government, both as to policy and as to justice, in the place or places (with God's help) to be conquered."[35] The Company issued a document known as the Articled Letter, which set out the various regulations, including criminal matters, whereby the Commandeur of whichever of its ships was in port would govern both the ship and the settlement. Although intended for their fellow settlers, the nature of criminal penalties prescribed were clear indicators of the brutal, authoritarian nature of Dutch colonial rule that developed in the Colony. According to colonial historian Sir Cecil Clementi,

> A fine was imposed for curses, oaths, blasphemy or mockery, dissatisfaction with rations, or for being absent from both morning and evening prayers without sufficient cause. Whoever drew a knife with intent to stab another was to be fastened by the knife through the hand to the mast (of the ship) and left to free himself. Wounding was punishable by kneel-hauling and loss of a month's wages. Murderers were to be tied to the corpse and thrown with it overboard and all their wages and prize money were to be forfeited.[36]

By the time of the capitulation to the British in 1803, this system of rule had evolved into the permanent Councils (or Courts) of Policy and Justice for Essequibo and Demerara that had been established to deal with all governmental and judicial matters. The Councils of Justice were responsible for all civil and criminal matters in the colony, and the Councils of Policy performed legislative, executive, and administrative functions as well as the business of the Dutch West India Company. Matters of defense were handled by a burgher militia system, based on what was in existence in Holland. Under this system every able-bodied settler who had taken the oath of allegiance and paid five guilders to become a citizen was required to take up arms for the defense of the colony or the repression of civil disturbances whenever ordered to do so by their Governor.[37] The seat of government at that time was located in Essequibo, which was divided into two districts. There was a separate burgher system for each district, and each company was commanded by a captain, assisted by a lieutenant and an ensign. It was these officers for the two burgher companies then in existence who constituted the first College of Kiezers (electors) formed by Governor Storm Vans Gravesande in order to nominate planter representatives to the Essequibo Council of Policy and Justice.[38] A similar militia system was established in Demerara.

The burgher officers also performed other interesting functions. Apart from conducting court martials for the trial of offenses, policing in the colony was effected by these officers who performed the duties of justices of the peace as well as constables. The burgher officers also found their way into the justice system before the formation of the Demerara Council of Justice, when the Essequibo Council of Justice decided in 1753 to establish a special court (recht bank) for the trial of petty offenses in Demerara subject to a right of appeal to itself. The Commandeur of Demerara presided in this court with two officers of the Demerara burgher militia. When the Demerara Council of Justice was formed in the same year, it was the six officers of the Demerara burgher militia (two captains, two lieutenants, and two ensigns) who, along with the Commandeur of Demerara as President, constituted the first Council of Justice for Demerara. The senior of the two burgher captains presided over the Council whenever the Commandeur and the Essequibo councilors were absent. There was no clear separation of powers under this system of Dutch administration, and this practice of overlapping the judicial and law enforcement functions, where the burgher officers acted as constables as well as justices, (in addition to their regular military functions) indicated a form of military rule and "muddied" the streams of justice for hundreds of years after Dutch rule ended.

These arrangements for governing the settlers in the Colony under Dutch administration had nothing to do with the majority of the population—African slaves who were brought to the Colony by Dutch slave traders to be utilized as a cheap source of labor for agricultural and industrial purposes. The Dutch had first tried native Amerindian slave labor, but this practice was discouraged by the metropolitan authorities in the Netherlands who imposed conditions upon early settlers requiring them not to "ill-treat the natives of the countries they visited, and not to injure them in any way in their persons, goods, women or children."[39] The penalty for settlers who broke the rules included fines and flogging. Treaties of peace were concluded with several Amerindian tribes, which precluded their enslavement. Most importantly, as will be discussed later, Amerindians were cultivated as valuable allies in policing the interior and in controlling the African slave population. Under Roman Dutch law, which prevailed in the Colony, the African slaves were considered to be property subject to the total control of the masters who owned them. During the Dutch administration of Guyana, there were no laws for the protection of slaves, and their only protection, according to historian James Rodway, was "a natural tendency (by the Dutch) to punishments that did not seriously injure the slave as a working animal."[40] A 1772 communication from the Prussian envoy in the Netherlands to Frederick the Great expressed the view that "the Dutch settlers in Surinam, Berbice and Essequebo . . . are rightly accused of treating their slaves more barbarously than is the case with the slaves in the Antilles."[41]

Some examples of extreme brutality to slaves by their Dutch masters are revealed by Rodway. As punishment for the attempted stealing of a bag of coffee, a Negro slave named Cato was publicly flogged to the point of bleeding, was branded, had both his ears cut off, and finally was made to work in chains for the rest of his life.[42] Another slave, a house woman named Mashy, was cruelly flogged by her Dutch mistress Elizabeth deWever, who later poured melted sealing wax into the wounds of the bleeding slave.[43] The slave population was governed by violence and coercion, and the burgher militia turned a blind eye to the atrocities committed against them. Other means of governing the slave population under the Dutch administration included a skillful tactic of separating the different tribes over wide territory, and also of separating individuals from their particular tribe in order to prevent communication and effective organization among them. Efforts by the slaves to resist the oppression were handicapped by linguistic barriers between tribes. Slaves were also denied the rights of speech and association, and were not allowed to give evidence in court.[44]

The Articles of Capitulation under which the British took possession of Guyana (the colonies of Essequibo, Demerara, and Berbice) provided, inter alia, as follows:

> The Laws and Usages of the Colony shall remain in force and be respected, the mode of taxation now in use be adhered to, and the inhabitants shall enjoy the public exercise of their Religion in the same manner as before Capitulation; no new establishments shall be introduced without the consent of the Court of Policy, as the Legislature of the Colony.[45]

The Dutch system of government was maintained with minor changes. Provision was made for six financial representatives to be elected by the College of Kiezers (electors) who would have the right of voting on taxation and other fiscal matters in the Colony and would sit with the Court of Policy as a Combined Court. In this way elected planter representatives could exert control over the affairs of the Colony. By 1812 the two Courts of Policy and Justice were merged and centralized in the capital city, Georgetown. Separate law courts were set up for the administration of justice in Berbice and Essequibo. Subject to the overriding power of the Imperial Parliament, the Colonial Governor, by Royal Instructions, was given full power to make laws for the good government of the Colony, with the advice and consent of the Court of Policy, and the College of Kiezers was eventually abolished. Under the British Administration, there was a noticeable relaxation of military and arbitrary rule. The emerging prominence of the anti-slavery movement in Britain precipitated the enactment of laws for the improvement of the condition of slaves, and a Protector of Slaves was appointed in the Colony. With the coming of emancipation, the individual planter was replaced by the law courts as the source of justice or punishment.

Compared to the slavery period, the immigration period was characterized by more open avenues of political mobility. A variety of shifts in the qualification for voting after 1834, from the possession of a number of slaves to the payment of direct taxes resulted in the enfranchisement of a larger percentage of the population, especially the middle class, consisting of the Portuguese and Chinese immigrants and the Coloreds or Mixed people. Table 3.3 gives an indication of the absolute increase in the electorate between 1850 and 1892.

By the year 1928, when the old Dutch constitutional arrangements were replaced by a new British Crown Colony Constitution, several small trade unions were in existence, such as the Bakers' Association, which had been formed in 1888 by the employees of bakeries, and the Mechanics Union. However, the first one to be formally recognized, the British Guiana Labour Union, was founded in 1919.[46] Incipient political organization was progressively replaced by mass political mobilization under a governmental system that was clearly authoritarian but yet allowed some degree of political participation through the exercise of the franchise.

The first major constitutional change allowing for increased popular participation and representation came in 1891 when qualifications for voting were

Table 3.3
Increases in the Guyana Electorate between 1850 and 1892

Year	Registered Electors
1850	916
1884	1,306
1886	1,233
1888	1,418
1889	1,599
1890	1,973
1891	2,044
1892	2,375

Sources: (a) *Annual Report of British Guiana.* H.M.S.O. 1884 through 1892.
(b) Sir Cecil Clementi. 1937. *A Constitutional History of British Guiana.* London: Macmillan & Co., pp. 365–68.

reduced from ownership of property to income valued at $480 per annum. In 1909, this sum was further reduced to $300, thereby allowing more persons to participate in the electoral process. Locally born Black representatives (descendants of slaves) appeared in the legislature for the first time, and these extensions in the franchise had the effect of further increasing the voting population from 1,973 in 1890 to 4,312 by 1915.[47] This period also saw the emergence of voluntary associations such as the League of Colored Peoples (LCP); the East Indian Association (EIA); the People's Association (consisting of the descendants of African slaves, usually referred to as "Creoles"),[48] and political parties such as The Popular Party, The British Guiana Labour Party, and The Political Affairs Committee, the last two becoming the nucleus of the later People's Progressive Party.

Under the new Constitution of 1928, however, the Court of Policy and the Combined Court were abolished and instead a Legislative Council was established consisting of thirteen *nominated* official and unofficial members, fourteen elected members and the Governor, the Colonial Secretary, and Attorney General as ex officio members. Subject to His Majesty's Instructions, the Governor retained the power to make laws for the "peace order and good government of the colony" with the advice and consent of the Legislative Council.[49] An Executive Council was also established that consisted of the Governor, the Colonial Secretary, the Attorney General, seven *nominated* members, and only two elected members of the legislature. The metropolitan power had effectively wrested control of the affairs of the Colony from the electorate, first, by the removal of the financial representatives who sat in the Combined Court and had hitherto "called the tune" through the exercise of fiscal power and by reducing the number of elected members; second, by providing (under Article 59) that *only* the Governor could initiate money measures; third, by seating a majority of the government's representatives in the Legislative and Executive Councils; and finally, by retaining the Governor's usual reserve executive power.

There was further constitutional reform in 1947 in response to intense political agitation by the diverse masses for a role in the making of decisions that affected their daily existence. Many more political parties had been formed, the most prominent of which was the People's Progressive Party (PPP) headed by a young, East Indian dentist, Dr. Cheddi Jagan.[50] There was a concerted effort by the PPP and many other political parties, voluntary associations, and trade unions that existed at that time to fight for greater participation in the political system. The bulk of the leadership of the existing political parties occupied similar leadership positions in trade unions.[51] By virtue of these alliances, political gains were made despite the oppressive nature of colonial rule. Cheddi Jagan was elected to the Legislative Council in 1947. He served in that capacity as an individual until 1953.[52] The literacy test and property qualification for voters were abolished in 1953, and universal adult suffrage was introduced.

Progressive constitutional gains continued to be made. By the 1953 elections a new constitution had been introduced (the Waddington Constitution) to implement a limited cabinet ministerial system intended to concede to an elected majority governance of the internal affairs of the Colony. The PPP (with a multiracial composition of mainly East Indians and Blacks) headed by Cheddi Jagan won the 1953 election. The PPP's ideological commitment to a combination of nationalist and Marxist strategies for the improvement of the society was anathema to the political style of the British colonial rulers. In short order British troops were making their way across the Atlantic to Georgetown. The Constitution was suspended and the PPP government Ministers were evicted from office exactly 133 days after being installed. The British Government issued a statement that said, inter alia, that

> Her Majesty's Government has decided that the Constitution of British Guiana must be suspended to prevent Communist subversion of the Government and a dangerous crisis both in public order and in economic affairs. . . . The faction in power have shown by their acts and their speeches that they are prepared to go to any lengths, including violence, to turn British Guiana into a Communist State. The Governor has therefore been given emergency powers and has removed the portfolios of the Party Ministers. Armed forces have landed to support the police and to prevent any public disorder which might be fomented by Communist supporters.[53]

Race relations in the colony took a downward dive when the PPP split along racial lines in 1955, and political rivalry between the leader, Dr. Cheddi Jagan, and his deputy, Forbes L. F. S. Burnham, an eloquent attorney (who was Black) escalated. Burnham formed the People's National Congress (PNC), the membership of which was mainly Black, and Jagan's PPP consisted mainly of East Indians. The British preferred the more moderate Burnham and, together with the United

States, used every means at their disposal to prevent the spread of communism in the region in general and the Colony in particular.

Nevertheless, in 1961 British Guiana achieved full internal self-government, and the PPP under the leadership of Dr. Cheddi Jagan, gained a majority in the Legislative Assembly. In 1962, a general strike erupted into violent riots, and British troops were called in to restore order in February, 1962, and again in 1963. In 1963, the general disorder in the society, which Jagan claims was engineered by Burnham, the British, and the United States's CIA in order to remove him from office, took on racial overtones and resulted in the worst race riots in the nation's history. Elections were held in late 1964 following constitutional conferences between Guyana and England in 1962 and 1963. The system of proportional representation was substituted for the "first-past-the-post" system by which parliamentary seats had been allocated.[54] When national elections were held in 1964, although the PPP received the most votes, they failed to gain a majority of seats in parliament. With the blessings of the British government, Forbes Burnham formed a coalition government with the United Force (a party consisting mainly of Portuguese and Colored elites). In 1965 the British Guiana Independence Conference met in London and a new, Independence Constitution was approved.

On May 26, 1966, Guyana was declared an independent nation and became a sovereign democratic state within the Commonwealth. Under the Independence Constitution, a Governor General was appointed by the Queen of England. In 1970, the final tie with Britain was severed when Guyana became a Republic and substituted a President to be elected by the National Assembly to replace the office of Governor General. Since 1966, Forbes Burnham's PNC won all the elections held in the country under questionable electoral practices, and the party remained in office, until international pressure was brought to bear on the government for "free and fair elections." The Carter Center monitored free elections in 1992 and Dr. Cheddi Jagan's PPP was returned to power by winning a majority of seats at the polls. The PPP has remained in political control of the country, having been victorious at all subsequent elections held to date.

CONCLUSION

Throughout the colonial era Guyana was plagued with public disorder, slave rebellions, strikes (mainly in the agricultural but also in the industrial sectors), civil strife, race riots, and political violence, all of which were the result of the social, political, and constitutional arrangements dictated by the plantation system. Having attracted European attention primarily because of its promise for plunder and profits, Guyana's social and political history is the history of a protracted struggle by transplanted populations mainly from Africa and Asia, and their descendants, for freedom from the oppression of the colonial condition.

The peculiar governmental arrangements established by the early Dutch settlers and planters, followed by the British, was to have a profound and lasting impact on the development of law and the administration of justice in the Colony. It was the denial of representation of the majority of the population in the closed system of government, even after emancipation (by franchise requirements of property, income, and literacy that could not be met) that fostered the political violence and civil strife that lasted throughout the colonial era. By the time adult suffrage was achieved in 1953, other forces were at work to keep the masses in disarray, as the British insisted on charting the future of the Colony that it would soon relinquish.

The seeds of the most painful divisions were sown early in the colonial era by the racially graded system of social subordination that was measured by degree of "Whiteness." The subjugation of the Africans under the slave system was enforced by brutality and coercion, as well as by ascriptive values and customs. Africans were considered to be inherently inferior and were relegated to the lowest strata of society. The East Indians, although coming to the country under the same conditions as the other immigrants of light complexion (Portuguese and Chinese), were relegated to the similar social status as the ex-slaves and were always treated as second class subjects.

Colonial Guyana was also a stratified society on the basis of the convergence of race and class. After emancipation, the plantation system ensured that the darker races, Africans and East Indians, remained at the bottom of the socio-economic ladder. Having settled mainly on or near the plantations, the East Indians were kept at a mere survival level by meager wages and onerous conditions of service, whereas the Africans were pressured by the colonial government, in collusion with the planters, to return to estate labor by measures such as high taxation for their lands and the denial of credit and licenses. At the same time, the Portuguese and Chinese were vigorously assisted in establishing themselves in business and commerce in the towns to which they had migrated from the estates. The majority of the population was therefore kept at the level of serfdom and became the forces of the public disorder that characterized these years. The interplay of all these factors produced the particular brand of policing that emerged in the Colony.

NOTES

1. *World Statistics in Brief.* 1995. Series V, No. 16. World Statistics Pocketbook. New York: United Nations Department for Economic and Social Information and Policy Analysis, p. 77.

2. Leo A. Despres. 1967. *Cultural Pluralism and Nationalist Politics in British Guiana.* Chicago: Rand McNally & Co., p. 3.

3. See Allan Young. 1958. *The Approaches to Local Self-Government in British Guiana.* London: Longman, Green and Co., pp. 9–23. Whereas in 1829, there were 100,000 slaves in the Colony, more than half of whom lived and worked on the sugar, coffee, and cotton plantations, by 1848 only 19,939 of them were to be found on the estates. See Despres, *Cultural Pluralism and Nationalist Politics in British Guiana,* pp. 45–47.

4. Brian Moore. 1987. *Race, Power and Social Segmentation in Colonial Society: Guyana After Slavery 1838–1891.* Philadelphia, Pa.: Gordon and Breach Science Publishers, Ltd., p. 35.

5. See Leo Despres, *Cultural Pluralism and Nationalist Politics in British Guiana,* pp. 59, 60.

6. The Government of India issued an Order under the Defence of India Act on March 12, 1917, ending Indian immigration. See M. Shahabuddeen. 1978. *Constitutional Development in Guyana: 1621–1978.* Georgetown, Guyana: Guyana Printers Ltd., p. 634.

7. See M. G. Smith. 1965. *The Plural Society in the British West Indies.* Berkeley: University of California Press; and Leo Despres, *Cultural Pluralism and Nationalist Politics in British Guiana.*

8. Moore, *Race, Power and Social Segmentation in Colonial Society*, p. 52.

9. Despres, *Cultural Pluralism and Nationalist Politics in British Guiana*, p. 63.

10. See Shahabuddeen, *Constitutional Development in Guyana: 1621–1978,* p. 592.

11. See Elsa Gouveia. 1971. "Change and Stability in a West Indian Slave Society." In *Readings in Government and Politics of the West Indies*, edited by Trevor Munroe and Rupert Lewis. Jamaica: Department of Government, University of the West Indies, pp. 21–29 (p. 21). See also R. T. Smith. 1988. *Kinship and Class in the West Indies.* Cambridge, Great Britain: University of Cambridge, pp. 82–109.

12. Arthur Stinchcombe. 1994. "Freedom and Oppression of Slaves in the Eighteenth-Century Caribbean." *American Sociological Review* 59:911–29.

13. G. W. Roberts. 1948. "Some Observations on the Population of British Guiana." *Population Studies* 2:185–218.

14. Arthur Stinchcombe, "Freedom and Oppression of Slaves in the Eighteenth-Century Caribbean," p. 923.

15. Elsa Gouveia, "Change and Stability in a West Indian Slave Society," p. 23.

16. M. Shahabuddeen, *Constitutional Development in Guyana: 1621–1978*, p. 593.

17. Shahabuddeen, *Constitutional Development in Guyana: 1621–1978*, p. 592.

18. Ibid., p. 594.

19. Moore, *Race, Power and Social Segmentation in Colonial Society*, p. 210.

20. This would mean the 32 cents and 48 cents per day for field and factory laborers that was paid during the apprenticeship period, which was introduced after the abolition of slavery in 1834 and lasted for four years.

21. Allan Young. 1958. *Approaches to Local Self-Government in British Guiana.* London: Longman, Green and Co., p. 16.

22. Walter Rodney. 1981. *A History of the Guyanese Working People, 1881–1905.* Maryland: John Hopkins University Press, pp. 65–69.

23. Ibid., pp. 90–102.

24. Shahabuddeen, *Constitutional Development in Guyana: 1621–1978*, p. 624.

25. Chandra Jayawardena. 1971. "East Indians and the Plantation System in Guyana." In *Readings in Government and Politics of the West Indies,* edited by Trevor Munroe and Ruper Lewis. Jamaica: Department of Government, University of the West Indies, pp. 31–33 (p. 31).

26. Ordinance No. 4 of 1864 and as amended.

27. Jayawardena, "East Indians and the Plantation System in Guyana," p. 33; and also Shahabuddeen, *Constitutional Development in Guyana: 1621–1978,* p. 629.

28. Shahabuddeen, *Constitutional Development in Guyana: 1621–1978*, p. 629.

29. Alvin O. Thompson. 1977. *Colonialism and Underdevelopment in Guyana, 1580–1803.* Bridgetown, Barbados: Carib Research and Publications, Inc., pp. 41–68 (p. 52).

30. See Shahabuddeen, *Constitutional Development in Guyana:1621–1978*, p. 21.

31. The Guyana Independence Act was passed on May 12, 1966.

32. See Despres, *Cultural Pluralism and Nationalist Politics in British Guiana,* p. 31, and M. Shahabuddeen, *Constitutional Development in Guyana 1621–1978*, pp. 22, 23.

33. See Rodney, *A History of the Guyanese Working People, 1881–1905*, p. 2.

34. M. Shahabuddeen, *Constitutional Development in Guyana: 1621–1978*, p. 21.

35. Ibid., p. 24.

36. See Sir Cecil Clementi. 1937. *A Constitutional History of British Guiana.* London: Macmillan and Company, p. 22.

37. Shahabuddeen, *Constitutional Development in Guyana: 1621–1978*, p. 28.

38. Ibid., p. 28.

39. Ibid., pp. 573, 574.

40. James A. Rodway. 1891. *A History of British Guiana from the Year 1668 to the Present Time.* (3 vols.). Vol. I, Georgetown, Guyana: J. Thompson, p. 166.

41. M. Shahabuddeen, *Constitutional Development in Guyana: 1621–1978*, pp. 600–01.

42. Rodway. 1891. *A History of British Guiana from the Year 1668 to the Present Time.* Vol. II, p. 22.

43. Ibid., p. 22.

44. Ibid., Vol. I, p. 225.

45. Clementi, *A Constitutional History of British Guiana*, pp. 411–23.

46. Rodney, *A History of the Guyanese Working People, 1881–1905*, p. 163; and Ashton Chase. 1964. *A History of Trade Unionism in Guyana: 1900–1961*. Georgetown, Guyana: New Guyana Company Ltd., pp. 48–50.

47. *Annual Report of British Guiana.* H.M.S.O. 1892, 1894; also R. T. Smith. 1964. "Ethnic Difference and Peasant Economy in British Guiana," in *Capital, Saving and Credit in Peasant Societies*, edited by Raymond Firth and B. S. Yamey. London: Allen & Unwin, 1964.

48. These associations were concerned primarily with advancing the interests of their members. See Ralph R. Premdas. 1975. "The Rise of the First Mass-Based Multi-Racial Party in Guyana." *Caribbean Quarterly* 20:5–20 at 6; also Rodney, *A History of the Guyanese Working People, 1881–1905*, pp. 175, 176.

49. See Shahabuddeen, *Constitutional Development in Guyana: 1621–1978*, pp. 457, 458.

50. Cheddi Jagan. 1972. *The West on Trial.* Berlin: Seven Seas Publishers, p. 98.

51. See Ralph R. Premdas. 1972. "Voluntary Associations and Political Parties in a Racially Fragmented State: The Case of Guyana." University of Guyana: Occasional Papers. No. 2, Feb. 1972, p. 5.

52. Jagan, *The West on Trial*, pp. 68, 69.

53. Ibid., p. 125.

54. For a discussion of the effect of the substitution of the proportional representation for the first-past-the-post system, see Edward Green. 1971. "The 1968 General Elections in Guyana and the Introduction of Proportional Representation." In *Readings in Government and Politics of the West Indies*, edited by Trevor Munroe and Rupert Lewis. Mona, Jamaica: University of the West Indies, pp. 134–36.

4

The Evolution of Policing in Colonial Guyana

Throughout their writings, the social philosophers Marx and Engels always stressed the importance of history—that continuous process of social movement and social change that holds the key to our existence. For them, there could be "no adequate explanation of any question facing man unless that question is viewed *historically*."[1] The utility of the historical approach has long been recognized in police studies,[2] and will be applied here in order to arrive at an understanding of how policing in Guyana, and in particular the propensity for police violence, was shaped historically by the social and political forces that influenced it.

The model of organized policing that was eventually implemented in colonial Guyana differed greatly from that of the home country of the European colonists who established permanent settlements in the territory.[3] As was the case of many other countries in the British colonial empire,[4] policing evolved out of the need for population control as the colonists pursued their solitary aim of speculative profiteering in a slave society. The distinctions between British policing style and policing in colonial Guyana, however, predate the establishment of organized police forces and can be traced to the earliest attempts at maintaining social control under the slave system.

Policing was initially developed in England in accordance with the Anglo-Saxon custom whereby citizens were mutually responsible for keeping the peace and upholding the law. This responsibility was usually assumed by the adult males in each community. During the Middle Ages (1066–1485), local noblemen appointed "Constables" to maintain law and order and arrest criminals, and the Statute of Winchester (1285) further provided for the appointment of "watch and ward" officers to guard the towns between sunset and daybreak. The constables retained sole control of law enforcement functions until the founding of the Marine Police Establishment in 1798. Despite agitation for a professional police force from the economically powerful middle class, it took decades before Sir Robert Peel (the Home Secretary) was able to successfully achieve police reform through the enactment by Parliament of the Metropolitan Police Act in 1829. By virtue of this Act, the old constabulary system was abolished and the London Metropolitan Police became the first organized professional police force in Britain.

A distinctive feature of policing under the constabulary system that existed before reform was the fact that the police services were staffed by persons who were very similar in socio-economic status to those they policed—the ordinary, poor folk of "low" status—who were often as corrupt as those they were charged with policing.[5] The constables were largely ineffective in controlling the escalation of property crime (mainly theft)[6] that accompanied the transition from feudalism to capitalism, when thousands were thrown out of work by the introduction of machinery to replace manual labor. Fear of public disorder was precipitated by the swelling ranks of the unemployed, and workers' protests at the introduction of machinery, but, as Gurr points out, there was little evidence of civil strife in London itself by the time the model designed by Sir Robert Peel was endorsed by the British Parliament (1829).[7] There is no doubt, however, that the rising merchant and middle classes wanted more efficient and reliable protection for their persons and property,[8] yet they were especially concerned that a centralized police force would interfere with their liberties and become an instrument of internal surveillance and repression as it had in the case of the heavily armed and militarized Gendarmerie of France (French police). The highly intimidatory posture of the Paris police, where according to Alan Williams, 1 in every 10 policemen worked in "investigation and intelligence,"[9] alarmed the English public. The weight of evidence suggests that despite the ever present threat of civil disorder in the pre-capitalist period, the institutionalization of policing in England under the model designed by Sir Robert Peel was primarily a means of achieving efficient and effective law enforcement, the protection of property, the prevention of crime, and the punishment of offenders.[10]

That the opposition to the reform movement toward the establishment of a professional police force was premised on concern for civil liberties and the rule of law is revealed in the report of the *Royal Commission on the Police Command (1728)* cited by Skolnick.[11] There, in answer to the expressed fear of the British upper classes that the establishment of a professional police force would result in tyranny, the Commission reassured the public that the police would be governed by the rule of law and would be answerable to a democratically elected Parliament.[12] Many assurances had to be given before police reform was able to succeed in 1829.

The circumstances surrounding the development of policing in colonial Guyana stand in sharp contrast to the factors outlined above. Even after the emancipation of slaves, and the establishment of a formal police force, there was never any attempt to make those responsible for policing accountable for their actions. In fact, the type of police repression feared at "home" (in Britain) was actively promoted in the Colony. The evolution of policing in colonial Guyana will be discussed under two broad historical periods, namely (a) the Slavery period, 1613 to 1834 when the Abolition Act, 1833, came into effect, and (b) the Post-slavery/ Colonial era, 1834 to 1966, when the freed slaves and a variety of immigrants were allowed varying degrees of participation in the governance of the Colony until independence was achieved.

THE SLAVERY ERA—POLICING THE POWERLESS

During the period of Dutch rule (which began around 1613, when the first settlements were established, and lasted until 1803, when the Colony was captured by the British), there were, in effect, two systems of policing in Guyana—one for the "free" settlers and one for the slaves on the plantations. Slave labor was used for all the agricultural and factory work on the plantations in order to cultivate and prepare mainly sugar, coffee, and cotton for export. Slaves were considered to be "property," and the master could do what he liked with them, except that a fine was imposed if it could be established that a slave died as a result of punishment he had received.[13] On the subject of the relationship between the Dutch planters and the African slaves in this regard, James Rodway had this to say:

> Their [the slaves'] evidence against a white man was not valid; an attempt to strike one of the favoured race was punished by death, and the masters and overseers not only had the power to inflict corporeal punishment, but if they killed a negro were only subject to a fine.[14]

It appears that there was no formal police organization in the Colony during the Dutch administration in the sense of a permanent agency involved primarily in the traditional law enforcement functions. Instead, under a burgher militia system fashioned after that in Holland, every able-bodied citizen (White settlers who had taken the oath of allegiance and paid five guilders) in the Colony was required to bear arms to defend the Colony in times of war and to restore public order in case of internal civil strife. The law required the burghers to take up arms whenever called upon to do so by their Governor.[15]

The Colony (which then consisted of the separate settlements of Demerara, Essequibo, and Berbice [united in 1831]) was divided into districts, and there was a separate burgher company for each district. Each company was commanded by a captain, a lieutenant, and an ensign. These officers were nominated by the Commandeur and his Council and "performed the duties of justices of the peace as well as those of constables."[16] It means therefore that in addition to being responsible for the nomination of planter representatives to the Councils of Policy and Justice (when constituted as the College of Kiezers [electors]), the burgher officers also sat as a court martial for the trial of offenses, and even, as was the case in Demerara, constituted, along with the Commandeur of Demerara sitting as President, the first Council (Court) of Justice for Demerara.[17] Provisions existed whereby the senior burgher captain could preside over the Council in the absence of the Commandeur. The Demerara Council of Justice had jurisdiction over all civil matters involving claims amounting to 150 guilders or less, subject to the right of appeal to the Essequibo Council of Justice.[18]

It would seem therefore that under the Dutch system of administration, the military, to wit, the burgher officers, penetrated society at every available level (policy, justice, defense, and law enforcement). In the free society, the burgher officers could therefore apprehend persons who violated the criminal law, then either nominate representatives of the planters to sit in the Council (Court) of Justice, or sit directly in the Court (as they did in the case of the Demerara Council of Justice) and thereby participate in the adjudication of guilt or innocence. Also, as members of the Council of Justice, and as justices of the peace in their own right, the burgher officers could adjudicate in civil matters as well. By virtue of a 1774 resolution of the States-General of Holland, the Councils of Justice were to be guided in their judgments by the laws of Holland and the Criminal Ordinance and Manner of Proceeding of Philip II of 1570.

This system of the administration of justice applied in theory to all persons in the Colony, but the evidence suggests that, in practice, slaves were confined to the plantations and were under the sole control of their masters and "as long as he (the master) did not kill them, it was no business of the Fiscals (prosecutors)."[19] The cases of the extra-judicial punishments awarded to the slaves Cato and Mashy by their masters[20] seem to further support the conclusion that masters dispensed summary justice to slaves who committed petty crime. However, Netscher[21] as well as Shahabuddeen[22] mention the existence of courts where slaves were tried for capital offenses, such as rebellion.

Under British administration in the Colony, a Police Board was established in 1812 for the towns of Georgetown and New Amsterdam, but it appears that persons employed by this Board were few in number and were responsible for performing the duties of watchmen, jail keepers, order maintenance in court, and the service of judicial process.[23] Regular policing was still conducted by the militia and on June 5, 1817, Militia Regulations were enacted by the Court of Policy providing for the establishment of three battalions in Demerara and two in Essequibo. Included in the Demerara battalions were "two companies of artillery . . . a troop of cavalry and a rifle company; to consist of such numbers and to be under such particular arrangements as the Governor may, from time to time, think proper."[24] Under Article IV of the Militia Regulations, all White and free Colored male inhabitants between the ages of 16 and 50 and capable of bearing arms were required to serve in the militia. As distinct from the situation under Dutch rule, however, the members of the Courts of Policy and Justice as well as the fiscals (prosecutors) were exempted from service in the militia until they had vacated their official positions. Article XIX of the Militia Regulations required members to turn out in case of "fire, *revolts on plantations,* or other disturbances," (italics mine) upon pain of punishment for those who dared to disobey their military superiors.

In addition, a special system of policing for the slaves in the Colony, which consisted of "slave patrols," was developed by the plantation owners and managers, who had absolute control over the conduct of their slaves. Slave patrols arose out of the need firstly, to protect the continuity of the labor supply that was constantly being threatened by the practice of slaves regularly escaping into the interior, where they would set up their own "bush settlements." In Guyana, ill-treated slaves regularly deserted via the Orinoco River into neighboring Venezuela, thereby necessitating an Extradition Treaty between Spain and the Netherlands in 1791. Many additional abscondments took place when slaves were sent into the bush to cut "troolies" for the construction of houses, and there was great need for a surveillance system, operated by persons familiar with the terrain, to find and capture runaways.

Second, an effective repressive machinery was needed because the slaves in Guyana never ceased in their efforts to gain freedom. Apart from suicide, rebellions and insurrections were common throughout the Slavery period. Slaves outnumbered their masters by more than ten to one and in some extreme cases, about fifty to one.[25] Despite efforts by the planters to prevent effective communication and organization among the slaves, and the work of White missionaries in fostering "subordination, industry, and happiness," there was constant fear that the slaves would revolt. Some of the African slaves were literate in Arabic and had occupied leadership positions in their social hierarchy at home.[26] Others had either been taught by the missionaries or had taught themselves to read English, and were aware of the anti-slavery movement in Britain.[27] Their abhorrence for the frequent whippings that constituted the main method of social control was illustrated by their willingness to risk their lives in trying to escape, knowing fully well that the punishment for desertion or rebellion was death.

Slave patrols were charged with finding and capturing runaway slaves and bringing them back dead or alive usually for a monetary reward of a few hundred guilders (a handsome sum at that time). In addition, the patrols were allowed to keep everything taken from the rebels or runways as "prize money." The slave patrols were encouraged to resort to deadly violence in order to capture runaways. If the slaves could not be brought back alive, the patrol would nevertheless be rewarded for proof that they were disabled or murdered, for which the display of the "severed right hand," or "black arm" of the slave was sufficient proof. Rodway cites many instances of slave patrols being charged by the Dutch with the capture of runaways where the reward was stated to be "400 guilders offered for every bush negro captured alive and half the amount for a severed right hand."[28] One infamous slave-patrolling expedition in 1795 was able to produce as many as 70 "black arms" upon its return.[29]

The problem of runaways also gained the attention of the Court of Policy, and in 1795 "orders" were issued requiring that all slaves found wandering about without passes were to be arrested and flogged. The free Colored people were ordered in June of 1795 to register themselves within 24 hours so that they could be employed in expeditions against the "bush Negroes." There is also evidence of the formation of a Negro corps by the government in 1796. Despite the disapproval of some planters, the "South American Rangers," were required, with the promise of freedom for good conduct, to assist the troops in expeditions against settlements of "bush Negroes." [30] In 1811 a proclamation was issued placing restrictions on the assembling of slaves at night. Regulations were made requiring planters to maintain a minimum number of Whites in relation to the number of slaves. An Essequibo Ordinance of 1784 required that a ratio of one White to every fifty slaves should be maintained. Despite some resistance from the Berbice Court of Criminal Justice, free Colored persons were regarded as Whites for the purpose of fulfilling these requirements in practice, until they were officially put upon an equal footing with Whites by a proclamation issued by the Governor in 1822. The violence that was routinely committed by the slave patrols was encouraged and condoned by the Colonial authorities, as concern mounted over the frequency of slave revolts and the intractable problem of the "bush Negroes."

The Dutch were careful to cultivate the native Amerindians, who knew the terrain well, as useful allies in the struggle to capture runaways and to crush slave revolts. They were richly rewarded with money and presents for their services. [31] The free Coloreds on the plantations, some of whom even owned their own slaves, were also effective allies of the British in their efforts to maintain control over the slaves. According to Raymond Smith, "in practice, the Whites depended upon them a great deal."[32] Not only did they enable the proprietors to satisfy the security requirements relating to the ratio of Whites to slaves on the estates, by being counted as Whites, but they also were useful against the slaves because they identified with the masters, and greatly valued the special positions they were allowed to occupy both by law and practice. In a petition to the Governor dated April 2, 1822, reaffirming their loyalty to the colonial administration, the Colored petitioners stated, in part:

> that your petitioners humbly beg leave to refer Your Excellency and the Hounourable the Council of Government of Berbice to the history of this colony and particularly to the dreadly revolt of 1763 in which Your Excellency and the Honourable the Council of Government will not discover among the discontented and rebellious one of the coloured, but, on the contrary, will find several of them employed in situations of trust and discharging them with fidelity.[33]

In addition to serving in "expeditions" to catch runaways, the free Colored people were allowed to take up commissions in the militia from around 1822.[34] The militia was primarily relied upon to crush slave revolts on the estates, assisted by the regular slave patrols consisting mainly of Amerindians and sometimes contingents of British troops from neighboring territories who were called in to deal with the more serious cases. The militia regularly received commendation from the authorities for their "efficiency" in executing summary justice on the rebels. After the initial uprising, the slaves usually fled the estates and the Amerindians would lead the militia "to one Negro camp after another" where the men would be surrounded and shot, their "black arms" being saved for the purpose of collecting the rewards that were offered usually by the Court of Policy and Justice.[35] Sometimes heads of the rebels killed would be cut off and stuck on staves along the river for the others to see. Women and children were usually taken prisoner. Rebel slaves who surrendered or were taken alive, especially ringleaders, were tried for their offenses in the Court of Justice and were usually burnt by slow fire, broken on the wheel, or hanged.[36]

The nature of "policing" done by the slave patrols and the militia reflected the seriousness of the settlers in keeping the slave population in its place, and in many instances went far beyond what was required to restore order in the Colony. Fourteen instances of slave uprisings were recorded by Pairadeau Mars from available historical sources of the Slavery period, eleven (78.5%) of which he classified as being serious enough to amount to rebellions.[37] In the case of the two main rebellions, one in 1763 in Berbice, when slaves resisted the authorities for a sustained period of about eleven months,[38] and the Demerara rebellion in 1823, extreme force was used to exterminate the rebels. The reason for the Berbice rebellion is best explained by a letter sent to the Dutch Governor by Cuffy, leader of the rebels, on 3rd April, 1763, where he declared

> that the Negroes sought no war but only broke into rebellion owing to the bad treatment of some of the masters: that they were prepared to give half the colony to the whites, if they would leave them the other half, but that in no case would they be slaves again.[39]

Of course, no such agreement was entertained and instead all the law enforcement forces of the Colony were mobilized to crush the rebels. A price was put on Cuffy's head as well as those of the other ringleaders, and money was allocated to reward patrol and militia men who captured, injured, or killed the estimated 2,000 rebels who had fled into the interior. Those who were brought in alive or who had surrendered were tried in the Court of Justice and many received the death penalty. The most painful method of death, believed to be burning by slow fire, was reserved for the leaders of the rebels, who according to the record, were tortured for several hours and endured their suffering with "courage" and "dignity."[40]

In the case of the Demerara rebellion of 1823, the slaves were allegedly reacting to rumors that emancipation had been granted to them by the British government in England, but the local planters were withholding their rights from them.[41] The slaves only used violence when threatened with resistance from the Whites with firearms. Several Whites were merely "put in stocks" to facilitate the escape of the slaves and were not harmed. However, martial law was quickly declared, and hundreds of slaves were shot. Mass executions and the display of dead bodies in chains, and heads mounted on spikes ended the gory affair. The militia had their allowances doubled during the period of martial law as a reward for their unflinching efforts to crush the slaves.[42]

The development of policing in the Colony during the Dutch and British occupations under the Slavery system reflected the violence of the social order, and shares many similarities with the way policing developed in the United States of America, especially in the southern states. Both Samuel Walker and P. L. Reichel traced the first attempt at American-style policing back to the infamous "slave patrols" legislated into existence by colonial state governments in the South during the first half of the 18th century to maintain order among the slaves and to deal with the problem of runaways.[43] The preamble to the 1757 Georgia law setting up police patrols states:

> [I]t is absolutely necessary for the Security of his Majesty's Subjects in this Province, that Patrols should be established under proper Regulations in the settled parts thereof, for the better keeping of Negroes and other Slaves in Order and the prevention of any Cabals, Insurrections or other Irregularities amongst them.[44]

Similar laws existed in all the Southern (Slave) States where it was felt that the threat of rebellion and violence against the minority White proprietors necessitated something more than the capricious militia system that existed for maintenance of public order. In Georgia, these patrols were made up of all free White males (between the ages of 16 and 60) and had full power to break open Negro dwellings in search of arms and ammunition and to inflict corporal or other punishment on any slave who was suspected of being a runaway, or who was disrespectful to the patrolmen.[45] Patrolmen were required to bring slaves who had committed criminal offenses before the magistrates' courts.[46]

The policing of the powerless in slave society was intended to fulfill the dual purpose of protecting the safety of the planters, and ensuring an uninterrupted labor supply on the plantations. In so doing, arrangements for the policing of the colony reflected the violence and brutality of the system that created it, and the emancipation of the slaves brought many changes in form, but few in substance.

THE POST-SLAVERY/COLONIAL ERA—POLITICAL POLICING

The Need for Population Control

The Ex-slaves

The transition from slavery to freedom for the African slaves in British Guiana did not come immediately upon the passing of the Abolition of Slavery Act of 1833. Instead, the Act provided for a compulsory apprenticeship period of either four or six years for nonpraedial and praedial laborers, respectively. By becoming apprenticed laborers, slaves, though free, were still bound to provide labor for the plantations. Their erstwhile masters became their employers and were given time to prepare for the inevitable attrition that would follow complete freedom. Equally important, however, was the need for a complete reorganization of the legal, social, and political framework of government to accommodate the inclusion of tens of thousands of people into the free society. When the African slaves were eventually freed with the termination of the apprenticeship system on August 1, 1838, there were more than 100,000 slaves in the colony.[47] Between 1838 and 1928 an additional 340,972 immigrants had been added to the population in order to fulfill the labor requirements of the plantation economy. In contrast, there were only a few thousand Europeans. According to the 1911 population census, they numbered only 3,937 at that time. In fact, the Europeans, who were in control of the political and economic sectors of government, were always in the minuscule minority.

The first order of business for the colonial government was to take steps to ensure the tranquility of the Colony while maintaining production on the estates. The judicial system had been designed to service only the relatively small, free population and had to be expanded to include the ex-slaves, who even during the apprenticeship period were subjected to the "informal" justice dispensed by estate managers and overseers. For example, a six-month report for the period July to December 1833 by the two Protectors of Slaves in the Colony indicated that despite their presence, about half of the entire male slave population in the Colony were still being flogged each year.[48]

The colonial government was faced with the task of assuming rightful control of the judicial system that the planter class had appropriated to itself. Slaves had now become apprenticed laborers who had to be *paid* as well as housed, clothed, and fed in return for their services. Mechanisms had to be put into place to resolve disputes between the masters–employers and the apprenticed laborers. A few months before the Abolition of Slavery Act came into force a system of appointing Justices of the Peace to dispense summary justice and administer punishment to the slaves had been implemented, but its effectiveness was doubtful since most of the appointees were either planters or attorneys. These Justices of the Peace performed the function of adjudicating in disputes between masters and the apprenticed laborers until 1835, when they were replaced by stipendiary magistrates.[49]

The failure of the colonial government to speedily put in place a fair system for the interpretation and enforcement of the conditions of apprenticeship that was mandated by the Abolition of Slavery Act resulted in much ambiguity, mistrust, and resistance by the laborers. Monica Schuler identifies issues of the exploitation of child labor, the length of the workday, and the differential treatment afforded to praedial and nonpraedial laborers, with regard to the length of the period of apprenticeship, as being the causes of the conflict that existed between masters and apprentices during the apprenticeship period.[50] The laborers frequently peacefully protested what they considered to be the injustices meeted out to them under the apprenticeship system, but the response from the government was often extreme.

The Justices of the Peace and later the stipendiary magistrates who were openly partial to the planters, interpreted the withdrawal of labor, and the agitation of the laborers usually for a shorter workday as an affront to lawful authority, and a threat to the social order. Martial law was often imposed and the protestors given a variety of punishments. In one recorded case, the leaders of nonviolent protest were indicted in the Supreme Court in the capital city of Georgetown for the crimes of sedition and riotous assembly. One protestor received the death penalty and was hanged, 4 were sentenced to transportation, and 32 to be flogged.[51] Both the Law Officers of the Crown and the Secretary of State reviewed and supported the severity of the punishments. The current Governor, Sir James Carmichael Smyth, forever remembered for his humanity and strong sense of justice abhorred the use of corporal punishment and incurred the wrath of the planter class when he granted mercy to the 32 to be flogged. He was accused of "encouraging the insubordination of the Negroes."[52]

After the termination of apprenticeship in 1838, the planter class pressured the colonial government through its control of the Colony's purse strings by its elected majority in the Combined Court, to use whatever coercive measures were necessary to force the ex-slaves to remain on the estates in order to alleviate the labor crisis that abolition had caused. The ex-slaves' apparent resolve to fight what they considered to be unjust practices and to demand fair wages was seen as a threat to the stability of the Colony, and the authorities placed great emphasis on force and repression as a means of social control.

The Indentured Immigrants

The situation with regard to the indentured immigrants was very similar to that of the ex-slaves. Found to be the most suitable for estate labor, the large contingent of East Indian immigrants who were imported into the Colony to replace the slaves (approximately 238,960 arrived between 1838 and 1917, and more than two-thirds remained) found themselves to be practically marooned on the estates by a variety of measures implemented by the colonial government. Their ascription to the soil and complete deliverance into the power of the estate managers was achieved by the provisions of the Consolidated Immigration Ordinance (No. 4 of 1864 as amended). Under this law, criminal sanctions were imposed for failure to perform work in a satisfactory manner and for absence from work without permission, which was defined as "desertion" if the period of absence exceeded one week. A pass system was implemented and immigrants who wandered away from the estates without permission from the manager could be arrested and prosecuted under the vagrancy laws. These offenses were punishable by hard labor, a fine, and/or imprisonment, and where a term of imprisonment was imposed it was added to the immigrant's period of indenture.

Criminal sanctions were used to enforce civil obligations under contracts of service. Added to this was the fact that until the situation was corrected by an amendment to the Immigration Ordinance in 1873, criminal defendants were not competent to testify on their own behalf,[53] and therefore the immigrants who were charged for labor offenses were convicted on the sole evidence of their employers. But even when the East Indian was allowed to give evidence, little importance was attached to it. They were frequently prosecuted for failing to work and invariably unable to discharge the burden imposed under the Immigration Ordinance (Section 3, Ordinance No. 9 of 1868), of proving reasonable cause therefor. Work, for the indentured laborer, was divided by law into "tasks" that often required superior qualities of physical endurance for fulfillment, and when the average immigrant failed to fulfill his tasks, he would be prosecuted under the labor laws. According to Raymond Smith, in 1875, complaints laid before the courts under the Immigration Ordinance amounted to 30.22 percent of the total number of indentured servants.[54]

The powerlessness of this large body of immigrants who were regularly overtasked and underpaid, was keenly felt even by some of those appointed by the colonial government to administer justice. Joseph Beaumont, who served as Chief Justice in the Colony during this period, had this to say of the general labor laws and the Immigration Ordinance of 1864, in particular:

> The Ordinary law of master and servant in Demerara is severe enough in all conscience, and unequal enough as between master and servant (to say nothing of the unequal mode of its administration) to satisfy the most exact demands of the former. It is, however, a liberal and just code as compared with what are specifically known as the "labour laws," i.e., the compulsory and penal provisions of the law for enforcing the immigrants to labour.[55]

The Immigration Agent General who was charged with the protection of the rights of the immigrants and their representation in the courts was largely ineffective in the face of sustained opposition both from the planters and the Governor. In addition, there are reports of immigrants who tried to complain to the Immigration Agent General being arrested on the way and jailed for desertion.[56] One major grievance of the immigrant laborers was that "the magistrates without exception were said to be entirely under the thumbs of the planters, so that it was impossible for coolies to obtain justice."[57]

The Effect of Civil Unrest

The use of the legal machinery as an instrument of exploitation and repression of the "coolies" and the free laborers resulted in numerous labor disturbances, stoppages of work, and strikes on the sugar estates, which were usually treated as riots or uprisings. Labor disturbances often involved the intervention of government troops, and at times the governor also had to personally intervene to pacify rebellious estate laborers. In 1869, for example, at both Plantation La Jalousie and Plantation Leonora in Demerara, labor disturbances provoked the intervention not only of the military troops and the governor, but also the Immigration Agent General and the Attorney General, after which the ringleaders were arrested and later imprisoned.[58]

Meanwhile there was also civil unrest in the towns and villages where the two main sections of the population, Blacks and East Indians, resided respectively. There was much poverty, unemployment, and crime in the towns, especially Georgetown. In the villages there was great opposition to the payment of property

Table 4.1
Civil Disturbances during the Post-slavery/Colonial Period: 1834–1970

Period	Protest/ Demonstration	Major Strike/ Riot	Rebellion/ Revolution	Total
1833–92	4	16	1	21
1893–1946	7	18	—	25
1947–70	83	62	1	146
Total *n*	94	96	2	192
Percent	49.0	50.0	1.0	100

Source: Compiled from data presented in Pairadeau Mars. *Political Modernization and Stability in A Developing State: The Guyana Example.* Unpublished Ph.D. thesis, Carleton University, Ontario, June 1975, pp. 133, 139, 156.

taxes, which were felt to be unjust. Court Marshals and police who came to the villages to execute levies were met with resistance. The immigration question was also a source of conflict, as the planters preferred to replace Black laborers on the estates with poorly paid East Indian immigrants, rather than pay the former a living wage. After the expiration of their period of indenture, thousands of East Indians remained isolated on the sugar estates practicing their own religion (mainly Hindu and Islam) and culture. Those who moved off the estates went into farming and trading and tended to cluster in villages of their own. By the year 1911, only about thirty percent of them had returned to India,[59] and those who remained knew little English and resisted attempts to "christianize" them.

Participation in civil disturbances became quite frequent, and the colonial government showed little tolerance for organized struggle and the resolution of industrial conflict. Table 4.1 gives a breakdown of the kinds of social unrest and numbers of incidents that characterized this period. As can be readily seen, there was a total of 192 incidences of civil unrest during the post-slavery/colonial period, the majority of which involved significant social disorder in the form of major strikes, riots, and, in a few cases, rebellions.

The Establishment of the Guyana Police Force

The Guyana Police Force was formally established in 1839 under the advice of the Commissioners of the London Metropolitan Police, but it is clear that order maintenance was uppermost in the mind of the colonial authorities. The duties of the police were as follows:

To aid, assist and obey the magistrates and to bring to justice all persons charged with or suspected of murders, robberies, thefts of all description, and misdemeanours, as well as all rogues, vagabonds, idle and disorderly persons, and *to suppress and prevent all tumults, riots, brawls, outrages and disorders, and all other offences of any kind whatsoever against the public peace and laws of this colony.*[60] [Italics mine]

Although the Guyana Police Force was initially established as a civilian force, this arrangement did not last long. As the need for a repressive means of social control increased, military influences were gradually incorporated, and the force was fully transformed from a civilian, but armed, body into a semi-military force in 1891, when British troops withdrew from the Colony.[61] The Force was then brought in line with those already in existence in other West Indian territories, which were modeled after the Royal Irish Constabulary, a fully militarized police force established by the British in Ireland.

The racial composition of the Force mirrored the concerns of the colonial government in maintaining loyalty and reliability based on race, color, and homogeneity. According to Brian Moore (1987) in 1987, the officer corps (both commissioned and noncommissioned) were still exclusively White, while the rank and file consisted of a small number of Whites (20), East Indians (67), and an overwhelming majority of Coloreds and Blacks, mainly from foreign countries (505).[62] It appears from its policy of recruiting foreigners to police the country, that the colonial government was concerned about maintaining social distance between its police forces and the local community. Great care was taken to ensure that local police were stationed outside their communities. The emphasis was placed on control rather than service functions.

As political instability in the Colony increased, so did the numerical strength of the police and the expenditure of the colonial government for their maintenance. Between 1850 and the 1870s the expenditure on the police force had increased from 19,363 to more than 50,000 pounds per year,[63] and a practice developed of swearing in special constables or rural constables to help put down disturbances. Up to the time of the 1856 or "Angel Gabriel" riots in Georgetown, the police were in possession of armories and other weapons but were not issued with them. After the riots, however, 300 muskets and 30,000 cartridges were supplied and not only were the police armed, but a system was created whereby muskets were issued to estate managers to arm overseers and other reliable agents of the manager.[64] In addition, an Ordinance was passed by the Court of Policy prohibiting the assemblage of more than five persons.[65]

The East Indians regularly received the fire power of the police when industrial action such as work stoppages were treated as "riots." Sometimes the Riot Act would be read and then the police would immediately open fire on the strikers. In other cases the Riot Act was not read before strikers were fired upon. In one instance at Plantation Anna Regina in 1872, 5 East Indian laborers were killed and 8 wounded when police opened fire on strikers.[66] In another incident at Plantation Non Pariel in 1896 4 immigrants were killed and 11 injured by police as a result of an industrial dispute, and in 1903 8 were killed and 5 wounded during a strike at Plantation Friends in Berbice.[67] Similar events occurred at Plantation Rose Hall and Plantation Ruimveldt. In 1913, at Plantation Rose Hall, workers resisted police as they tried to arrest one of their number. One policeman was killed and several constables wounded, but in return police fired on the crowd, killing 15 workers. At Plantation Ruimveldt in 1924, mounted police brutally attacked a crowd of workers who were allegedly beating drums and waving sticks; the death toll was 13 killed and 18 wounded. Of the 147 workers subsequently prosecuted, 127 were convicted of offenses connected with the disturbance.[68] These are by no means all of the instances where police opened fire on sugar estate workers. Magistrates could be depended upon to impose the harshest punishments on alleged rioters, especially the much-feared flogging with the "cat-o-nine tails." Locally born Blacks (called "Creoles") who had drifted into the towns in large numbers received similar treatment from the control-oriented colonial police. Peter Fraser sums up the problems of the "Creoles" in the Colony at the turn of the century as follows:

> In the early years of the twentieth century the Creole population had suffered nearly thirty years of unrelieved depression. Their replacement as estate labourers by Indians and as factory workers by machines, the failure of their villages because of legal problems, the high price of land, difficulties with drainage and irrigation, and the failure to find a profitable export all contributed. The gold industry provided temporary relief to some. . . . This long depression concentrated the minds of the Creoles on economic problems and the search for an explanation for their condition.[69]

In addition to labor disputes, inter-ethnic friction between East Indians and Blacks brought the subordinate population of the Colony in open confrontation with the police repeatedly, and in many instances these confrontations ended in violence and the loss of life. Unsatisfactory social and political conditions were identified with colonialism and White dominance, and when the trade union movement got underway, workers pressed not only for an improvement in their work conditions, but also for the dismantling of the colonial system.

Two civil disturbances, the 1905 Riots and the Enmore Riots (1948), will be discussed in some detail, as the exhaustive records left with respect to these incidents clearly demonstrate not only their historical importance, but also their utility in capturing the dynamics of policing during the post-slavery/colonial period.

The 1905 Riots and the "Centipedes"

The 1905 Riots began on November 28, 1905, in the city of Georgetown when stevedores on the wharf at a shipping firm called Sanbach went on strike, demanding an increase of wages. The strike quickly spread to other shipping firms in the city, and workers traversed the waterfront trying to persuade others, sometimes forcibly, to join the strike. The next day, porters employed at Plantation Ruimveldt also began a strike for better wages. Simultaneously, other sugar estates on the East and West Banks of Demerara, including Diamond Estate, experienced industrial unrest and strikes as sugar estate workers protested the deplorable conditions of work and the starvation wages they were receiving. By Thursday,

November 30, hundreds of striking workers were joined by their unemployed relatives and friends as they took to the streets of Georgetown. There was no rioting, but the workers actively tried to prevent others from breaking the strike and vowed not to return to work until their demands for better wages were met. The colonial government responded to the escalating situation by issuing an *Extraordinary Official Gazette* containing a proclamation by His Excellency the Governor Sir Frederic Hodgson, which read, in part:

> Whereas certain persons who feel aggrieved as to the rate of pay granted to them for work as porters in the loading and unloading of vessels have disturbed the peace and order of the town by tumultuously assembling on the streets and interfering with peaceable citizens:
>
> I hereby proclaim that it is my intention to put an end to all riotous proceedings by force. Orders have been issued for all riotous assemblies to be dispersed. If necessary the Riot Act will be read, and the powers conferred by Law will then be used.
>
> I earnestly call upon all peaceable citizens to avoid joining assemblies and crowds as by so doing they will run the risk of being injured or even losing their lives.[70]

The intention to resort to official violence was therefore clearly spelled out, but it appears that the strikers did not take the Governor at his word. On the evening of November 30, 1905, the city magistrate read the Riot Act in Georgetown, after which the crowds dispersed, resolving to continue their industrial action the next day. It is clear that the mere presence of workers when assembled together was interpreted by the Governor as a "riotous assembly" and a proper occasion for the use of force, including deadly force. The police were equipped with very powerful Martini-Enfield rifles (converted) and the militia used the magazine Lee-Enfield. These rifles had an extreme firing range of 3,500 yards and were considered to be too powerful for use in the suppression of crowd disorder. According to the Government Secretary, in order to stop the penetration of a bullet (.303) fired from these weapons "the following thicknesses of materials are necessary: sand, 20 inches; oakwood, 27 inches; earth, 28 inches." Buckshot, apparently in vogue at this time, was considered to be most appropriate for the dispersal of crowds with the least amount of physical injury, but His Excellency the Governor was unfavorably disposed to this method of crowd control as "it spoils the rifle."[71]

The next day, Friday, December 1, 1905, matters came to a head at Plantation Ruimveldt on the outskirts of Georgetown when cane-cutters struck for better wages. According to the cane-cutters' version of events, on that fateful day, having made up their minds to ask for an increase in wages, about twenty-five to thirty of them, men and women, ceased work and approached the manager on their way from the fields. One of their number, George Henry, went up to the manager and laid his hand on his shoulder saying "We want to speak to you, sir, about our pay." The manager told the crowd to disperse and that he would have nothing to do with them, and he sent for the police. When the heavily armed police arrived under the command of Inspector De Rinzy, the manager alleged that he had been assaulted by the cane-cutter, and the police then proceeded to arrest George Henry in a brutal manner. His "cutlass" (the cane-cutter's working implement used to cut the canes) was taken away from him and he was handcuffed and deposited in the manager's yard to await transportation to the Brickdam police station in Georgetown.

Inspector De Rinzy, who was White, posted his artillery men around the manager's residence and told the crowd consisting of Black and East Indian canecutters "You children, go away from here, it would be a pity if you got destroyed." The crowd apparently did not take him seriously and gathered on the road in front of the manager's yard and replied "We ent come to you; we come to the manager. We ent rowing [quarreling]. We only come to seek for price, and we cannot go."[72] The crowd then made an effort to take the truck-line bridge leading into the manager's yard, but were prevented by the policemen on duty with fixed bayonets. Without further warning Inspector De Rinzy instructed his men to open fire. Pandemonium broke out in the crowd as people started running for cover. Some remained rooted to the ground in disbelief. As the firing continued "one man drop, then another, then another." Many workers were wounded and four subsequently died of their injuries. Instead of being taken to the nearby estate hospital, the bleeding bodies of the wounded were put on a cart and paraded through the city on their way to the colonial hospital in Georgetown as a warning to the others of the fate that awaited them.

The large crowd of strikers in Georgetown, instead of being cowed as was intended, erupted into frenzied anger and converged on all the symbols of colonial authority and oppression. Portuguese businesses (known for their exploitation of the poverty of the masses), and vehicles carrying members of the judiciary (the Chief Justice and magistrates) were attacked. The crowd invaded the Public Buildings, the official seat of the Governor, rushed about in search of Colonel Lushington, who had allegedly killed a bystander at Brickdam, and vented their frustration even on individual members of the ruling class, mainly Whites. More police and fire power were brought in, and the police fired on the crowd at different points in the city—mainly Thomas Street and Brickdam—and by dusk, seven persons had lost their lives, and more than seventeen had been seriously wounded. The police claimed that the mob had pelted them with stones, and had refused to disperse. Many of the victims were innocent people who were mere spectators of the protest.

The militia was called out and special constables were supplied by the employees of the merchant class and immediately sworn in to assist the police. Two British warships, the Diamond and the Sappho, arrived in Georgetown on December 4 and 5. By December 6, 1905, the strike was over, eight people had been killed and more than thirty persons wounded.[73] No increases in wages were granted to the waterfront or the estate workers. Hunger and deprivation, which had prevailed throughout the depression of the late nineteenth century, and the absence of any means of subsistence, resulted in the inevitable trek back to the same atrocious conditions of work and wages that had precipitated the strike. But the workers were not to be allowed reprieve to mourn their dead and wounded. The colonial government immediately mobilized the legal machinery to teach the strikers a lesson.

The Riots were felt to be the work of the large group of Black, unemployed persons who resided in Georgetown under conditions of extreme deprivation and had seized the opportunity to create public mischief. In fact, however, many of these people were the casualties of the deliberate policy of the plantocracy in collusion with the colonial government, of replacing Black laborers with indentured servants who were forced to accept lower wages because of their contracts of service. Despite the availability of a large unemployed labor force, the colonial government continued to import indentured servants from India until the early twentieth century, and this was the cause of much animosity between East Indians and Blacks in British Guiana.[74] For many of these men, women, and youths there was no regular work to be had, and children were left to wander the streets in search of a means of existence. As a result, vagrancy and petty crime was prevalent in Georgetown during this period, and these persons were felt to be mainly responsible.

There is evidence that a pervasive practice developed among the "colonists" and even members of the emerging middle class of Coloreds and educated Blacks, of referring to these people as "centipedes," which in the tropics are considered to be despicable, nocturnal creatures of sluggish habits. All upward-bound members of the local population joined with the colonists in condemning this class. Punitive legal measures and vigorous enforcement of the vagrancy laws were widely supported. The contempt for this class of persons seems to have been fostered by the status differentiation and social stratification that was perpetuated under slavery. These persons were mainly Black and poor and as such represented everything that the local middle class wanted to distance itself from. The newspaper records of the 1905 Riots are replete with references to the evil and violent disposition of the "centipedes" and lays the blame for all the trouble during the riots squarely on them. Apart from a few members of the middle class who had been elected to the Court of Policy and were clearly outraged by the action of the colonial authorities, members of the middle class drew a distinction between the "strikers" and the "centipedes," and joined in the castigation of the latter. This derogatory name calling received approbation even in the highest forum of colonial administration, the Court of Policy. In defending the frequent use of flogging as punishment for the rioters, during debates in the Court of Policy on the subject of the disturbances, the Attorney General had this to say:

> The answer to the question why was the law administered in respect to flogging was a simple one. There was a large number of "centipedes" here, and last year a law was passed to deal effectively with this undesirable class. But (I) cannot see why the Hon. Member has objected to the application of the law to the very class of people whom it was passed to meet.[75]

According to this definition of the situation by colonial authorities, what was in effect a working-class protest for better wages and conditions of work had been transformed into a class struggle between the forces of good and evil. Careful scrutiny of the sequence of events reveal, in the case of the 1905 Riots, that the frenzied physical attacks and destruction of property were occasioned by the direct action of the police in firing indiscriminately into the crowd of peaceful protestors. The police themselves had precipitated the riot, and then claimed to be responding to it. According to the Government's figures, fifty-eight constables were injured and one died as a result of a beating he received from the rioters.[76]

The proceedings of the colonial government and the exercise of the judicial function in the aftermath of the 1905 Riots are very instructive in understanding the nature of the rule of law and the purpose of policing during the colonial era. The evidence of collusion by the executive and the judiciary in the illegal and illegitimate abuse of police power to use deadly force was indisputable. During the Riots the Governor had openly proclaimed himself to be the protector of "the property and interests of the mercantile community" and stated that such interests justified the taking of life.[77] With regard to the police he said that "they did not discharge their rifles on any occasion except when ordered by their officers to do so, and they were in fact fully under control (and) deserved praise."[78] In open violation of promises made to redress the grievances of the strikers, the Governor personally intervened to compel several estates' authorities to abandon the implementation of increased rates of wages, which they had agreed to grant to the workers. He visited the estates and threatened to withdraw security forces if wages were increased. This happened both at Plantation Schoonord and Plantation Ruimveldt among others where, even though the managers had already agreed to the increases, they had to revert to the old wages. The Governor promised that "If any disorder should again arise . . . a sufficient force would be available for its suppression."[79]

Strikers were relentlessly prosecuted for offenses in connection with the disturbances. Hundreds of persons were charged with having committed Summary Conviction Offences, even where they had allegedly committed Indictable Offences so that they could be flogged under the Summary Conviction Offences Ordinance. It is noteworthy that very few arrests were made *during* the riots when the police alleged that they were being assaulted and attacked. After the strike ended no stone was left unturned to find and prosecute persons identified as having committed offenses during the riots. Several accounts are given in the *Daily Chronicle* of persons being surrounded in the street and taken into custody by armed police solely because they are suspected of being in the "centipede" class, and then being charged with offenses in connection with the riots.

Information supplied by the colonial government to the Court of Policy, which met on December 29, 1905, indicated that 105 persons had been convicted in Georgetown and 9 in the West Coast of Demerara of offenses in connection with the riots. The alleged rioters were invariably convicted on the basis of evidence proffered by the police, and corroborated mainly by Whites and members of the merchant class. Most of the offenses were for carrying stones or sticks "to cause alarm to the public," throwing stones to the danger of the public, unlawfully carrying a cutlass (the implement of a cane-cutter's trade), insulting and/or assaulting the police, or unlawful assembly and refusal to disperse when required to do so by a police officer. Penalties were severe and included varying terms of imprisonment, hard labor, and several lashes (usually twenty-four) with the cat-o-nine tails, a greatly feared, barbaric, whipping device that was capable of inflicting crippling spinal injuries.

A grievous penalty, hair cropping, was reserved for the women, mainly of African descent, and was usually attached to a term of imprisonment. This involved the removal of all the hair on the head by a barber the day before release from prison. The effectiveness of this form of punishment dated back to African tradition whereby a female with her head shaved was looked upon as an outcast. The law permitting hair cropping was very effective because the tradition had somehow survived the slave system, and Black women were greatly offended by this form of punishment. Hair cropping was therefore a means of specific and general deterrence, as well as a mechanism for labeling these women as societal outcasts.

The police force was strengthened with the addition of forty mounted police, and six sub-inspectors of police to be mounted. Mounted police with properly trained horses were expected to be very effective in controlling future rioters. Additionally, the volunteer force, which had been defunct for several years, was resuscitated "to assist in the preservation of order," and consisted of two companies of eighty men. The Government Secretary refused to reveal the strength of the police force at the time of the riots in answer to a question in the Court of Policy. He said, however, that the militia consisted of a total of 375 men, and the reserve force, 238 men. Additional funds were approved by the Court of Policy to finance the expansion of the police force and the reformation of the volunteer force, and to equip the police with superior horses to be imported from the United States.

The elected representatives in the Court of Policy, the most vocal of whom was Patrick Dargan, took the colonial government to task over the killing of civilians by the police during the Riots. Dargan was a locally born attorney of Mixed race and represented the Georgetown District. Dargan accused the Governor of being a racist and of deliberately excluding Coloreds and Blacks from the newly formed Volunteer Force. During debates in the Court of Policy on the issue of the Volunteer Force, Dargan confronted the Governor with a statement he had allegedly made, in the presence of witnesses, to the effect that "the Black man was not going to rule this place."[80] The Governor denied making the statement. The fact that only White men were invited to join the Volunteer Force seems to support Dargan's contention.

Dargan was deeply moved by the events of the 1905 Riots and immortalized himself among Guyana's greatest sons by his tireless work to get justice for the relatives of the victims. He was incensed at the verdict of the jury at the Coroner's inquest that the victims "met their death from gunshot wounds at the hands of the police shooting on the 1st December in the lawful execution of their duty after the Riot Act had been read and the people duly warned."[81] After the colonial government refused to cause an inquiry to be made into the causes of the riots and whether the shootings were justified, Dargan created history in the Colony by bringing private criminal prosecutions against the policemen involved, including the Inspector General, on behalf of the relatives of the victims. The following excerpts from a letter written by Mr. Dargan to the *Daily Chronicle* on December 16, 1905, eloquently captures the essence of the controversy concerning the police use of deadly force in the 1905 Riots. His legal reasoning clearly set out the common law with regard thereto, and shows why the use of force was unreasonable and excessive:

> I have stated that from the evidence it appeared that the Riot Act was read at Ruimveld only. Mr. De Rinzy states in his evidence that he read the Riot Act. If he did do so, section 321 of the Indictable Offences Ordinance points out his duty. It is this: If the people did not disperse within 15 minutes after the Riot Act was read he had, with the assistance of his men . . . to cause the persons in the mob to be apprehended and carried before a Magistrate, and if in causing them to be apprehended any one or more of the mob is killed, the person ordering the apprehension and the persons executing the order are indemnified.
>
> To shoot a man because he threw stones at you would be using excessive and unnecessary force, which the law does not permit, even in the case of a riot. The law was clearly laid down in the Featherstone disturbances in 1893 by Lord Justice Bowen and Mr. Haldane, Q.C. In the report it is stated that:
>
> > "The taking of life can only be justified by the necessity for protecting persons or property against various forms of violent crime, or by the necessity of dispersing a riotous crowd which is dangerous unless dispersed, or in the case of persons whose conduct has become felonious through disobedience to the provisions of the Riot Act and who resist the attempt to disperse or apprehend them."
>
> Neither of these things appear to have happened . . . and if they did not happen, the killing of the several persons at these places cannot be justified.[82]

Dargan's criminal prosecutions of the police were eventually dismissed by the court, as expected. The Governor reiterated his congratulation of the police force for the excellent way in which they handled the riot. The merchants and other colonists in Georgetown presented the sum of $1,074 to the noncommissioned officers of the police force as an expression of their gratitude for the protection afforded to them during the riots.[83]

Importance of the 1905 Riots as an Illustrative Example

The 1905 Riots are discussed in such great detail because this single event captures all the essential forces at work in policing during the colonial period. Firstly, it provides the context for the use of official violence as a means of population control. In so doing, it illustrates the utility of the conflict perspective in providing the theoretical framework for the analysis of police violence during the colonial period.

As discussed in Chapter 1, this study relies on the contextual definition of the situation in its attempt to find an explanation for police violence both during the colonial and post-colonial periods. Applying the conflict perspective to the analysis of the facts, we may conclude that at the time of this event, there were two diametrically opposed groups in society. One group consisted of the minority colonial rulers, plantation owners, and business people, and the other comprised the majority of mainly agricultural, factory, and other blue-collar workers. The latter group was engaging in what it perceived as lawful activity, agitating for better wages and working conditions. For the minority ruling class, this amounted to the creation of a potential insurrection that had to be swiftly and effectively crushed. The scenario points to a perception of social threat that calls forth the proverbial preemptive strike in the form of official violence. This society consists of a culturally diverse population that lacks social cohesion and it is held together by coercion and the threat of force.

The fact of the matter with regard to the 1905 Riots is that it was the use of deadly force by police that precipitated the rioting that took place. The facts show that the power to open fire on a riotous mob was used long before the mob became riotous. Dargan's discourses in the Court of Policy as to lack of justification for the use of deadly force is corroborated by newspaper accounts of what actually happened. But instead of punishment for the officers involved, there is commendation, and all attempts to gain justice for the victims were thwarted. The colonial Governor refused to constitute a Commission to enquire into the events, and Patrick Dargan's private prosecutions against the police on behalf of the relatives of the deceased victims, were dismissed. The rule of law was ineffective in bringing the police to justice, while, at the same time, it was vigorously enforced against suspected "troublemakers," who were actively pursued and severely punished.

Actions taken by the colonial state authority to strengthen the law enforcement establishment are also instructive. First of all, there was an increase in the numerical strength of the police, the addition of mounted police, reformation of the volunteer (reserve) force, and the allocation of more money for the acquisition of weapons of war. These factors characterize authoritarian and repressive colonial rule that required the use of force to enforce and maintain the status quo. As Patrick Dargan repeated over and over in his discourses in the Court of Policy, this was a police force that "did not know what its duties were."[84] Ironically, this was not a civilian, but a militarized force that since 1891 had been trained and equipped to perform the exact same duties it was performing—population and crowd control.

The Enmore Riots, which took place more than four decades later, illustrate how little changed in Guyana with regard to the policing of the local population during the lengthy period of British colonial rule.

The Enmore Riots (1948)

On April 22, 1948, cane-cutters at sugar estates on the East Coast of Demerara went on a general strike over the system of cane cutting (cut and load as against cut and drop). There were many other grievances between the cane-cutters and the managers at that time, including the failure to recognize their union, the Guiana Industrial Workers Union (GIWU), as the proper bargaining agent for both field and factory workers. Among some of the deplorable conditions under which estate workers toiled were poor housing and sanitation, the lack of potable water, the exploitation of child labor, and the inability to gain redress for industrial grievances.[85] Between 1942 and 1948 there had been numerous stoppages of work at estates on the East Coast of Demerara due to industrial disputes between workers and managers, and widespread discontent mounted over unresolved issues.

According to the police version of the events, on the morning of the day in question, a crowd of about 400 striking workers tried to enter the factory at Enmore. There is no evidence to support a finding that the workers posed a deadly threat to the police or anyone else. However, the police claimed that they had to open fire to prevent themselves from being overpowered by the strikers, and to protect the factory and those who were working therein from destruction. After the initial bullets were discharged by the police, the workers took evasive action, but the firing continued even after they began to flee from the scene. Five sugar workers who have become known as the Enmore Martyrs, were killed, and fourteen were wounded by police during the confrontation.[86]

Although this incident was not as complex and controversial as the 1905 Riots, it bears many similarities therewith. In both cases, the police were responding to an industrial dispute, and it was clear that the crowds could have been dispersed by other nonlethal means. At the time of the Enmore riots, tear gas was the popular method for crowd dispersal, but it was not used to prevent the workers from entering the factory compound. Yet the Commission of Enquiry in this case concluded that the police had acted justifiably in opening fire on the crowd. They were constrained to note, however, that several of the workers had been shot from behind, and when in actual flight and that there was an excessive use of deadly force.[87]

In the days that followed, 138 persons were prosecuted for rioting (mainly assaults and stone throwing). Of this number eighty-six were convicted, fined, and imprisoned. The police were praised for their handling of the disturbances, one was awarded a medal for meritorious service, and several were promoted.[88] None of the policemen who were involved in the shooting were prosecuted by the Crown in respect of the incident, but several private prosecutions were brought on behalf of the relatives. The response of the executive and the judiciary to the arbitrary and excessive use of deadly force by police was similar to that of the 1905 Riots, which had taken place decades earlier.

CONCLUSION

The development of policing in colonial Guyana was shaped by the ever-changing social and political conditions in the society. Beginning with slave patrols, which were put together on an ad hoc basis to quell slave rebellions and capture runaways, policing in the Colony was adapted to deal with the new social order that emerged as a result of the abolition of slavery and the importation of immigrant labor. The militarization of the first permanent police force was a direct response of the political system to the actual and perceived threat of incendiary conflict generated by the massive laboring population in the Colony. The composition of the force also reflected the concerns of the metropolitan power in maintaining loyalty from the force, and perpetuating the divide-and-rule policies that had become an indispensable part of the social order.

Three distinctive characteristics of policing in the Colony emerge from the available historical evidence. These are (1) the emphases on control and coercion rather than service as the primary function; (2) the legitimation of police behavior, however reprehensible, by the executive and judiciary; and (3) the indiscriminate resort to violence, that is, the use of deadly force as a means of social control and especially crowd control. All these characteristics are evident from the specific duties, functions, and modus operandi of the police in the Colony. In the case of the 1905 and the 1948 (Enmore) riots in particular, the police adopted the "show of force" rather than the "containment" strategy of suppression. The use of deadly weapons, rather than other methods of crowd control, showed little respect for human life. These characteristics distinguish the type of policing that evolved in Guyana during the colonial period as one where weapons were used as a preferred means of communication between the police and the public.

NOTES

1. Howard Selsam, David Goldway, and Harry Martel, eds. 1970. *Dynamics of Social Change: A Reader in Marxist Social Science.* New York: International Publishers, p. 26.

2. George L. Kelling and Mark H. Moore. November 1988. "The Evolving Strategy of Policing." *Perspectives on Policing,* No 4. Washington, D.C.: National Institute of Justice and Harvard University; and Hubert Williams and Patrick V. Murphy. January 1990. "The Evolving Strategy of Police: A Minority View." *Perspectives on Policing,* No 13. Washington, D.C.: National Institute of Justice and Harvard University.

3. The first settlements were established by the Dutch in the early seventeenth century and the territory was eventually ceded to Britain by the Treaty of Paris of May 30, 1814. See Alvin Thompson. 1987. *Colonialism and Underdevelopment in Guyana, 1580–1803.* Bridgetown, Barbados: Carib Research and Publications, Inc., pp. 15, 41–64, and passim; James Rodway. 1891. *A History of British Guiana from the Year 1668 to the Present Time* (3 vols.), Vol. II. Georgetown: J. Thompson, pp. 2–32, 116–162, 213, 284.

4. David M. Anderson and David Killingray. 1991. "Consent, Coercion and Colonial Control: Policing the Empire, 1830–1940." In *Policing the Empire, Government, Authority and Control, 1830–1940.* David M. Anderson and David Killingray, eds. Manchester, U.K.: Manchester University Press, pp. 5–15.

5. Ted Robert Gurr. 1976. *Rogues, Rebels and Reformers: A Political History of Urban Crime and Conflict.* London: Sage, pp. 120, 121.

6. According to Gurr, in London in 1840 there were 2,271 convictions for robbery, burglary, larceny, and receiving stolen goods. See Gurr. Ibid., pp. 43, 45.

7. Gurr, Ibid., p. 122.

8. See Stanley H. Palmer. 1988. *Police and Protest in England and Ireland, 1780–1850.* Cambridge, U.K.: Cambridge University Press, pp. 6–11, 376–429, esp. at 427. Also, see Sir

L. Radzinowicz. 1948–68. *A History of English Criminal Law and Its Administration from 1750* (5 vols.), New York: Macmillan, for a full discussion of police and protest in England.

9. Alan Williams. 1979. *The Police of Paris, 1718–1789.* Baton Rouge: Louisiana State University Press, pp. 65, 103–112.

10. Palmer, *Police and Protest in England and Ireland, 1780–1850*, pp. 277–315.

11. See Jerome Skolnick. 1975. *Justice Without Trial.* 2nd ed. New York: John Wiley & Sons, p. 3.

12. Ibid., p. 45.

13. See M. Shahabuddeen. 1978. *Constitutional Development in Guyana, 1621–1978.* Georgetown, Guyana: Guyana Printers Ltd., p. 612.

14. Rodway, *History of British Guiana From the Year 1668 to the Present Time,* Vol. I (1668–1781), p. 225.

15. Shahabuddeen, *Constitutional Development in Guyana, 1621–1978*, pp. 28, 31, 60.

16. Ibid., p. 28.

17. Ibid., p. 31.

18. The seat of government was located in Essequibo at this time.

19. Shahabuddeen, *Constitutional Development in Guyana, 1621–1978*, p. 600.

20. This was previously discussed in chapter 3.

21. P. M. Netscher. 1888. *History of the Colonies Essequibo, Demerary and Berbice: From the Dutch Establishment to the Present Day.* Translated by W. E. Roth. Gravenhage, Provincial Utrecht Society of Arts & Sciences, p. 110.

22. M. Shahabuddeen. 1973. *The Legal System of Guyana.* Georgetown, Guyana: Guyana Printers, Ltd., pp. 70, 71.

23. W. A. Orrett. 1951. *The History of the British Guiana Police.* Georgetown, Guyana: The Daily Chronicle Ltd., Printers and Publishers, p. 3.

24. Guyana government document. *The Local Guide: Demerara-Essequibo*, 1821. p. 10.

25. Rodway, *History of British Guiana from the Year 1668 to the Present Time*, Vol. I, p. 174; Vol. II, p. 173.

26. Shahabuddeen, *Constitutional Development in Guyana, 1621–1978*, p. 602.

27. R. T. Smith. 1980. *British Guiana.* Westport, Conn.: Greenwood Press, pp. 31–33.

28. Rodway, *History of British Guiana from the Year 1668 to the Present Time*, Vol. II, pp. 78, 79.

29. Ibid., p. 79.

30. Ibid., p. 121.

31. Ibid.

32. Smith, *British Guiana*, p. 27.

33. Shahabuddeen, *Constitutional Development in Guyana, 1621–1978*, p. 594.

34. R. T. Smith gives the date for allowing Mulattoes to take up commissions in the militia as 1823 in Berbice; See Smith, *British Guiana*, p. 27. Shahabuddeen, however, gives the date as 1822; see Shahabuddeen, *Constitutional Development in Guyana, 1621–1978,* p. 595.

35. Netscher, *History of the Colonies Essequibo, Demerary and Berbice*, pp. 98, 99, and passim.

36. Ibid., pp. 110, 111.

37. Pairadeau Mars. 1975. *Political Modernization and Stability in a Developing State: The Guyana Example.* Unpublished Ph.D. Thesis, Carleton University, Ontario, pp. 123, 124.

38. See Alvin O. Thompson, *Colonialism and Underdevelopment in Guyana, 1580–1803*, pp. 153–174.

39. Netscher, *History of the Colonies Essequibo, Demerary and Berbice,* p. 97.

40. Ibid., p. 111, 91–113.

41. See Emilia Viotti da Costa, 1994, *Crowns of Glory, Tears of Blood, The Demerara Slave Rebellion of 1823*, New York: Oxford University Press, for a very insightful account of this rebellion.

42. Rodway, *A History of British Guiana from the Year 1668 to the Present*, Vol. II, p. 248; also, Smith, *British Guiana*, p. 36.

43. See Samuel Walker. 1977. *A Critical History of Police Reform: The Emergence of Professionalism.* Lexington, Mass.: Lexington Books, pp. 4–6; also, P. L. Reichel, 1988. "Southern Slave Patrols as a Traditional Police Type." *American Journal of Police*, Vol. III, no. 2, pp. 51–77.

44. A. Candler, ed. 1910. *The Colonial Records of the State of Georgia.* Vol. 18, Atlanta: Chas. P. Byrd, State Printer, p. 225.

45. B. Wood. 1984. *Slavery in Colonial Georgia.* Athens: University of Georgia Press, pp. 123–24.

46. P. S. Foner. 1975. *History of Black Americans: From Africa to the Emergence of the Cotton Kingdom.* Westport, Conn.: Greenwood Publishers, p. 206.

47. Leo A. Despres estimated that there were approximately 100,000 slaves in the Colony in 1829. No accurate count of the exact figure at the time of emancipation could be found, but the population had probably increased by that time. See Leo A. Despres. 1964. "The Implications of Nationalist Politics in British Guiana for the Development of Cultural Theory." *American Anthropologist* 66:1051–77 (p. 45).

48. William A. Green, Jr. 1969. "The Apprenticeship in British Guiana, 1834–1838," *Caribbean Studies* 9(2):44–66.

49. Ibid., p. 49; See also Monica Schuler. 1988. "Plantation Labourers, the London Missionary Society and Emancipation in West Demerara, Guyana." *The Journal of Caribbean History* 22:100.

50. Monica Schuler, "Plantation Labourers, The London Missionary Society and Emancipation in West Demerara, Guyana," pp. 100–2.

51. See Green, "The Apprenticeship in British Guiana, 1834–1838," pp. 49, 50; and Monica Schuler, "Plantation Labourers, the London Missionary Society and Emancipation in West Demerara, Guyana," pp. 101, 102.

52. Green, "The Apprenticeship in British Guiana, 1834–1838," p. 50.

53. M. Shahabuddeen. 1973. *The Legal System of Guyana.* Georgetown, Guyana: Guyana Printers, Ltd., p. 323.

54. Smith, *British Guiana*, p. 47.

55. Chandra Jayawardena. 1971. "East Indians and the Plantation System in Guyana." In *Readings in Government and Politics of the West Indies*, Trevor Munroe and Rupert Lewis, eds. Mona, Jamaica: Dept. of Government, University of the West Indies, pp. 31–33 (31) .

56. Ibid., p. 32.

57. Rodway, *A History of British Guiana from the Year 1668 to the Present Time.* Vol. III, p. 197.

58. Ibid., pp. 193, 194.

59. G. W. Roberts. 1948. "Some Observations on the Population of British Guiana." *Population Studies* 2:211.

60. Orrett, *The History of the British Guiana Police*, p. 5.

61. Sir Charles Jeffries. 1952. *The Colonial Police.* London: Max Parrish & Co., p. 64.

62. Brian Moore. 1987. *Race, Power and Social Segmentation in Colonial Society, Guyana After Slavery 1838–1891.* London: Gordon and Breach Science Publishers, p. 205.

63. Ibid., pp. 205, 206.

64. Orrett, *The History of the British Guiana Police,* p. 12.

65. Rodway, *A History of British Guiana from the Year 1668 to the Present Time,* Vol. II, p. 118.

66. Ibid., p. 201.

67. Orrett, *The History of the British Guiana Police,* pp. 26, 32.

68. Ibid., pp. 37–48.

69. Peter D. Fraser. 1981. "The Immigration Issue in British Guiana, 1903–1913: The Economic and Constitutional Origins of Racist Politics in Guyana," *Journal of Caribbean History,* Vol. 4, pp. 25, 26.

70. 1905. *The Riots in Georgetown 1905. Details of the Outbreak, its Cause, and the Measures Taken for its Suppression. Inquest on the Victims and Punishment of the Rioters.* Reprinted from *The Daily Chronicle,* Georgetown, Demerara: Estate of C. K. Jardine, Dec'd., Printers, Publishers and Bookbinders.

71. Extracted from proceedings of a meeting held in the Court of Policy on December 13, 1905, between His Excellency Sir Frederic Hodgson, the Government Secretary, Captain Tothill, of H.M.S. Diamond, Captain Hodges of H.M.S. Sappho, Colonel Lushington and several members of the merchant class to discuss the formation of a volunteer force for "the preservation of order in the city in time of emergency."

72. *The Riots in Georgetown 1905.*

73. Ibid.

74. Peter D. Fraser, "The Immigration Issue in British Guiana," pp. 20–23.

75. "The Riots in Georgetown," 1905. *The Daily Chronicle,* 1905. Georgetown, Demerara: Estate of C. K. Jardine, Dec'd., Printers, Publishers, and Bookbinders.

76. Ibid.

77. Extracted from Governor Hodgson's speech to strikers at the Public Buildings, Georgetown, December 1, 1905, *The Riots in Georgetown, 1905.*

78. *The Riots in Georgetown 1905.*

79. Ibid.

80. Ibid.

81. Ibid.

82. Ibid.

83. Orrett, *The History of the British Guiana Police,* p. 34.

84. *The Riots in Georgetown 1905.*

85. Ashton Chase. 1964. *A History of Trade Unionism in Guyana: 1900–1961.* Georgetown, Demerara: New Guyana Company Ltd., p. 142.

86. *Report of the Enmore Enquiry Commission,* 1948. Georgetown, Demerara: British Guiana Legislative Council No. 10/1948.

87. Ibid.

88. Orrett, *The History of the British Guiana Police,* p. 69.

5

The Socio–Political Environment and the Rule of Law

The nature of policing and police violence in the post-independence period in Guyana was as much a product of social and political forces as it had been during the colonial era. This chapter will illustrate how the tradition of colonial-type policing was built upon, strengthened, and expanded to accommodate new social, economic, and political conditions that developed as the society achieved self-rule, entered the modern era, and had to rely on its own resources to resolve endemic internal conflict and achieve social control. Evidence will be presented to show that although the nature of the social threat and the source of repression changed with independence, the use of police power primarily to maintain political power and that "ugly face" of authority that exists in a society held together by coercion,[1] continued until quite recently. Currently, although political repression and authoritarian rule has apparently ended, old habits die hard, and the question that needs to be asked is whether the police are assuming a new and independent role determined primarily by their own definition of society's requirements. That question will be answered in the next chapter when available statistical data on police-caused homicide during the period 1980 to 1994 will be analyzed. This chapter focuses on the dynamics at work in the modern period that created the context for police violence.

In keeping with the schematic presented earlier, the discussion of the impact of the contemporary socio–legal environment as a determinative factor in perpetuating social control by coercion rather than consensus, and the use of police power to rule by force and the threat of force, will focus on the extent to which the following issues created the context for police violence in the post-independence period:

1. The nature of social conflict
2. Social control and the police
3. The rule of law and the police

THE NATURE OF SOCIAL CONFLICT

The theoretical framework for this study is grounded in the conflict perspective in so far as structural conditions generate social conflict, and a threat to the social order, resulting in the use of force to maintain social control. Dahrendorf's *coercion theory of society* focuses on power and authority relations as a source of social conflict and is felt to be especially relevant for understanding the nature of social conflict in Guyanese society that has generated police violence in the post-independence period. This section will show how the nature of social conflict in Guyana at the beginning of the independence period and thereafter was directly related to the struggle for political power during the immediate pre-independence period between groups sharply divided along ethnic and class lines, occasioned by the impending departure of the British. In the course of this struggle, the police emerged as a strategic and deadly weapon in the hands of the political rulers, who found it expedient to maintain the legacy of colonial policing for the purpose of public intimidation, order maintenance, and internal surveillance.

Before discussing the social conflict generated by the struggle for political power in Guyana, the question of economic factors as a source of social conflict must be addressed. Several empirical studies already referred to have focused on various economic indicators of social conflict to explain police use of excessive force.[2] Foremost among them is the research of Jacobs and Britt, who found empirical support for economic inequality as an indicator of social conflict to explain police homicide in the United States.[3] Sorenson and others, more than a decade later, also found empirical support for a positive relationship between economic inequality and the police homicide rate in the United States.[4] In order to understand the context of police violence in the post-independence period in Guyana, it is important to investigate, first, whether socio–economic conditions existed separately and distinctly from the political dimension of conflict. Second, the question needs to be asked as to whether such conditions were sufficiently conflict-producing so as to create a situation of social threat and call forth a coercive governmental response in the form of the use of excessive police force.

The Socio–Economic Perspective

The lack of adequate socio–economic data for empirical analysis is a serious handicap to this study. Data from which to calculate a measure of economic inequality such as the gini index of income inequality were not available for Guyana. In this regard, there is merit in a new approach that has been used in the technical literature to examine the socio–economic context in a different way that, though not useful for the purpose of the testing of hypotheses and the prediction of police homicide rates, could still shed light on whether the socio–economic conditions at the beginning of the independence period fostered social conflict and the likelihood of social threat that lead to a repressive governmental response.

The approach was used by Paul Chevigny,[5] who posited that indexes "that correlate social conditions or changes in social conditions with social turmoil or rebellion" though not definitive as viable explanations for social upheaval, are nevertheless useful as indicators of social dissatisfaction and unmobilized social conflict, the awareness of which may provoke official violence and repression. The importance of this type of inquiry, according to Chevigny, lay in whether social conditions are so conflict-generating that a sense of apprehension pervades the social atmosphere that could be interpreted by political rulers as a *risk of social unrest* or unmobilized social conflict. This in turn provokes a need for the official show of force or the threat of force to prevent the latent dissatisfaction and conflict from becoming manifest.

Chevigny[6] updated an index prepared by Duff and McCamant[7] as an indicator of social dissatisfaction and conflict that could lead to violence and repression in Latin American countries; he created a scale to measure the "perceived *threat* of unrest" in the societies he investigated. As explained in an earlier chapter, this scale was interpreted to represent the *likelihood* of social unrest and was arrived at by calculating a differential based on the social mobilization and social welfare ranking of the individual countries.[8] The factors on which the social mobilization ranking was based included the presence of newsprint per capita, radios per thousand persons, television sets per thousand persons, and urban population as a percentage of the total population. The presence of these factors tend to raise the demand for economic goods and social services. The social welfare ranking was based on the literacy rate, calories per diem, doctors per capita, and GNP per capita. The presence of these factors indicate the ability of the government to meet the needs and wants that are associated with higher levels of economic development and consumption patterns. The level of social discontent or social dissatisfaction could be measured by the differential between the two, and the stronger the negative differential the greater the dissatisfaction that in turn could lead to violence and/or government repression and the converse. Based on these considerations, the index updated by Chevigny was used to help explain the existence of problems in the societies he investigated (Jamaica, Argentina, and Brazil) that could create the need for governmental repression in the form of police violence.

Chevigny also examined South American and Caribbean countries, including Guyana, for purposes of comparison. With reference to Guyana, based on data compiled in the mid 1980s, Chevigny arrived at a positive welfare-mobilization differential of .19, thereby suggesting that indicators of social welfare exceed social mobilization, or that want satisfaction is modestly greater than want generation. This therefore means that socio–economic conditions, if taken alone, are not a likely source of the social dissatisfaction or unmobilized social conflict that could call forth official violence in Guyana. Such a finding, in spite of high levels of police homicide, also occurred in the case of Brazil, which produced a somewhat favorable social welfare–social mobilization differential (.37). This demonstrates the limitations of his explanation. Chevigny attributed this favorable indicator in the case of Brazil to the distortions in the statistical data and explored other factors that could generate the very high police homicide rate in that country, which is known for its infamous death squads and dismal human rights record.[9] In the case of Guyana, it should be noted that this social welfare–social mobilization differential relates to dissatisfaction that is based only on socio–economic factors; this translates into the inability of the political system to satisfy popular demands for required goods and services. There is not much indication of high expectations among a population that has experienced a consistent decline in living standards.

Another way of assessing the importance of economic factors is to investigate the extent to which rapid social change could generate social conflict. Some modernization theorists, who suggest a strong positive relationship between socio–economic variables and social conflict, contend that the rapid pace of economic and social change tends to impose strains on the relationship between groups in the political process and to undermine the capability of the government to function effectively.[10] Eisenstadt,[11] for example, contends that industrialization and urbanization are likely to increase the scope of conflict between different groups and classes in the political system because it tends to create high expectations, social disorganization, anomie, and frustration. These conditions could lead to social instability and civil strife as the gap widens between the "haves" and the "have nots." Huntington goes so far as to conclude, citing historical evidence, that not only is rapid social and economic modernization a predictor of instability, but also that the "degree of instability is related to the rate of modernization."[12]

In the case of Guyana, however, there is also evidence to support the conclusion that the country has not experienced the rapid industrialization and urbanization associated with the development of high economic expectations that could lead to social conflict. The overall statistical profile of the economic situation during the modern period shows very little in terms of social and economic modernization trends. The economic picture is rather one of poverty and economic decline. Since independence, the economy of Guyana has experienced a consistent downward trend, resulting in its current ranking among the poorest nations of the world with sixty to eighty percent of the population living below the poverty line.[13] The United Nations Development Programme published a world league table showing the most- to the least-developed countries in 1992, and Guyana was ranked at 104th place. This assessment was corroborated by the World Bank in a 1992 Economic Report on Guyana. While lamenting the paucity of socio–economic data on the basis of which the extent of poverty in Guyana could be reliably ascertained, the World Bank reported that "official" estimates indicate that sixty-seven percent of the population was existing below the poverty line.[14] Meanwhile, the disbursed total external debt that was still outstanding representing the sum of long-term and short-term external debt and the use of International Monetary Fund (IMF) credit, increased from 1,486 million dollars in 1985 to 1,995 million by the end of 1994.[15]

The socio–economic data on Guyana presented in Table 5.1 and covering the period 1961 to 1994 gives a more concrete picture of the background against which the discussion of the economic perspective of social conflict is being conducted. Although the GDP and GDP (per capita) seemed to have recovered from the periods of decline in the decade of 1981 to 1990, as Table 5.1 shows, the figures for Guyana have always been very modest. Economic growth has been marginal from the time of independence until 1991, when improvement is apparent. Guyana is one of the few countries of the world where the population is decreasing. The absence of growth and the steady decline in population shown in Table 5.1 from 1981 onward may be an indication that the country's high rates of migration is having some effect (along with other factors such as high infant mortality rates and low life expectancy), on the country's population trends. The number of persons emigrating from Guyana is estimated at about 5,000 to 7,000 per year, and during the decade leading up to 1993, it was estimated that 70,000 Guyanese citizens emigrated to the United States and Canada alone.[16] The other economic indicators—total consumption, gross domestic investment, and exports of goods and services—all support the overall picture of steady decline rather than the macroeconomic trends associated with high industrial development and strong performance both domestically and in the export sector.

Focusing on the questions raised as to the impact of social change and modernization as a catalyst for social conflict, it does not appear likely that Guyana experienced the kind of rapid social change that would create the conditions for social conflict as described above. As Table 5.2 shows in the period leading up to independence in 1966 and shortly thereafter, the three indices of modernization adopted for Guyana, per capita income, urbanization, and educational enrollment, only gradually increased. Per capita income in local currency, the percentage of the population attending educational institutions and the percentage of the population living in urban areas showed very gradual increases between 1947 and 1968 and this trend has continued throughout the post-independence period. With regard to urbanization in particular, increases between 1947 and 1968 reveal a very slow pattern of social change. As Table 5.1 demonstrates, by dividing the period 1961 to 1990 into three decades, the average annual growth rates for the urban population has still been consistently marginal, though experiencing some improvement in 1991 and 1992. Data collected from the *Statistical Yearbook for Latin America* provides corroboration. For example, the urban[17] population

Table 5.1
Selected Average Annual Growth Rates
(Constant 1988 Prices 1961–1994)

	1961–1970	1971–1980	1981–1990	1991	1992	1993	1994
1. GDP*	3.6	0.9	–3.3	6.0	6.5	8.2	8.5
2. GDP (Per Capita)	1.0	0.3	–3.3	6.2	6.6	—	—
3. Population (Total)	2.5	0.4	–0.1	–0.1	–0.1	—	—
4. Population (Urban)	0.4	2.0	0.6	3.2	3.2	—	—
5. Total Consumption	3.6	1.2	–4.1	1.1	N.A.	—	—
6. Exports	3.3	2.9	–2.6	17.0	18.4	—	—

*Gross Domestic Product. Figures for 1993 and 1994 represent the *real* gross domestic product at factor cost.

Sources: (a) Inter-American Development Bank. 1995 Report. *Economic and Social Progress in Latin America*, p. 107.
(b) Clive Y. Thomas. 1993. "The State of Poverty and Poverty Studies in Guyana." In *Poverty in Guyana: Finding Solutions.* Georgetown: Institute for Development Studies, University of Guyana, p. 17.

Table 5.2
Aggregate Modernization Trends in Guyana 1947 to 1970

		Percent Population	
Year	Per Capita Income ($ Guyana)	*Urbanization*	*Educational Enrollment*
1947	266	20	19
1953	342	20	19
1957	397	19	23
1961	421	18	24
1964	424	21	28
1968	528	30	27

Sources: (a) *Annual Reports of British Guiana*, 1947–1963.
(b) *Yearbook of the West Indies and the Caribbean*, 1964–1968.
(c) *Annual Statistical Abstract*, Ministry of Finance, Georgetown, 1970.

expressed as a percentage of the total population for Guyana for the years 1970, 1980, 1985, and 1990 were 29.5, 30.5, 32.5, and 34.6, respectively.[18]

Rates of industrialization have also been relatively static, if not in decline, over time. To the extent that sugar plantations are regarded as industrial concerns and the major industrial concern for Guyana, it could be observed that the country witnessed at least a contraction if not an actual decline in the expansion of this industry over the years. Employment statistics on sugar estates reveal that a much greater proportion of the work force represents field rather than factory workers.[19] As Clive Thomas pointed out in his report on the sugar industry to the International Labor Office (Geneva) some years ago, a multitude of problems in the sugar industry have prevented the mechanization and technical development that was expected, and rather than expansion there has been a reduction of factories operating in the industry since 1949.[20] There has also been a consistent decline in output in the sugar industry over the years. This trend has been followed to a greater or lesser extent in the case of all other major industries in Guyana, as Table 5.3 shows.

In the case of gold and bauxite, fluctuations in output do not show a steady pattern of decline but clearly, except for the years 1990 and 1991, there has been no sustained growth in those industries and no noteworthy attempts to modernize. The production of alumina was discontinued in 1983 and the entire plant has been abandoned. Bauxite production has fluctuated and in recent years has continued to fall, experiencing a twenty percent decline in output in 1994.[21] Nationalization of all the major industries such as bauxite and sugar has had a negative impact on productivity and competitiveness on the world market.

The economic profile of the post-independence period presented herein does not support a finding of modernization as a source of social dissatisfaction and conflict, since Guyana did not experience the rapid social change that accompanies high rates of industrialization and modernization. Rather, the economy has been characterized by poverty and decline until around 1991, when some

Table 5.3
Output of Major Products—1980 to 1991

	Sugar ('000 Tonnes)	Rice ('000 Tonnes)	Timber ('000 Cubic Metres)	Bauxite ('000 tonnes)			Gold ('000 Ounces)
				Calcined	*Dried*	*Alumina*	
1980	270	169	173	601	1,027	246	11
1981	301	166	124	531	498	170	19
1982	292	182	247	392	784	73	7
1983	256	148	236	345	744	—	9
1984	246	180	155	517	754	—	11
1985	247	156	170	487	1,050	—	10
1986	249	183	121	441	979	—	14
1987	224	147	189	426	883	—	21
1988	170	130	164	401	904	—	19
1989	167	142	147	298	919	—	17
1990	132	93	146	288	1,107	—	39
1991	163	151	151	331	1,015	—	59

Source: Adapted from C. Y. Thomas. 1993. "The State of Poverty and Poverty Studies in Guyana." In *Poverty in Guyana: Finding Solutions.* Georgetown: Institute of Development Studies, University of Guyana, p. 20.

improvement could be discerned. It would seem, therefore, that based on this limited scrutiny of the economic indicators for the post-independence period, other sources of social threat and social conflict need to be examined. The significance of ethnicity and class as a source of social conflict and social threat will now be discussed.

The Ethnicity–Class Perspective

Long before independence was achieved in Guyana, the groundwork had been laid for what was to become a society plagued by ethnic and class conflict. The setting for this conflict has been identified by plural society theorists as "cultural pluralism," whereby under colonialism the forced migration of different peoples or ethnic groups resulted in congeries of separate cultural units, which co-exist without combining to form an integrated social whole. Plural society theorists M. G. Smith and J. S. Furnival,[22] in defining culture as the observance of distinct and unique institutional practices, posit that the source of conflict between these groups lie in their cultural specificity; the incompatibility of their institutional practices and customs; and the loyalties of each of these groups to the countries of their origin rather than to their new home. According to Smith, a plural society exists "only when there is a small dominant group that is preoccupied with maintaining power over culturally discrete sections of a society."[23] The potential for violent conflict between these groups intensifies in the political arena when the small, dominant group prepares to withdraw from the scene, and a single cultural section strives for dominance of governmental power.

The tendency toward the occupation of different geographic regions, and a strict division of labor among the different ethnic groups, increased the potential for inter-group conflict in Guyana. The situation was exacerbated by the effect of class divisions, and social stratification based on skin color. As was discussed earlier, colonial society was highly stratified, with Whites occupying the dominant positions in government, the public service, and in the plantation economy, where they were the owners and managers. The Portuguese, Chinese, and the Colored or Mixed population occupied the middle class and held positions in trade, commerce, business, middle management in the public service, and professions such as medicine and law. At the bottom of the social ladder were the dark-skinned groups, the Black and East Indian workers. The Blacks tended to occupy the entry level positions in the public service, factory, and unskilled positions in the business and service sectors, as well as providing labor for the gold and mining industries and the balata fields in the interior. A sizeable proportion remained in subsistence farming, and a handful were able to obtain jobs in the teaching profession after being educated abroad. Blacks tended to migrate to the cities and urban areas.

East Indians replaced the Blacks as the major source of labor on the sugar plantations and tended to establish their villages near the plantations and to engage in agricultural pursuits (e.g., the cultivation of rice) for their livelihood. The Amerindians, the only indigenous people of Guyana, resided in isolated villages in the interior or "hinterland," and engaged in subsistence farming and hunting, while providing labor for the logging and forest industries. They were considered to be among the lower classes also. Eventually, East Indians and Blacks replaced Whites in the public service, entered the professions, and eroded the Portuguese and Chinese monopoly of the commercial and trading sectors. But as the British prepared to withdraw from the scene, the problems of racial, cultural, and class divisions provided "grist for the mill" in an intense struggle between the two leading political parties, divided along racial lines, for control of the political process. The role played by the contradictions inherent in the authority structure, and the mechanisms employed for maintaining social control deserves separate discussion.

The manipulation of ethnic and class divisions in society for the purpose of authoritarian rule was an indispensable component of the colonial state. Under a "divide-and-rule" policy, it was important to foster divisions among the non-White population so as to prevent coalitions of anti-state agitators. This was also crucial for colonial governance, especially in the security forces, because Whites were always the numerical minority and had to rely on non-Whites to police other non-Whites. The ever-present concern about inter-ethnic cleavages and the skillfulness of the colonial authority in using ethnic and cultural differences to their advantage is exemplified by the effectiveness of the Black West India Regiments in protecting the interests of the slave owners throughout the British Caribbean during the eighteenth and nineteenth centuries. Howard Johnson quoted Roger Norman Buckley on the subject as follows:

> Although the West India Regiments were composed chiefly of recruits from various African nations, as well as a diminishing number of Creoles, no apparent attempt was made to form companies of Africans belonging to a single national or language group, or even of Creole soldiers. On the contrary, the *Description and Succession Books* show that companies were heterogeneously formed of, for instance, Ibos, Hausas, and Creoles. The reason for this organization was, no doubt, the time-honored principle of divide and rule.[24]

Enloe[25] also discusses the skillful use of ethnicity by European colonizers in Africa for the purpose of managing resistance to state rule, where the colonial authorities not only nurtured the existing cultural and ethnic differences, but implemented policies geared toward widening the gap between ethnic groups.

The effect of a deliberate "divide-and-rule" policy could also be discerned in the economic sphere, where East Indians were the preferred source for plantation labor, and policies were implemented to keep them almost "captive"on the sugar estates. They were discouraged from migrating to the urban centers and given incentives to remain on the plantations. When the Compulsory Education Act mandating school attendance for children under the age of fourteen years was passed, it was not enforced against East Indians. East Indians, who were willing to accept smaller wages, were used on the sugar plantations to drive wages down, and were the preferred choice to the free Blacks, who insisted on being paid a living wage. This preference for East Indian labor on the plantations generated much animosity between them and the Blacks, the other major ethnic group in the Colony.

According to Fraser, the colonial authority, at the behest of the planters, allowed the continued importation of East Indian immigrants to provide labor for the sugar estates and the imposition of tax measures to pay for immigration, despite widespread poverty and economic depression in the Colony, and a large surplus of unutilized Black labor. By the early twentieth century, the anti-immigration movement led by representatives of the Black population had degenerated into a cultural attack on the East Indian immigrants, as is evident from statements made in a memorandum submitted by the People's Association (an organization representing the interests of the local Blacks) to the Sanderson Committee, which was investigating immigration, in 1909:

> It is well known . . . that the wage which suffices to maintain the East Indian in comparative comfort would mean a starvation pittance to the black man. The latter's civilization is essentially British in its characteristics. The negro has been Christianized and educated in accordance with British ideas and conceptions; his tastes in food and clothing approximate to those of the British, and he has been trained to think and to act in harmony with the particular civilization of which he is a product. On the other hand, the coolie on the sugar estates is content for the most part with a loin-cloth and a frugal diet consisting chiefly of rice. The rate of wages, therefore, upon which an East Indian immigrant can subsist would be inadequate for need of the African race. And it is the East Indian under indenture who fixes the rate of wages rather than the free labourer.[26]

Fraser expresses the view that the degeneration of the discussion of the effects of the sugar industry on the Guyanese economy into personal animosity and attacks between the two major ethnic groups, Blacks and East Indians, laid the groundwork for the ethnic animosity and violence that characterized the decade of the 1960s in Guyana.

There is no doubt that the powerful planter class had a vested interest in promoting ethnic animosity. As one of the more influential planters, Henry Barkley, said in his evidence concerning the conditions in the colony as early as 1848:

> The presence of a few Africans, Coolies and Portuguese, have on this occasion (of the strike) proved the salvation of the colony?— I think entirely; the planters themselves attribute the preservation of their lives to it. From one of the letters it is clear that the different races in the colony is one great cause of the confidence they feel in their personal safety. They look upon the Portuguese and Coolies as their friends in any struggle which might take place.[27]

By far, the most insidious and conflictful use of ethnicity for political purposes by the colonial authority was evidenced by the ethnic composition of the security forces. The governing colonial regime was also adept at augmenting the strength of the military forces by utilizing the services of ethnic groups different from that of the population in uprising. During the slavery period for example, the Dutch military regime relied on the services of the native Amerindian population to help put down African slave insurrections, or to capture runaway slaves in hiding in the dense forested regions of Guyana.[28] The treatment of the free Colored people (who were partially of African ancestry) as a separate, privileged class and the use of their services in the militia to police slaves and put down rebellions has already been discussed. Again, during the Angel Gabriel Riots of 1856, East Indians were used to police Africans.[29]

When the first centralized police force was established in 1839, restrictive and discriminatory requirements for entry ensured that the East Indians were excluded. In the beginning, this pattern was not readily discernible, as the need for social distancing from the population resulted in only a few constables being recruited locally; all other members of the force were recruited either from other West Indian Islands, the United Kingdom, or other countries. But even well into the twentieth century, when all constables and some non-gazetted officers (sergeants and inspectors) were recruited locally, Blacks were given preference in the selection process, and the force was predominantly Black. East Indians laboring on the sugar plantations frequently engaged in industrial actions such as strikes and demonstrations against unfair conditions of work, and the question of reliability and loyalty of East Indian police in suppressing these disturbances weighed heavily on the minds of the colonial masters. In keeping with the old "divide-and-rule" policies, stipulations as to age, height, medical fitness, marital status, and educational standards were effective in excluding East Indians, even though they comprised the numerical majority among all racial groups in the Colony. As G. W. Roberts explained in his research on the population of British Guiana dating back to the nineteenth century, East Indians as a group have always had higher fertility and reproduction rates than other segments of the population.[30]

Table 5.4 shows the racial distribution of the population dating back to 1841, until 1980, and it can be easily discerned that since their introduction into the Colony of British Guiana as indentured servants, the East Indians have increased in numbers more rapidly than any other racial group. From a figure of 105,463 in 1891, the number of East Indians steadily grew over the years to reach the figure of 377,256 in 1970, an increase of 271,793 (72 percent). Meanwhile, Blacks, the second largest ethnic group in the country, had only increased by 111,503 (49 percent) during the same period. In 1970, East Indians accounted for 51 percent of the total population, whereas Blacks accounted for only 30.7 percent, and by 1980 there were 389,760 East Indians in Guyana, compared to 231,330 Blacks. East Indians are estimated to have since increased their numerical representation in the total population, which today stands at 834,000.[31]

In 1965, the International Commission of Jurists (ICJ) in Geneva, Switzerland, was invited by the government of Guyana to undertake an "impartial inquiry into the question of racial imbalance in all significant areas of Governmental activity and all other relevant areas of public life in which racial imbalance may be harmful to the welfare of the community and to the public's interest generally."[32] Included among the "significant areas of governmental activity" was the police force, and the findings of the Commission were very illuminating with regard to the question of the relative under-representation of East Indians in the police force.

Table 5.4
Racial Distribution of the Population of Guyana according to the Censuses of 1841 to 1980*

Census Year	Portu-guese	White	Negro	East Indian	Chinese	Mixed	Other	Total
1841	2,619	—	—	343	—	—	—	—
1851	7,529	—	—	7,682	—	—	—	—
1861	9,859	—	—	22,081	2,629	—	—	—
1871	12,029	—	—	48,363	6,880	—	—	—
1881	11,926	—	—	79,929	5,234	—	—	—
1891	12,166	4,558	115,588	105,463	3,714	29,029	374	270,865
1911	10,084	3,937	115,486	126,517	2,622	30,251	243	289,140
1921	9,175	3,291	117,169	124,938	2,722	30,587	659	288,541
1931	8,612	2,127	124,203	130,540	2,951	33,800	352	302,585
1946	8,543	2,480	143,385	163,434	3,567	37,658	285	359,379
1960	8,346	3,217	183,950	267,797	4,074	67,191	302	534,877
1970	9,668	4,056	227,091	377,256	4,678	84,077	576	707,402
1980	—	770	231,330	389,760	1,842	83,763	3,266	—

Note: Censuses prior to that of 1891 gave distributions by place of birth and not by race; in this table entries in respect of these early censuses represent persons born in Madeira, India, and China. From the censuses of 1891 to 1960 full racial breakdowns are available. The number of Portuguese entered for 1960 is provisional.

*Amerindians are excluded from this table. The census of 1960 was the first that effected a complete enumeration of Amerindians in the interior. Because of incomplete coverage prior to 1960, published numbers of this group vary considerably from census to census, and could not therefore be included in this table. According to the 1960 census the total number of Amerindians was 25,453, that meant that the population of the country as a whole stood at 560,330. According to the 1970 census, the total number of Amerindians was 32,794, which meant that the population of the country as a whole stood at 740,196. According to the 1980 census, the total number of Amerindians was 39,867.

Sources: (a) *Population Census of the Commonwealth Caribbean*, 1970.
(b) *Population Census of the Commonwealth Caribbean, 1980–81,* (Guyana), Vol. 3, Table D 10.
(c) Memorandum presented by the Government of British Guiana to the International Commission of Jurists, *Report of the British Guiana Commission of Inquiry: Racial Problems in the Public Service,* October 1965, p. 16

A government memorandum prepared by G. W. Roberts (who was at that time a Professor of Demography, Department of Sociology, University of the West Indies) traced the ethnic composition of the police force for the benefit of the Commission, and revealed that reference to census data on occupation among East Indians supports a conclusion that as early as 1891 members of the police force recruited from this ethnic group were relatively few in number. Census data revealed that there were sixty-six East Indians engaged in policing as an occupation in 1891, twenty-four in 1911, and twenty in 1921. In 1931, police figures were combined with those of the militia and the prison service and a total of thirty-eight East Indians were tallied holding these occupations.[33]

This census data corroborate the findings of historians W. A. Orrett and Brian Moore, both of whom referred to the disproportionate representation of East Indians in the police force during the latter half of the nineteenth century. Orrett gave a figure of forty-seven members of the police force who were of East Indian descent in 1883,[34] and Moore estimated that in 1887, the sixty-seven East Indian police amounted to only 10.7 percent of the force's strength.[35] The census data showing the small number (sixty-six) of East Indians engaged in policing as an occupation in 1891, despite their substantial representation in the general population (38.7 percent) according to the data presented in Table 5.4, reflects the continuation of an earlier trend that persisted into the twentieth century.

The ICJ's findings with regard to the racial composition of the British Guiana Police Force in 1965, including the Special Constabulary, the Rural Constabulary, and the Supernumerary Police are presented in Tables 5.5 and 5.6. As can be seen from Table 5.6, Blacks make up 74.9 percent, or approximately three-quarters of the British Guiana Police Force, while East Indians comprise only 18.4 percent. Those in the category called "Mixed," which would include Mulattoes and Coloreds, are the third largest group, comprising 5.3 percent, whereas the other ethnic groups combined account for the remaining 1.3 percent. Compared to their percentage in the population, which may be estimated at around 50 percent in 1960, East Indians are very much under-represented in the police force. Blacks are grossly over-represented if their representation in the total population is estimated at around 35 percent at that time. When the police force is considered along with the auxiliaries consisting of the Special Constabulary, Supernumerary Police, and the Rural Constabulary, as shown in Table 5.5, Blacks still lead numerically, comprising 71.9 percent, while East Indians account for only 20.7 percent.

The disproportionate representation is also reflected in the hierarchical rankings in the police force, as shown in Table 5.6. Among the highest ranks, the Officers, the great majority (69 percent) are Blacks, while about 12 percent are Mixed. As expected, Whites are over-represented (considering that they comprised around only 1.5 percent of the population at that time). Also, as was to be expected under the colonial system, they were holding all the dominant positions in this rank. The commissioner, deputy commissioner, and two of the four assistant commissioners were White. East Indians were the numerical minority in this rank, representing only 8 percent of the total. The preponderance of Blacks is repeated among the ranks of Inspectors as well, accounting for a hefty 80 percent, while East Indians only comprise 12.7 percent. Of the 106 Sergeants in the Force, Blacks again account for the majority, as they do for every other rank.

In summary, the Commission found that as of 1965, of the slightly under 1,600 men in the police force, about 75 percent were Black, about 18 percent were East Indian, and 5 percent were Mixed. The Committee's conclusions concerning ethnic imbalances in the police force were prophetic. The Commission stated, in part:

Table 5.5
Racial Composition of British Guiana Police Force (June 30, 1965)

Body	European	East Indian	Amerindian	Black	Portuguese	Chinese	Others	Total
B. G. Police Force	6	287	10	1,160	5	2	83	1553
Special Constabulary	1	119	3	290	2	1	13	426
Supernumerary Police	—	98	—	230	13	—	10	—
Rural Constabulary	—	106	18	442	8	1	43	618
Total	7	610	31	2,122	28	4	149	2,951

Source: Adapted from International Commission of Jurists, *Report of the British Guiana Commission of Inquiry Racial Problems in the Public Service.* October 1965, p. 50.

Table 5.6
Proportional (%) Distribution of British Guiana Police Force by Rank and Race, 1965

Rank	White	Portuguese	East Indian	Chinese	Black	Mixed	Amerindian
Officers	10.2	—	8.2	—	69.4	12.2	—
Inspectors	—	—	12.7	—	80.0	7.3	—
Sergeants	—	1.9	5.7	—	86.8	5.7	—
Corporals	—	1.0	8.7	1.0	80.1	8.2	—
Constables	—	0.1	21.9	—	72.8	4.3	0.9
Total	0.3	0.3	18.4	0.1	74.9	5.3	0.6

Source: Memorandum presented by the Government of British Guiana to the International Commission of Jurists, *Report of the British Guiana Commission of Inquiry: Racial Problems in the Public Service.* October 1965, p. 170.

In a society such as that of British Guiana today, where racial divisions are an important factor in political life, it is essential that the police force should broadly reflect the different races of the population . . . the reason being that a preponderance of any one racial group in the police force may be harmful to the public interest in that members of the racial group or groups which are inadequately represented may have little trust or faith in the impartiality of the force and may perhaps even fear them. It is thus desirable that the Police

Force of British Guiana should broadly reflect the racial composition of the population if it is to command general confidence and support.[36]

The Commission then made several recommendations for increasing the intake of East Indians into the police force, including the reduction of height and chest measurement requirements, and the waiver of such requirements when the applicants are so young as to be likely to continue to develop physically. There is no independent evidence to support the view that the Commission's recommendations were diligently pursued and for how long. Using a "name discerning method," however, Danns perused the lists of names of members of the police force during the period 1970 to 1977 to determine their ethnicity and concluded that of the 2,408 recruits whose names he examined, 2,221 or 90.2 percent appeared to be Blacks, and 187 or 7.8 percent appeared to be of East Indian descent. Danns concluded that there was a reduction of between 13 and 17 percent in the number of East Indians being recruited during this period as compared to 1965.[37]

Although this method of analysis is a questionable one, statistics on the racial composition of the force are not available, and, at least, one can conclude that there is no impartial basis upon which a finding could be made that the situation has improved since 1965. Further, during a taped interview with the researcher, which was conducted in Georgetown in August, 1995, the Hon. Minister of Home Affairs admitted that there was still an under-representation of East Indians in the Guyana Police Force and further stated that at the present time there is no official policy to increase the number of East Indians by the use of racial quotas or other such measures. The Minister confirmed that entry to the Guyana Police Force is still being done on the usual competitive basis from the pool of applicants they receive, regardless of race.

This ethnic imbalance in the police forces emerged as a contentious factor that exacerbated the social conflict that persisted at the time of independence in Guyana. The divisions that were fostered between East Indians and Blacks during the colonial period matured into an association between ethnicity, and organized political movement in the pre-independence period and became the source of social conflict and extreme violence. As defined by Huntington, the situation between Blacks and East Indians during this period can be described as one of ethnic polarization, where each of the two separate ethnic communities is more self-conscious of its own identity than about its role on the broader national level.[38]

Ethnicity was also used by political leaders to garner popular support. As opportunities for local participation in the political process increased with constitutional developments in 1947, 1953, 1957, and 1964[39] (which removed the literacy and property qualifications for the exercise of the franchise, granted universal adult suffrage, and subsequently, internal self-government for Guyana), various political organizations emerged that often appealed to racial sentiments to influence the outcome of local elections for seats in the legislative assembly. "Apanjaht" (vote for your own kind) became the rallying cry of political leaders, and each blamed the other for creating racial divisions in the population.[40] As Leo

Despres pointed out, the immediate pre-independence period witnessed the most violent and bloody clashes between the East Indian and Black cultural sections not "by chance . . . (but) because certain individuals and groups have decided that something can be achieved by making them clash."[41] Table 5.7 shows the class and ethnic representation of the dominant political parties in Guyana at this time.

As can be seen, the three parties that dominated the political scene at that time—the People's Progressive Party (PPP), headed by Dr. Cheddi Jagan, an East Indian dentist; the People's National Congress (PNC), led by Mr. Forbes Burnham, a Black lawyer; and the United Force (UF), led by Mr. Peter D'Aguiar, a Portuguese businessman—all had their separate ethnic and class bases of leadership and support representative of the racial and class cleavages in society. As the Table 5.7 shows, the class nature of the state had shifted from the metropolitan colonial rulers to the locally born professional, intellectual, and business elites who had all been educated abroad. Both Forbes Burnham and Cheddi Jagan practiced racial politics, with people of African descent supporting Burnham and people of East Indian descent supporting Jagan. The United Force, which has always been very small in size, was controlled by the European and light-skinned elites and business people.

The PPP dominated the political arena between 1957 and 1964 mainly through ethnic voting. Cheddi Jagan served as Premier under the system of internal self-government, much to the dismay of the colonial authorities, with whom ultimate authority rested,[42] and the United States, which viewed Jagan as a dangerous communist threat to the stability of the entire Caribbean region.[43] The British consid-

Table 5.7
Class and Ethnic Representation by Political Parties in Guyana between 1950 and 1964

Major Political Party	Date of Birth	Ideology	Class Basis of Leaders	Class Basis of Support	Ethnic Basis of Leaders	Ethnic Basis of Support
People's Progressive Party (PPP)	1950	Marxist	Professional/ Intellectual	Rural/ Agrarian Proletariat	East Indian	East Indian
People's National Congress (PNC)	1958	Nationalist/ Socialist	Professional/ Bureaucratic	Urban Proletariat/ Service Sector	African	African
United Force (UF)	1962	Colonialist/ Capitalist	Commercial/ Landlord	Commercial/ Landlord	Portuguese Mixed	Portuguese Colored Mixed

Source: Perry Mars. 1990. "Ethnic Conflict and Political Control: The Guyana Case." *Social and Economic Studies. 39*:65–94, p. 76.

ered the more moderate Forbes Burnham to be the lesser of the two evils and preferred that Burnham be the one to lead Guyana to independence. They therefore stalled on-going negotiations with Jagan for a firm date for independence, and instead, with the help of the CIA, embarked on a covert destabilization campaign to remove Jagan from office.[44] Meanwhile, a desperate struggle was being waged between the PPP and the PNC to lead Guyana to independence and inherit full political power from the colonial authorities.

During the years 1962 and 1964 the latent conflict between the two largest ethnic groups in Guyana, the East Indians and the Blacks, exploded into open warfare. In each of these years anti-government strikes called by the PNC with the support of the UF against the PPP government, turned into riots involving looting, bombings, arson, and murder. Terrorist and counter-terrorist attacks by these two ethnic groups engulfed the entire country, as the violence spread from village to village, with every attack by one ethnic group against another being visited with an equal or greater reprisal. The disturbances resulted in the injury or death of several hundred persons, the displacement of almost three thousand persons of East Indian and African descent, and millions of dollars in property damage. Cheddi Jagan lays the blame for this sad chapter in Guyana's modern history squarely on the shoulders of the governments of the United States and Britain (CIA financing and infiltration of labor unions with the collusion of Britain, and the colonial government's failure to take action to put down the riots, being the main allegations).[45] But none of this could have occurred if the groundwork for racial animosity had not been laid during the colonial period and exploited as a political weapon by the local aspirants for state power.

Meanwhile, in preparation for the 1964 election, Britain passed the British Guiana (Constitution) Order in Council to introduce a new system of voting (proportional representation) to ensure the defeat of Cheddi Jagan at the polls. As expected, despite ethnic voting, political power passed to a PNC–UF coalition in the 1964 elections. Burnham subsequently ousted the UF and since 1968, through questionable electoral practices, the PNC ruled Guyana uninterruptedly until 1992, when power passed to the PPP under free and fair elections.

The loyalty of the police force to the colonial authorities, as well as the ability of the latter to use the force in pursuance of its own political agenda, was demonstrated during the disturbances that took place immediately preceding independence (1962–64). As stated earlier, this was a predominantly Black force, which since 1891[46] had been transformed into a semi-military outfit modeled after the Royal Irish Constabulary, with training and equipment of the army type. Also remember, this force had demonstrated its superior ability for crowd control and the putting down of peaceful demonstrations and riots with the use of deadly force on several occasions during the colonial period. During the period 1962 to 1964, despite the granting of internal self-government to Guyana, the British government maintained tight operational control over the security forces, including the police, through the colonial governor. The most senior officer in command was an Englishman, the result of an old system of direct recruitment of the top echelon of the force from the United Kingdom.[47] Cheddi Jagan repeatedly gives instances where his government, through the Minister of Home Affairs, *begged* the colonial governor to call out the police or have them intervene to save the lives of innocent people, including children, who were being raped and murdered in the ethnic violence, but all to no avail. In exasperation, the Minister of Home Affairs resigned in protest on June 1, 1964.[48]

Black police witnessed atrocities being committed against East Indians, and vice versa, and turned a blind eye. The laws of unlawful assembly and rioting were not enforced against unruly crowds, who were left to roam the streets and do as much damage as they wanted. Human life was freely expendable in the interest of political expediency. The police only took *defensive* action when forced to confront rioting mobs, often being attacked, stoned, and beaten. One superintendent of police was even shot and killed by rioting mobs in the 1962 disturbances. In no instance during the disturbances was deadly force used against those committing the crimes that would have justified it, such as murder, arson, rape, and the like. Cheddi Jagan's desperate pleas for troops from the United Kingdom were ignored by the authorities until a good deal of damage had already been done.[49]

In view of the preponderance of Blacks in the force, there was a general feeling of distrust and abandonment in the East Indian community, who felt that Black police would not intervene to help them. But the inactivity of the police was not only a result of racial cleavages, because the predominantly Black police force did not intervene to help *anyone* unless they received orders from the colonial administration, and such orders were often not forthcoming in a timely manner. The ethnic imbalance in the force resulted in a widening of the rift that had always existed between the police and the general population, of which East Indians were the majority, and it was to be used skillfully as a political weapon in the hands of the first ruler of an independent Guyana, the PNC's Forbes Burnham.

This discussion of ethnic conflict in Guyanese society has shown that at the time of the departure of the British, the society was recovering from the worst violence it had ever experienced, and the population was separated along racial and ethnic lines. Many persons had lost relatives or friends, or suffered financial ruin as a result of the violence. There was much distrust and hatred among Blacks and East Indians, and the political leaders were facing the challenging task of somehow picking up the pieces in a society totally lacking in social cohesion. Ethnic violence between Blacks and East Indians had subsided, but the *threat* of more conflict was an ever-present reality because of the possibility of reprisals and frontier justice to avenge wrongs that had been done.

The remainder of this chapter will describe how, during the post-independence years, Forbes Burnham took control of the security forces, including the police, in response not only to a *perceived* threat but also a *real* threat of social conflict in Guyanese society, as well as for the purpose of maintaining political power. In so doing, he perfected a process that had been started in 1891, when the police were first transformed into a quasi-military force. Like his colonial predecessors Burnham chose to rely on coercion rather than consensus as a means of social control.

The definition of police powers under the rule of law will also be discussed to show how all these factors worked together to create the context for police violence, the effects of which are still being experienced today.

SOCIAL CONTROL AND THE POLICE

The question of social control weighed heavily on the mind of Forbes Burnham when he was victorious at national elections held in 1964, but even more so when the British officially departed in 1966, with the attainment of independence. Ever conscious of the fact that the wounds had not yet healed following the deadly political rivalries, ethnic conflict, and violence that had immediately preceded independence, Burnham's PNC adopted the slogan "Peace Not Conflict" and at a mass open air meeting in Georgetown after winning the allegedly fraudulent 1968[50] elections, issued a warning to the political opposition as follows:

> We do not deny the right of the opposition to oppose, but as a government we will not permit the disruption of our national life in any manner. We are equipped materially and psychologically to deal firmly, impartially and swiftly with all who by any means or in any guise may be so ill-advised as to seek to spoil our record of peace and tranquility to gratify their puerile ambitions.[51]

In the same speech, Burnham described his relationship with the leader of the PPP as being one of "political conflict" and laid out his plans for the country:

> Let us now turn our eyes to the future for there is much to be done. First of all we must rid ourselves of all vestiges of colonialism. The process of decolonization now barely begun must be accelerated. There must be decolonization both of institutions and of minds. . . . We must overhaul our legal system. We must lay a solid foundation for a new society functioning in freedom. . . .
>
> And when I use the word decolonization I include in that concept the veritable creation of a new man. I include in that concept a complete break with past attitudes of subordination and differentiation.
>
> The problem of racial cleavage has been considerably lessened since the PNC took over the administration in 1964. . . . Nonetheless, we do realise that much work remains to be done in the area of race relations. The realisation of a national identity requires a resolution of this problem. . . .
>
> I want to tell you tonight that the forging of national unity and the decolonization of our minds are as important as our economic problems. They are important because they are related to the ideological position we take as we prepare to go forward. The identification of our ideological position is important because it is this identification which will determine our future in the psychological as against the statistical sense.
>
> Comrades and friends, the question in issue before us all is: What do we want for ourselves? Do we want to remain a mere residue of a colonial past? . . . Do we want to continue aping the ways of our former masters? I am fully aware of course that the means of communication in this twentieth century have had a tremendous influence on our ways of thinking, and that it is only too easy for us to forget our origins and fall into the cultural trap of our times, the trap which has made cardboard Europeans of so many of us.[52]

This lengthy quotation is intended to show that Burnham, an inveterate anti-colonialist, was obsessed with the attainment of two major objectives: (a) the dismantling of the colonial system, and (b) the maintenance of unchallenged political control of the country.

The Dismantling of the Colonial System

Although it seems that Burnham was sincere in his campaign to dismantle colonialism in all its forms, there was no better rallying cry to unite the nation across ethnic and class lines than the call for decolonization. It was a theme that everyone, especially the new middle-class elites of all races and political allegiances, could identify with. (Radicals and liberals at the University of Guyana and the University of the West Indies still give Burnham credit for helping to awaken some sense of national identity in the Caribbean.) Anti-colonialist rhetoric is a recurrent theme in most of the thirty-nine public speeches and statements presented in the selected discourses of the Prime Minister published as *A Destiny To Mould,* in 1970. In 1965 he had established an *Institute of Decolonization* at his PNC party headquarters in Georgetown.

But it was not decolonization alone that interested Burnham, he also wanted to replace "the colonial mentality," as it is popularly called, with something else. He wanted to create a new cultural identity to replace the "cultural trap" of colonization. He wanted a complete change of attitudes and values. He wanted a new ideology for the country, but most of all he wanted loyalty not only to the country, but to the PNC and ultimately to him as the leader of the PNC. And this loyalty included the loyalty of all the agencies of government, especially the security forces—the army and the police. Nothing short of the creation of a new political culture would have sufficed for Burnham.

The development of political culture involves the deliberate structuring of political beliefs, values, and attitudes toward the existing political system. Through political culture, the individual's position toward the state, political behavior, and political beliefs may be redefined. Sydney Verba, in his discussion of the nature of political culture, referred to the deliberate manipulation of basic beliefs as being a common strategy of political elites of new nation states who "have taken upon themselves the task of remaking the basic belief system in their nations as part of their overall task of nation building."[53] According to Lucian Pye, political culture also has an emotional dimension that may include commitment to national identity and political loyalty.[54] Burnham was not only a brilliant lawyer and eloquent speaker, but also an astute politician. In articulating what was, in effect, the belief system of a new political culture, he emphasized the need for a new national identity to replace the false consciousness that had been created by decades of colonial rule. He often thundered against notions of White superiority, and the evils that had been visited upon the population during colonial rule, vowing to revolutionize society through the "decolonization of behavior and attitude" and the adoption of socialist ideology.[55] If we deconstruct some of Burnham's speeches, we find that the question of loyalty was constantly on his mind. He also constantly spoke of the need for national unity and national discipline, all of which were lacking in Guyana.[56]

The Maintenance of Political Control

To achieve success at the polls in 1968, in spite of ethnic voting, Burnham had allegedly indulged in questionable electoral practices, but having obtained power, he had to deal with a formidable and disgruntled PPP opposition leader who, through ethnic alliances, had the support of the numerical majority of Guyanese (East Indians), many of whom had suffered irreparable losses during the years of ethnic violence. These factors created uncertainty and the perpetual threat of impending conflict that seemed to make Burnham want to prepare himself to make a preemptive strike, if necessary. National security and social control were matters of the utmost urgency, and as Burnham turned his attention to the security forces, including the police, it became clear that his warning to the political opposition quoted previously was no idle threat.

Burnham specifically targeted the police for what can be called "cultural infiltration," which was totally inimical to their supposed role as impartial servants of the public. The opportunity to reverse the damage that had been done under British colonialism, and to recreate policing in accordance with the traditional civilian model, was forever lost as Burnham drafted the entire security forces into his master plan for the creation of a new society. He had already vastly extended the police force's powers of arrest, search, and seizure by passing the National Security Act (to be discussed later), shortly after independence was achieved. We will now examine how Burnham, conscious of the uneasy peace prevailing in society, and the perpetual conflict he faced with his political opponents, enlisted the loyalty and support of the police force and helped to create the context for police violence in contemporary Guyanese society.

The Politicization of the Police

Under the independence constitution, although the Minister of Home Affairs had responsibility for the police, final control rested with the Prime Minister. When Burnham appointed himself to the rank of Executive President under the 1980 constitution, he appended to that position a new title called "Commander-in-Chief" of the armed forces, with responsibility, inter alia, for appointing the Commissioner of Police and the Deputy Commissioner of Police as follows:

> 89. There shall be a President of the Co-operative Republic of Guyana, who shall be Head of State, the supreme executive authority, and Commander-in-Chief of the armed forces of the Republic.
>
> 211. (1) The Commissioner of Police and every Deputy Commissioner of Police shall be appointed by the President acting after consultation with the Police Service Commission.[57]

In addition to the title of "Commander-in-Chief," Burnham donned special ceremonial attire symbolic of a rank superior to that of Commissioner of Police, and penetrated the police force with party ideology reflective of the new political culture.

Under his infamous policy initiative known as the doctrine of "Paramountcy of the Party," Burnham defined the relationship between the PNC party and all the agencies and employees of government, as one of complete loyalty and subservience of the latter to the former. This doctrine was first announced at a special PNC congress in 1973, where the ruling party was declared to be superordinate to the government. The legislative, executive, and judicial branches of the government were all declared to be the "executive arm" of the PNC. Burnham rationalized this unusual state of affairs, which was inconsistent with Westminster-style parliamentary democracy, as being a necessary process for the reorganization of society and the achievement of socialist goals. The political socialization of government employees, including the police, was also imperative for the proper functioning of the new society. In 1975, Burnham clarified the position as follows:

> It is the Party that formulates policy on the basis of its ideology, strategy and tactics. It is the Party that mobilizes, educates and appeals to the people on the basis of its programmes. It is the Party that then selects the members of the political government to execute the former's policy which has been carefully debated and then presented.[58]

The Guyana Police Force, which, as has been pointed out, had never been treated as an independent and impartial service organization, had no trouble in adapting to the new role defined for it by the PNC Party. The tenets of the new political culture—of loyalty, decolonization of attitudes, and nation building—resonated with the police who were repeatedly exhorted to be in the forefront as guardians of the revolution and implementers of Party policy. The following quotation, from a speech given by Burnham to the members of the force attending a Junior Officers Course in 1976, captures the essence of the new role that was defined for the police and the extent of political indoctrination that took place:

> You cannot enforce law and order in vacua. Law and order have to be enforced within a particular context of values and objectives . . .
>
> You therefore have to understand what type of society we are pledged, as a community and as a nation, to build . . .
>
> Therefore to understand and accomplish this I say, without apology, that you have to understand the meaning of socialism and its tenets. I say without apology *because there are still some who would say that the police force must be apolitical; it must not be interested in ideology or in the type of society; it must merely enforce the law.*
>
> It was part of our brainwashing to make us believe that we were apolitical when we served colonial masters; but if a group of our own, seeking to raise us out of the mire of colonialism and all the degradation that goes with it, sets out a particular code, is that wrong?
>
> *Policemen are citizens first and then vocationally policemen. Therefore it is commendable that there are political subjects, dealing with ideology and attitudes, to be discussed during the*

course of this three-month exercise. Nevertheless, having finished this course, even understanding what you have discussed in intellectual terms does not qualify you to be a *leader*...

It seems to me, therefore, that not only is this course the beginning of good things in terms of showing our capacity and ability to train our own people, but, if some of the words and sentiments I have uttered mean anything in terms of fitting you for *real leadership in the socialist Guyana,* which at least verbally you claim to support...

You will be judged by your performance not only professionally, but as a citizen, as a man, *as a builder of a new society.*[59] (Italics mine)

As can be discerned from the above quotation, the role defined for the police was primarily a political one and it was part of a deliberate strategy which resulted in a complete distortion of the police function. Members of the force were encouraged to see themselves as loyal "leaders" of the socialist revolution, at the disposal of the government and political party in power, rather than the entire society as a whole. The relevance of training in "political subjects dealing with ideology and attitudes" for the purpose of regular police work is baffling to say the least. The extent of the political indoctrination that took place in the police force is illustrated by the following "Special Greetings" sent to Forbes Burnham who was then the Prime Minister of Guyana, at the opening of the Third Biennial Congress of the People's National Congress on August 22, 1979, as follows:

I bring you greetings from the Management Team and all members of the Guyana Police Force, an institution which has been in the saddle of law enforcement and *national security* for over 140 years.

We congratulate you on the occasion of your Third Biennial Congress, and feel confident that out of your deliberations will come the usual well conceived programme for the furtherance of the social, political, economic and intellectual development of our state and people.

We have genuine and complete confidence in the dynamic leadership of the Party in Government, and wish to re-affirm our pledge of support in the struggle toward our socialist goals.

Move on to a successful Congress.

LONG LIVE OUR COMRADE PRIME MINISTER!

LONG LIVE THE PEOPLE'S NATIONAL CONGRESS!

LONG LIVE THE CO-OPERATIVE REPUBLIC OF GUYANA![60] (Italics mine)

Apart from verbal pledges of loyalty, the police force displayed PNC posters on the walls in police stations, and some members even wore PNC caps and Burnham buttons![61]

The United States Department of State had this to say about the partiality of the police forces in its *Country Report on Human Rights Practices* for 1982:

The belief that the state security forces have become the private protectors of the ruling party has done more to undermine political activism than any other single factor. Disenchantment, fear, despair, and apathy characterize the attitudes of the majority of Guyanese toward politics.[62]

The doctrine of "Paramountcy of the Party," and the politicization of policing, produced a force that was completely at the disposal of an increasingly authoritarian and unpopular government that had to rely on coercion and repression to maintain political power and social control. The goals Burnham defined for the police were political and nationalist goals, and had nothing to do with the prevention of crime and the enforcement of the law. The emphasis on loyalty and subservience to the party made it impossible for the police *not* to react against political opponents of the regime. These strategies were vital for the use of the police in the repression of the political opposition that was to characterize Burnham's rule. In short, the police in Guyana after independence did not know what their duties were. We will now turn to the more serious and violent component of the control function that was perfected under Burnham—the intimidation of the general population, and especially political opponents.

The Increased Militarization of the Police Force

Political and national security received much attention from Burnham until he died in 1985. Apart from the threat of racial conflict, Burnham constantly received criticism from opposition political parties, especially the PPP, all of whom accused him of rigging national elections to remain in office. The increasingly deteriorating economic situation was blamed on the PNC party's corruption and ineptitude in running the affairs of the country. A popular grassroots organization called the "Movement Against Oppression" was formed in 1970 "to protect the human rights of under-privileged and oppressed Guyanese." This organization was born out of the fatal shooting of a 15-year-old, unarmed youth named Michael Hendricks by police in Georgetown on Christmas day in 1970.[63] The organization claimed to be the voice of the people crying out for justice, and they were very vociferous in their campaigns against the government.

Added to this, a new political party had emerged in 1974, the Working People's Alliance (WPA), led by intellectuals and radicals from the University of Guyana and the dynamic, world-renown Guyanese scholar and historian, Dr. Walter Rodney. Rodney attracted both the local and foreign-based Guyanese elite as well as the urban working class, which was previously the domain of Burnham. Although Rodney was Black, the leadership of the WPA was multi-ethnic, and the party attracted a mixed following that could potentially break the pattern of racial voting in free and fair elections. Rodney emerged as a viable and very likeable choice for Guyanese who were disenchanted with the politics of both Burnham and his long-standing rival, Cheddi Jagan.

Against this background, Burnham felt it necessary to further militarize the police to effectively perform its role as leaders of the socialist revolution. Since 1891 the British Guiana Police Force was "transformed from a civilian, but armed, body into a semi-military force definitely modeled upon the Royal Irish Constabulary and available for defense as well as for strictly police purposes."[64] From around 1940, subsequent attempts had been made to demilitarize the force by title changes and other cosmetic factors,[65] but demilitarization did not effectively take place. For example, under the Police Act, which was passed in 1957 and still remains on the statute book today (as amended), the police "shall" perform military duties as may be required by the Minister of Home Affairs, and their duties include the preservation of the peace and the repression of internal disturbance. They may also be issued arms and ammunition for military purposes.[66]

The increasingly authoritarian administration of Forbes Burnham premised on fierce competition for political power and mass discontent, as predicted by Stone, Gittens, and Thomas, poured resources into preparing all the security services, including the police, for internal strife. Between September 1976 and May 1979, 4,000 gas grenades and projectiles were acquired from the United States under the Commercial Sales program, at a cost of U.S.$187,000.[67] Guyana also received foreign assistance from the United States, both monetarily and in the provision of training to members of the Force. Between 1950 and 1979, a total of 9.6 million U.S. dollars had been received by Guyana, in military subsidies awarded to threatened pro-U.S. regimes, from the United States Economic Support Fund, formerly known as the Security Supporting Assistance Program.[68]

With regard to training, the United States participated in a "counter-insurgency" campaign with Guyana, which was implemented through the Office of Public Safety (OPS) of the Agency for International Development (AID). Jenny Pearce quotes David Bell, a former AID administrator, as providing the following rationalization of the program to the Foreign Assistance Appropriations Committee in 1965:

> (T)he police are a most sensitive point of contact between government and people, close to the focal points of unrest, and more acceptable than the army as keepers of order over long periods of time. The police are frequently better trained and equipped than the military to deal with minor forms of violence, conspiracy and subversion.[69]

Between 1966 and 1970, 921 Guyanese police officers were trained under the OPS program at their Latin American facilities. By the end of 1973, fifty-three other members of the Force had been trained under the Public Safety Program in the United States at a cost to the United States of U.S.$1,299,000.[70] In addition to this, regular courses were offered to members of the Force at the International Police Academy operated by the Central Intelligence Agency (CIA). Top-ranking members of the Force, including past Commissioners were allegedly trained by the CIA's proprietary, the International Police Services, Inc., (INPOLSE) from a residential townhouse in Washington, D.C.[71] There is also evidence that at least one officer was given training in assassination, arson, and bombing by the infamous Texas Border Patrol, an organization "that was so dirty that even the Department of Defense refused to staff the operation."[72]

The police force that Burnham had so diligently crafted became indispensable to his campaign of internal surveillance and the silencing of all dissenting voices. Records of police abuses in the use of force, brutality, and torture are piecemeal for the years preceding 1980, when the Guyana Human Rights Association started to collect data on human rights violations. This information is not available from the police or through any other known source. There is reference however, to the occurrence of police killings in the petition issued by the Movement Against

Oppression to the government in 1970, calling for an inquest into the fatal shooting of Michael Hendricks by police. It stated in part:

> The reported circumstances surrounding his (Michael Hendricks') death give rise to anxiety and concern. It is clearly a matter of great public importance because *there have been a number of such incidents, many of which were not reported in the Press and to which the general society has remained blind.*[73]

Based on this document it appears that the use of fatal force by police was being questioned before the Guyana Human Rights Association published its first report in 1980. However, other forms of police brutality regularly occurred throughout the tenure of office of the PNC. The powers possessed under the National Security Act were routinely used to carry out searches and seizures and to impose a reign of terror directed primarily at the political opposition. Arrests, beatings, and torture regularly took place and opposition political meetings were routinely broken up by using police violence and intimidation.[74]

Burnham seemed to be particularly angry at Walter Rodney and the intellectuals at the University of Guyana who made up the leadership of the WPA. He referred to them as "counter-revolutionaries" and issued a warning that few took seriously at the time, but was soon to become tragic reality. In his address to the Third Biennial Congress of the PNC in August 1979, Burnham had this to say about the WPA:

> In March, 1979, they purported to draft a programme for the so-called Working People's Alliance, but have not dared to publish it. It could have been written by a group of untutored under-graduates, and says nothing original.
>
> The People's National Congress is a Party of Peace Not Conflict, but we will not buy peace at the cost of bowing to the counter-revolutionary agents of Imperialism.
>
> *The gauntlet has been thrown down. We have picked it up. The battle is joined. we ask no quarter and we shall give none. We shall use every weapon at our disposal. Let there be no weeping or complaints.*
>
> We must be committed and resolute. No wall must be too high to scale, no citadel too strong to take. The People must win under the leadership of the vanguard People's National Congress.[75] (Italics added)

And in the same speech, in referring to an incident where the Party headquarters was set on fire, the act, he said, of "counter-revolutionaries" and "enemies of the people," Burnham issued the following warning to his political opponents:

> I readily concede that our state of physical alertness and security at the time was not as high as it ought to have been, but, as was the case at Pearl Harbour and Hitler's invasion of the Soviet Union, *they have awakened a sleeping giant who will not sleep again, and who will not rest again until his enemies are crushed and utterly destroyed.*[76] (Italics mine)

WPA officials were given particularly brutal treatment, and several members of the WPA were killed by police under suspicious circumstances. Eusi Kwayana mentions the killing of WPA activists Ohene Koama (November 18, 1979) and

Edward Dublin (February 1980) by police under suspicious circumstances.[77] Other party members were charged with treason (Ivan Sookram and others) and tortured to obtain information.[78] Walter Rodney himself was continually harassed, arrested, imprisoned, and prosecuted until finally on June 13, 1980, he was assassinated by bomb blast under circumstances allegedly orchestrated by the PNC with the assistance of the military. Several intellectuals from the University of Guyana, known to be opposed to the Burnham regime, subsequently fled the country in fear for their lives. The United States State Department in its *Country Report* for that year (1980) concluded that "available information indicates that the government was implicated in the June 13 death of WPA activist Walter Rodney and in the subsequent removal of key witnesses from the country."[79]

The police, as well as the other security forces, transformed the society into a hostile and uncertain environment for those who would not support the tyranny of the PNC. Violence was legitimized as the appropriate means of communication between the police and the public, especially when the public consisted of political opponents to the ruling PNC government. After Rodney's untimely death, the WPA was effectively destroyed as a viable political alternative, and there was a marked increase in migration rather than agitation for political change. The militarization of the Force, coupled with the large expenditure of money on training and weapons of war and the emphasis on counter insurgency all prepared the police for the role they played in charting the political history of the country. These events resulted in the suppression of political dissent "in ways that maximize the deterrent impact upon potential offenders, that is everyone else."[80] The law also served to facilitate police violence in Guyana through the expansion of police powers to use deadly force. The final section of this chapter will show how the law promotes police violence in Guyana.

THE RULE OF LAW AND THE POLICE

"My lectures," wrote A. V. Dicey to James Byrce more than a hundred years ago, "will I feel greatly disappoint you. They are simply lectures and intended to explain very elementary matters to students who seem to me in need of guidance."[81] Little did Dicey know at the time that his "lectures," in which he set out the fundamental principles of limited government in terms of British parliamentary sovereignty, the rule of law, and the requirements of constitutional conventions, would have an enduring influence on the unending debate concerning the administration of law and order vis-à-vis the exercise of governmental power.

The idea of the rule of law can be traced as far back as the discourses of Aristotle,[82] but it was Dicey, in his *An Introduction to the Study of the Law of the Constitution* as his celebrated "lectures" were called when published in book form, who explained how the awesome powers of government could be checked by the rule of law. The "first meaning" of the rule of law, according to Dicey, was that "no man is punishable or can be lawfully made to suffer in body or goods except for a distinct breach of law established in the ordinary courts of the land."[83] Laws were laid down by Acts of Parliament (and Parliament would only make "good" laws) in accordance with constitutional conventions that placed a duty of compliance on the government under the principle of parliamentary sovereignty. But writing as he did in the latter part of the nineteenth century in the United Kingdom, Dicey could not have contemplated the reality of the concept of the rule of law when governmental action, *though lawful*, overrides the concept of limited government under parliamentary democracy and contravenes the fundamental principles of the constitution regarding individual rights and freedoms, the right of political opposition and dissent, and the right of citizens not to be deprived of their lives save and except under the jurisdiction of a competent court.

This discussion raises the question of the meaning of the rule of law when, as in Guyana, the law is used as an instrument of repression to "legalize" the abuse of power and the excessive use of force by the police under a formal political system of British-style parliamentary democracy. Under such a political system, however, Parliament does not always make "good" laws, and it is doubtful whether the mere enforcement of the law would be sufficient for the rule of law in such a case. To find a definitive answer to this dilemma we must move beyond Dicey and enquire into the true relationship between legality and justice under the rule of law.

Lon Fuller, in formulating his eight "principles of legality" or "principles of the rule of law" called attention to the relationship between legality and morality. Speaking of the internal and external morality of law that he considered to be preconditions for "good law," he arguably stopped short of disassociating abuse of governmental power and the making of unjust laws from the true meaning of the rule of law.[84] There seems to be merit in the claim of his critics that his requirements for the morality of law are merely conditions of efficiency rather than morality.[85] Hadley Arkes emphasized the importance of seeking the "principles of moral reasoning" that lie behind the United States Constitution in order to make sense of its provisions,[86] but he did not discuss the requirements for what could be called "moral" or "good" law that is implicit in ideas of the rule of law dating back to Dicey.

However, much can be learned about the requirement for justice that is included in the meaning of the rule of law by the broad content the concept has been given by the International Commission of Jurists at Athens in 1955, when the Commission declared that:

1. The state is subject to the law.
2. Governments should respect the rights of the individual under the Rule of Law, and provide effective means for their enforcement.
3. Judges should be guided by the Rule of Law, protect and enforce it without fear or favour and resist any encroachments by governments or political parties on their independence as judges.
4. Lawyers of the world should preserve the independence of their profession, assert the rights of the individual under the Rule of Law and insist that every accused is accorded a fair trial.[87]

This formulation makes the rule of law a dynamic concept so that it involves not only the subordination of the state to the law, but also the protection of individuals from the tyranny of unbridled state power. By requiring that governments should respect the rights of the individual, it impliedly forbids the making and enforcement of unjust laws. It requires the preservation of rights and freedoms that are often enshrined in that part of the constitution called the "Bill of Rights," because we hold these rights to be indispensable to the right to be human. Most of all, however, by exhorting judges and lawyers to preserve their independence, to avoid political interference, and to strive for fairness, it thereby incorporates rigorous standards of justice within the meaning of the rule of law.

This theme is also to be found among contemporary legal theorists who have debated the meaning of the rule of law in relation to the ideological orientation of the state. Abel makes the interesting observation that "most successful capitalist nations have grossly violated the rule of law" citing the United States as well as countries that are considered to be dictatorships, such as developing countries in Latin America, Asia, and the Arab world.[88] Abel focused on the inability of capitalist nations to provide equal justice under the law, which he insisted is an essential requirement of the rule of law. Krygier, stressing the "majesty" of the law and the precedence the law should take over politics, criticized the instrumental uses of law that took place in communist States professing Marxist ideology, the tenets of which he argued are not only antithetical to the requirements for the rule of law, but also dispense with the need for law altogether.[89] Skapska, agreeing with Krygier, focused on the subordination of the law to political authority and the use of law as an instrument of repression in Eastern European communist states before the collapse of communism.[90] What all these legal theorists seem to agree on, however, and what is pertinent to our discussion, is the fact that the mere presence of laws do not necessarily mean that the rule of law is alive, and that regardless of political ideology, the rule of law requires that governmental abuse of power be restrainable by law and that all be given the protection of the law and the use of an impartial legal system to correct injustice.

Policing is an essential governmental function in all civilized societies, and the police are barometers of the societies they serve. In a society governed by the rule of law, the police, as enforcers of the law, are required to conform to rigorous standards of justice and to be subject to legal restraint in the exercise of their awesome powers, especially the power to use deadly force. The discussion of the extent and exercise of police power to use deadly force in Guyanese society will focus on this broader meaning of the rule of law. The question therefore is not solely whether the police, as agents of the state, are acting in accordance with law, but even where the police are acting in accordance with law, whether such law, and their actions, are in keeping with the requirements that are imposed upon the state in a society that gives true meaning to governance under the rule of law. The extent of police powers under the law with regard to the use of force, especially deadly force, during the modern period in Guyana will now be examined.

Police Power to Use Force, and the Law

At the time of independence, the Constitution of Guyana made provision for the protection of fundamental human rights, such as the right to life; protection from torture and inhuman treatment, slavery, forced labor, arbitrary arrest, or detention; protection of private and family life and home; freedom of conscience; freedom of expression; freedom of assembly and association; freedom of movement; protection from discrimination on grounds of race, place of origin, religion, or political opinion; and protection from the deprivation of property without compensation. [91] Article 13 provided for the enforcement of these fundamental rights by the Supreme Court, which was thereby given an original jurisdiction to hear and determine applications by any person alleging that these rights "have been, is being or is likely to be contravened" in relation to him or her, and to determine any such questions that may be referred to it by a lower court.

With regard to the protection of the right to life, however, the Constitution created an exception where death results from the state's use of force in the certain circumstances. The entire article is reproduced below for ease of reference:

> 1. (1) No person shall be deprived intentionally of his life save in execution of the sentence of a court in respect of a criminal offence of which he has been convicted.
>
> (2) Without prejudice to any liability for a contravention of any other law with respect to the use of force in such cases as are hereinafter mentioned, *a person shall not be regarded as having been deprived of his life in contravention of this article if he dies as a result of the use of force to such an extent as is reasonably justifiable in the circumstances of the case—*
>
> (a) for the defence of any person from violence or for the defence of property;
> (b) in order to effect a lawful arrest or to prevent the escape of a person lawfully detained;
> (c) for the purpose of suppressing a riot, insurrection or mutiny; or
> (d) in order to prevent the commission by that person of a criminal offence; or if he dies as a result of a lawful act of war.[92]

Apart from the exceptions regarding instances of capital punishment and war, the remaining circumstances where the deprivation of life by the state will not be unconstitutional all relate to the exercise by the police of the power to use deadly force. In so far as the police are concerned, therefore, the use of deadly force will be lawful under the circumstances specified in Article 1.(2)(a),(b),(c), and (d) which, in effect, not only codified the English common law relating to the use of deadly force but dangerously extended it by allowing the use of force by the police first, in defense of property only (Article 1.(2)(a)), and secondly to prevent the commission of minor crime, which is included in the vague term "a criminal offence" (Article 1.(2)(d)).

Under the Police Act of 1957, as amended, the rights and powers of the police under the English common law were made applicable to the members of the Guyana Police Force as follows:

> 15. Every member of the Force, so long as he continues to be a member thereof, shall have all such rights, powers, authorities, privileges and immunities and shall be liable to all such duties, responsibilities and penalties as any member of the Force duly appointed now has or is subject or liable to, either by the common law or by virtue of any law which now or may hereafter be in force in Guyana.[93]

Under the English common law, as received into the country under British colonial rule, the use of deadly force by the police is protected under the law of justifiable homicide in the four situations specified by Article 1.(2)(a), (b), (c) and (d), but police homicide committed under these circumstances must also satisfy certain requirements in order to be considered lawful.

In the case of the situation codified by Article 1.(2)(a), the use of deadly force by police under the English common law is justifiable where the conduct of the victim involves an attempt to commit a felony against a person (including the officer), against property, or against the society at large.[94] In the case of property, however, the felonious threat has to be also accompanied by a threat of death or serious bodily injury, there being no independent right to use deadly force in defense of property only. Article 1.(2)(a) of the constitution makes no such distinction, and the use of deadly force by police is therefore justifiable to protect property only, irrespective of whether the property crime was accompanied by the threat of personal injury.

With regard to Article 1.(2)(b), which deals with the apprehension of criminals, under the English common law deadly force could be used under the "fleeing felon rule" to prevent the escape of suspected felons provided that it is absolutely necessary for that purpose, and the amount of force used was *reasonable* according to the circumstances of the case.[95] The use of deadly force had to be essential in order to effect the arrest, there being a great deal of certainty that less-drastic means would not have sufficed. The use of deadly force was never permitted in order to effect the arrest of a misdemeanant or someone who had only committed a petty crime.

This fleeing felon rule, which is really now an historical anachronism, reflected the situation in fifteenth-century England, where all felonies such as murder, rape, robbery, sodomy, mayhem, burglary, and arson were punishable by death. In the absence of an organized police force and the advances of modern technology, apprehending a fleeing felon meant a chase on foot and hand-to-hand combat with the assistance of primitive weapons such as swords and knives. The desperation of a person facing death, and the slim chance of recapture once the felon escaped, required the use of as much force as necessary to effect the arrest which it was felt was justifiable because the felon had already forfeited his life by committing the crime. Today, the death penalty has been abolished in England, and British police are largely unarmed!

With regard to Guyana, the reception of the English common law means that the fleeing felon rule is still alive and well, there being no attempt so far to legislate the rule out of existence. Diligent attempts to unearth judicial guidelines with regard to the application of this rule were fruitless during field research in Guyana in July and August of 1995. In a taped interview with the Honorable Chancellor of the Judiciary, however, the researcher was referred to the case of *The State v Evelyn Dick and Alwyn Dodson Evelyn*, Criminal Appeals Nos. 42 and 43 of 1983, where the Court of Appeal of the Supreme Court of Judicature reviewed the English common law with regard to the meaning of excessive force. Although in delivering the leading judgment of the Court the Hon. Chancellor was dealing with the use of excessive force in the context of self-defense, it is submitted that in the absence of judicial guidelines with regard to force used in the apprehension of suspects, the general principles laid down by the Court will apply.

In the instant case, the defendants were convicted of murder at the Demerara Assizes, and the second-named defendant claimed that he had acted in self-defense when he fired a gun in the direction of the deceased, who had a chair upraised and was advancing toward him. The Court of Appeal had to determine, inter alia, whether directions given to the jury by the trial judge on the question of self-defense and the degree of force used were erroneous. In reviewing the English common law, the Court endorsed and adopted the restrictions placed on the use of force that are contained in the *Report of the Criminal Code Bill Commission (1879)* and had been given approbation by Kenny in his treatment of justifiable homicide.[96] The pertinent passage in the *Report* is as follows:

> We take one principle of the common law to be that, though it sanctions the defence of a man's person, liberty and property against illegal violence, and permits the use of force to prevent crimes, to prescribe the public peace and bring offenders to justice, yet all this is subject to the restriction that the force used is necessary; that is, that the mischief sought to be prevented could not be prevented by less violent means; and that the mischief done by, or which might reasonably be anticipated from the force used, was *not disproportionate to the injury or mischief of which it was intended to prevent.*[97]

The reference in the above passage, which was approved by the Court, to the use of force "to prevent crimes, to prescribe the public peace and bring offenders to justice," tends to suggest that the principles laid down by the Court with regard to the use of force were made in contemplation of not only the circumstance of self-defense but in the generality of circumstances where the English common law permits the use of force. The court held that the element of "proportionality" is an intrinsic requirement for the legitimate use of force and phrased the question that must be answered in assessing whether excessive force was used as follows:

> (W)as there imminent danger to the prisoner's (person using the force) life or limb or the person he sought to defend, and if so, was there reaction by the prisoner, *proportionate* to it?[98]

The force used must also bear "reasonable relationship" to that of the impending attack. Based on the decision of the Federal Supreme Court of the Caribbean (Hallinan, C. J., Rennie, and Marnan, JJ. A.) in the Guyanese case of *John DeFreitas v The Queen* (1960) 2 W.I.R. 522, which was approved by the Judicial Committee of the Privy Council in the celebrated decision of *Palmer v The Queen* (1971) 1 All E.R. 1077, the Court held that the objective standard ought to be used in making the determination as to whether the use of force was reasonably necessary and proportionate to that of the imminent attack. This the Court described as "the officious *Bystander's Test*" of whether in the normal course of things, the force was justifiable, having regard to all the circumstances of the case.[99]

Returning to the extent of the power given to police by the Independence Constitution in conjunction with the English common law, these judicial guidelines on the use of force seem to suggest that the court will only sanction the use of *deadly force* by the police in situations where there was imminent threat of bodily injury *in proportion* to the force being used, which in this case would mean *serious* bodily injury or death. In order to reconcile this position with the common law exception of the fleeing felon rule, which does not require a confrontational situation between the felon and the officer but only that the felon was *fleeing*, it would seem that, at least, the crime for which the arrest is being made or in respect of which the escape is being prevented, must be proportionately serious to the injury that may be inflicted by the use of deadly force. The rule the Hon. Chancellor affirmed is still considered to be in existence in Guyanese jurisprudence. There seems to be no legal authority, therefore, for the departure in practice by the Guyana police from the common law situation requiring that the suspect be a fleeing *felon*, and for the use of deadly force to effect the arrest of fleeing persons who are only suspected of having committed petty crimes or who are escaping from lawful detention in respect of a petty crime or misdemeanor.[100] The inhumanity of this practice was given judicial notice in *Head v Martin* (1887) 85 Ky. 480, at 483–84, when the Court had this to say, "Human life is too sacred to admit of a more severe rule . . . [T]o permit the life of one charged with a mere misdemeanor to be taken when fleeing from the officer would, aside from its inhumanity, be more productive of abuse than good . . ." Judicial review of the fleeing felon rule is urgently needed so that the loss of life through police homicide in the course of making an arrest or preventing the escape of a suspect would be outlawed not only where the crime is a misdemeanor, but also where the suspect poses no threat of serious bodily injury or death.

This has been the position in the United States since 1985 when the U.S. Supreme Court outlawed the use of deadly force against nondangerous, unarmed, fleeing felony suspects in the case of *Tennessee v Garner*, 471 U.S. 1 (1985). Some legal scholars claim that the decision created a constitutional right to run for felony suspects, others that the fleeing felon rule has been laid to rest. The more balanced view is that in the United States the common law fleeing felon rule has been modified to bring it more in line with the Model Penal Code guidelines whereby the police may only use deadly force against fleeing violent felony suspects who are considered dangerous or who pose an imminent threat to the life or limb of another, including the officer.[101]

Article 1.(2)(c) is on all fours with the English common law, which has always recognized the state's right to use deadly force to prevent a breach of the peace. Finally, with regard to Article 1.(2)(d) the right of the police to use deadly force and deprive someone of their life also extends under the English common law to the prevention of crime but is similarly limited to crimes that amount to serious felonies against the person such as murder, robbery, house-breaking in the night-time, rape, mayhem, or arson.[102] As early as 1882 the courts singled out the type of felony that could be prevented by the use of deadly force when it declared it "would be shocking to the good order and government to have it proclaimed, with the sanction of the courts, that one may in broad daylight, commit a willful homicide in order to prevent the larceny of an ear of corn" (a felony at that time) *Storey v State* (1882). No distinction is made in the Guyana independence constitution based on the degree of seriousness of the "criminal offence," and the supremacy of the constitution means that it is controlling. The deprivation of life by virtue of police use of deadly force therefore would not be unconstitutional if it is done to prevent the commission of any criminal offense, regardless of degree of seriousness, and this would include misdemeanors and petty crimes.

The position outlined above with regard to the powers of the Guyana police to use deadly force under the laws of Guyana remained unchanged after the last constitution was adopted in 1980. The provisions of Article 1 of the Independence Constitution were reproduced verbatim in Article 138 of the new *Constitution of the Cooperative Republic of Guyana*, which replaced the Independence Constitution in 1980.

The National Security Act

In addition to the circumstances discussed previously, where the exercise of the power to use force, including deadly force, is legitimated under existing law, the police were given the license to use force against civilians under the provisions of the National Security Act, which was passed shortly after independence was achieved in 1966. This Act, the long title of which states, "An Act to make provision for divers matters touching on national security," is the first and only one of its kind to be enacted in the Commonwealth Caribbean. The relevant provisions that expanded police powers and gave them the right to use force in pursuance of those powers will now be discussed.

First, the Act empowered the Minister of Home Affairs to make orders directing the preventive detention of persons suspected of acting in any manner prejudicial to the pubic safety or public order or the defense of Guyana. Such orders came into force upon the making thereof whereupon the police may summarily arrest the persons named in the order without a warrant and detain them in "such a place and under such conditions as the Minister may from time to time direct."[103]

Second, a policeman not below the rank of inspector, except if he is in charge of the nearest police station, accompanied by such persons as he thinks fit, may in the interest of public safety or order enter, examine, and search any premises or place for firearms, ammunition, or explosives, and seize and detain any firearms, ammunition, or explosives found if he reasonably suspects that an offense has, been or is about to be committed.[104]

Third, the Minister may, by order, declare certain areas of the country to be "protected areas" and restrict the entry of persons into those areas. Persons who enter "protected areas" in defiance of the order of the Minister may be removed by any member of the police force or any soldier or officer of the Guyana Defence Force.[105]

Finally, under the provisions of this Act, any policeman may stop and search any person whom he finds in any street or other public place and reasonably suspects of having any firearm, ammunition, or explosive in his possession, or of having committed or being about to commit any other offense prejudicial to public safety or order. Any firearm, ammunition, or explosive or other article found in the person's possession in connection with the exercise of the power to search may be seized.[106]

In the exercise of all these powers, "any policeman may . . . take such measures as are reasonably required, *including the use, with any assistance, of force to any extent which is reasonably justifiable in the circumstances*."[107] (italics mine) "Force to any extent" implies that deadly force is also included and this amounted to a chilling expansion of the power of the state to lawfully deprive citizens of their lives. The legislature left no doubt that these powers were incremental when it provided that "the powers conferred by this Act shall be in addition to, and not in derogation of, any powers conferred by any other law" and "in the case of any conflict between any provisions of this Act . . . and any other law . . . that other law shall, in so far as it conflicts with the said provisions, be of no effect."[108] The Act does not impose any safeguards to ensure that these awesome powers would not be abused, but rather it seems that the legislature was concerned that the police not be hindered in their work.

This was the state of the law until 1989 when the National Security Act was repealed after many years of agitation by the political opposition and the Guyana Human Rights Association. Despite this, however, the lawful powers of the police in Guyana with regard to the use of force, and especially deadly force, under the existing constitution represents the transference of the state's monopoly on the use of force to the police in a wide variety of circumstances, without apparent regard for the sanctity of human life and the need for accountability and restraint. The police are in a unique position. Whereas the state, through the judicial system may only impose the penalty of death, after due process of law, as punishment for heinous crimes such as murder and treason, the police are given the license to kill in an instant long before the guilt of the victim could ever be ascertained.

In a society governed by the rule of law, justice requires that this power be sparingly exercised. In Guyana we find that not only have the common law rules been expanded to permit more situations where force, including deadly force, may be used, but also, until recently the floodgates were open for the police to kill whom they pleased under cover of the law. When the state fails to guard the lives of citizens by imposing adequate legal restraint on the use of force in policing, then it is questionable whether the rule of law is alive. When the state makes laws to legalize the arbitrary use of force in questionable circumstances, then the law becomes an instrument of repression rather than an instrument of justice and it is debatable whether and to what extent society gives true meaning to the rule of law.

CONCLUSION

This chapter has discussed the context of police violence and the use of excessive and deadly force in the post-independence period. Based on the theoretical framework of the conflict perspective, the social and political forces at work in contemporary Guyanese society have been explored. First, economic factors that have been empirically associated with police-caused homicide in the technical literature have been discussed in order to show that the likelihood of these factors significantly influencing the existence of social conflict was minimal.

However, an alternative source of the "perceived threat of social unrest" was located in the presence of the potential for ethnic conflict based on the historical relationship between the two largest ethnic groups in the country, East Indians and Blacks, that had been fostered by colonial "divide-and-rule" policies. The development of ethnic animosity leading to open warfare between these two groups during the period preceding independence, and the impact of continued racial politics, all resulted in the perpetual potential for social unrest. This was exacerbated by the ethnic imbalance in the police force that was allowed to continue despite the warnings of the International Commission of Jurists in 1965.

Added to the ethnic dimension, fierce political rivalries and the authoritarian rule imposed by the PNC added to social discontent and for the government the perception of impending social disorder, as the PNC held onto political power allegedly by rigging elections. Burnham identified the police force for specific cultural innovations, which coupled with increased militarization and extensive powers under the law, was transformed into a formidable political weapon. The opportunity to create traditional civilian policing in Guyana was forever lost as the indiscriminate use of police force and brutality became a daily reality in Guyana.

Although Burnham's reign of terror ended with his sudden demise in 1985, and the PNC government repealed the National Security Act in 1989, whether it can be said that the rule of law is alive in Guyana is an open question. The PNC continued to rule Guyana until 1992 when the PPP won the first allegedly free and fair elections held in Guyana since independence, with the help of the Carter Center and other international observers. The police, however, still possess all the powers they had short of those under the National Security Act, and they are still a formidable source of unbridled power, which seems to be beyond the restraint of the East Indian–dominated government.

The next chapter will examine whether the alternative explanation offered by the community violence hypothesis could account for the high incidence of police-caused homicide that was found to exist in Guyana based on data collected for the period 1980 to 1994. The question to be answered is whether police violence is a function of community violence as is argued by some researchers, or whether it is a result of the coercive rule of the state and the state's legitimation of violence in police work.

NOTES

1. Ralf Dahrendorf. 1968. *Class and Class Conflict in Industrial Society.* Stanford, Calif.: Stanford University Press, pp. 206–40.

2. See the studies discussed under "Theoretical Perspectives and Literature Review," Chapter 1.

3. David Jacobs and David Britt. 1979. "Inequality and Police Use of Deadly Force. An Empirical Assessment of a Conflict Hypothesis." *Social Problems* 26:403–12.

4. See discussion in Chapter 1 as well as Jonathan R. Sorenson, James W. Marquart, and Deon E. Brock. 1993. "Factors Related to Killings of Felons by Police Officers: A Test of the Community Violence and Conflict Hypotheses." *Justice Quarterly* 10:417–40.

5. Paul Chevigny. 1990. "Police Deadly Force as Social Control: Jamaica, Argentina, and Brazil." *Criminal Law Forum* 1:389–425.

6. Ibid., pp. 399–405.

7. Ernest A. Duff and John F. McCamant. 1976. *Violence and Repression in Latin America.* New York: The Free Press, pp. 56–93.

8. See Chapter 1 as well as Ernest A. Duff and John F. McCamant. 1976. *Violence and Repression in Latin America.* New York: The Free Press, pp. 56–93.

9. Chevigny felt that a great deal of distortion occurred in the computation of the scale because of the country's large GNP. See Paul Chevigny. 1990. "Police Deadly Force as Social Control: Jamaica, Argentina, and Brazil."

10. See Neil J. Smelser. 1962. *Theory of Collective Behavior.* New York: The Free Press, p. 55; Lucian Pye. 1966. *Aspects of Political Development.* Boston, Mass.: Little, Brown & Co., p. 47; Samuel P. Huntington. 1964. "Political Development and Political Decay." *World Politics* 3:386.

11. S. N. Eisenstadt. 1966. *Modernization, Protest and Change.* Englewood Cliffs, N.J.: Prentice Hall, p. 22.

12. Samuel P. Huntington. 1968. *Political Order in Changing Societies.* New Haven, Conn.: Yale University Press, p. 45.

13. Caribbean Conference of Churches. 1993. *Who's Included? A Survey of Poverty in Guyana,* Bridgetown, Barbados: Caribbean Conference of Churches, p. 7.

14. World Bank. 1992. *Guyana: From Economic Recovery to Sustained Growth,* Washington, D.C., p. 80.

15. Inter-American Development Bank. 1995. *Economic and Social Progress in Latin America.* Washington, D.C., p. 301.

16. Thomas J. Spinner, Jr. 1984. *A Political and Social History of Guyana, 1945–1983.* Boulder, Colo.: Westview Press, p. 142; Also, Caribbean Conference of Churches. November, 1993. *Who's Included? A Survey of Poverty in Guyana,* p. 7.

17. The term "urban" is considered to mean the conglomeration of a population of more than 10,000 in one locality. Guyana has only two urban centers: Georgetown and New Amsterdam.

18. Economic Commission for Latin America and the Caribbean. *Statistical Yearbook for Latin America and the Caribbean.* 1994. New York: United Nations, p. 8.

19. See Edwin P. Reubens and Beatrice G. Reubens. 1962. *The Sugar Industry of British Guiana.* Mona, Jamaica: Institute of Social and Economic Research, pp. 23, 24.

20. Clive Y. Thomas. 1984. *Plantations, Peasants and State (A Study of the Modes of Sugar Production in Guyana).* Institute of Development Studies/International Labor Office, Geneva, p. 136.

21. *Economic and Social Progress in Latin America.* 1995. *Special Report: Overcoming Volatility.* Washington, D.C.: Johns Hopkins University Press, p. 105.

22. J. S. Furnival. 1948. *Colonial Policy and Practice.* London: Cambridge University Press; and M. G. Smith. 1960. "Social and Cultural Pluralism." In *Social and Cultural Pluralism in the Caribbean.* Vera Rubin, ed. New York: Annals of the New York Academy of Sciences, pp. 763–85.

23. M. G. Smith. 1960. "Discussion: Multiracialism and the Plural Society." *Annals of the New York Academy of Sciences* 83:912–14.

24. Howard Johnson. 1986. "Social Control and the Colonial State: The Reorganization of the Police Force in the Bahamas 1888–1893." *Slavery and Abolition* 7: 46–58 (p. 50) quoting from Roger Norman Buckley. 1979. *Slaves in Red Coats: The British West India Regiments, 1795–1815.* New Haven, Conn.: Yale University Press, p. 117.

25. Cynthia Enloe. 1980. *Police, Military and Ethnicity: Foundations of State Power.* New Brunswick, N.J.: Transaction Books Inc., pp. 166–70.

26. Peter D. Fraser. 1981. "The Immigration Issue in British Guiana, 1903–1913: The Economic and Constitutional Origins of Racist Politics in Guyana." *Journal of Caribbean History* 14:18–45, p. 37.

27. Cited from the *British Parliamentary Papers,* 1847–48, xxiii, p. 199 in Madan N. Gopal. 1992. *Politics, Race and Youth in Guyana.* New York: Edwin Mellen Press, p. 35.

28. James A. Rodway. 1891. *History of British Guiana from the Year 1668 to the Present Time.* Vol. I, Georgetown, Guyana: J. Thompson, p. 256.

29. W. A. Orrett. 1951. *The History of the British Guiana Police.* Georgetown, Guyana: The Daily Chronicle Ltd. Printers and Publishers, p. 11.

30. G. W. Roberts. 1948. "Some Observations on the Population of British Guiana." *Population Studies* 2:185–218.

31. United Nations Department for Economic and Social Information and Policy Analysis. *World Statistics in Brief.* Series V No. 16. 1995. New York.

32. Quoted from the text of the letter written by the then Prime Minister, Forbes Burnham, to the International Commission of Jurists requesting the setting up of a special Commission of Inquiry. See *Report of the British Guiana Commission of Inquiry on Racial Problems in the Public Service.* Geneva, Switzerland: International Commission of Jurists, p. 9.

33. Memorandum presented by the Government of British Guiana to the International Commission of Jurists. *Report of the British Guiana Commission of Inquiry: Racial Problems in the Public Service.* Geneva, Switzerland: International Commission of Jurists, October 1965, p. 150.

34. Orrett, *A History of the British Guiana Police,* p. 18.

35. Brian Moore. 1987. *Race, Power and Social Segmentation in Colonial Society: Guyana After Slavery, 1838–1891.* New York: Gordon and Breach Science Pub. Ltd., p. 205.

36. *Report of the British Guiana Commission of Inquiry: Racial Problems in the Public Service.* Geneva, Switzerland: International Commission of Jurists, October, 1965, p. 41.

37. George K. Danns. 1982. *Domination and Power in Guyana.* A Study of the Police in a Third World Context. New Brunswick, N.J.: Transaction, Inc., p. 121.

38. Samuel P. Huntington. 1968. *Political Order in Changing Societies.* New Haven, Conn.: Yale University Press, p. 415.

39. See chapter 3, on the "Social and Political History of Guyana."

40. Cheddi Jagan. 1972. *The West on Trial.* Berlin: Seven Seas Publishers, pp. 288–304.

41. Leo A. Despres. 1964. "The Implications of Nationalist Politics in British Guiana for the Development of Cultural Theory." *American Anthropologist* 66:1051–77, p. 1074.

42. The colonial governor still sat in the Executive Council with three other Englishmen who held the most important portfolios. He also had the power to appoint additional ministers to counter the influence of the five PPP elected minsters. The governor was also entitled to appoint 11 members to the Legislative Council.

43. Discussed more fully in the Chapter on the "Social and Political History of Guyana."

44. See discussion in chapter 3, on the "Social and Political History of Guyana." Also, "Guyana: The Faces Behind the Masks." In *Covert Action Information Bulletin.* No. 10, August–September 1980, pp. 18–25; Jagan, *The West on Trial*; Spinner, *A Political and Social History of Guyana,* pp. 89–131.

45. Jagan, *The West on Trial,* pp. 248–339.

46. See the Chapter on the "The Evolution of Policing in Colonial Guyana." Also, Sir Charles Jeffries. 1952. *The Colonial Police.* London: Max Parrish & Co., pp. 63–65.

47. Jeffries, *The Colonial Police,* pp. 165–78.

48. Jagan, *The West on Trial,* pp. 205–312, and passim.

49. Ibid., pp. 188–247.

50. Ibid., pp. 389–94; Spinner, *A Political and Social History of Guyana,* pp. 121–28.

51. C. A. Nascimento and R. A. Burrowes, eds. 1970. *A Destiny to Mould: Selected Discourses by the Prime Minister of Guyana.* Trinidad and Jamaica: Longman Caribbean Ltd., p. 61.

52. Ibid., pp. 61, 62.

53. Lucian W. Pye and Sidney Verba, eds. 1965. *Political Culture and Political Development.* N.J.: Princeton University Press, p. 521.

54. Ibid., p. 9.

55. Nascimento and Burrowes, eds. *A Destiny to Mould,* pp. 59–64, 120–25, 152–60, and passim.

56. Ibid., pp. 121, 122, 153, 154, 199, and passim.

57. *Constitution of the Cooperative Republic of Guyana, 1980,* Articles 89 and 211.(1).

58. Forbes Burnham. 1975. *Toward the Socialist Revolution.* Georgetown, Guyana: People's National Congress, p. 8.

59. Opening Address by Prime Minister Forbes Burnham, First Junior Officers Course held on July 12, 1976.

60. *Report of the Third Biennial Congress of the People's National Congress,* August 22–26, 1979, Vol. 1.

61. Spinner, *A Political and Social History of Guyana,* p. 190.

62. *U.S. Department of State.* 1982. *Country Reports on Human Rights Practices.* Washington, D.C.: U.S. Government Printing Office.

63. *Collection of Papers: Movement Against Oppression.* Unpublished document.

64. Jeffries, *The Colonial Police,* p. 64.

65. For example, the assumption of responsibility for traffic control and licensing, the building of new stations and quarters, substituting riot drill for army drill, the modernization of the Criminal Investigations Department, appointing a police rather than a military officer to take charge of training and providing sport and recreation facilities. See Jeffries, *The Colonial Police*, pp. 64–65.

66. *The Police Act, 1957*, Sections 3.(2), (3).

67. Michael T. Klare and Cynthia Arnson. 1981. *Supplying Repression.* U.S. Support for Authoritarian Regimes Abroad. Washington, D.C.: Institute for Policy Studies, pp. 56–59, 118–19.

68. Ibid., pp. 112–13.

69. Jenny Pearce. 1981. *Under the Eagle.* Boston, Mass.: South End Press, pp. 52–53.

70. *Covert Action Information Bulletin: Destabilization in the Caribbean.* No. 10, August–September, 1980, p. 20; Also Pearce, *Under the Eagle*, p. 55.

71. *Covert Action Information Bulletin: Destabilization in the Caribbean.* 1980. No. 10 (August–September). Washington, D.C.: Covert Action Publications, p. 20.

72. Ibid.

73. Petition to Government by Movement Against Oppression. *Collection of Papers: Movement Against Oppression.*

74. Press Releases from the *Working People's Alliance*, Georgetown, Guyana; See also, Eusi Kwayana. 1991. *Walter Rodney.* Wellesley, Mass.: Calaloux Publications.

75. *Report of the Third Biennial Congress of the People's National Congress*, August 22–26, 1979, Vol. 1, pp. 115–16.

76. Ibid., p. 109.

77. Kwayana, *Walter Rodney*, pp. 37–40.

78. Ibid.

79. *United States Department of State Country Report on Human Rights Practices, 1980.*

80. Austin Turk. 1982. *Political Criminality.* The Defiance and Defense of Authority. Beverly Hills, Calif.: Sage Pub. Ltd., pp. 121–22.

81. Patrick McAuslan and John F. McEldowney, eds. 1985. *Law, Legitimacy and the Constitution: Essays Marking the Centenary of Dicey's Law of the Constitution.* London: Sweet & Maxwell, p. 39 quoting from a letter from A.V. Dicey to James Byrce, dated September 2, 1884.

82. Ian Shapiro, ed. 1994. *The Rule of Law.* New York: New York University Press, p. 121.

83. Sir Norman Anderson. 1978. *Law, Liberty and Justice (The Hamlyn Lectures, Thirtieth Series).* London: Stevens & Sons, pp. 11–12.

84. The internal morality of law refers to the substantive aims of the law and the relationship between legality and justice. The eternal morality of the law refers to the congruence between official action and the law governing such action. Lon Fuller. 1964. *The Morality of Law.* 2nd ed. New Haven, Conn.: Yale University Press, pp. 33–91, 157, and passim.

85. Robert S. Summers. 1984. *Lon L. Fuller (Jurists: Profiles in Legal Theory).* Stanford, Calif.: Stanford University Press, pp. 33–41.

86. Hadley Arkes. 1990. *Beyond the Constitution.* Princeton, N.J.: Princeton University Press, pp. 1–49, 245, and passim.

87. Quoted in Anderson, *Law, Liberty and Justice*, p. 14.

88. Richard L. Abel. 1990. "Capitalism and the Rule of Law: Precondition or Contradiction?" *Law & Social Inquiry* 15:685–97, p. 692.

89. Martin Krygier. 1990. "Marxism and the Rule of Law: Reflections After the Collapse of Communism." *Law & Social Inquiry* 15:633–63, pp. 647, 663.

90. Grazyna Skapska. 1990. "The Rule of Law from the East Central European Perspective." *Law & Social Inquiry* 15:699–706.

91. *Constitution of Guyana, 1966*, Articles 1–12.

92. *Constitution of Guyana, 1966.* Article 1.

93. The Police Act, 1957 as amended, section 15. *Laws of Guyana: Chapter 16:01.*

94. J. C. Smith and Brian Hogan. 1965. *Criminal Law.* 1st ed. London: Butterworths, pp. 230–38. See also 3rd ed. 1973, pp. 259–65.

95. Smith and Hogan, *Criminal Law;* see also commentary on the English common law in "Justification for the Use of Force in the Criminal Law." *Stanford Law Review* (1961) 13:566–609, pp. 569–71.

96. See C. S. Kenny. 1965. *Outlines of Criminal Law.* (19th ed. by J. W. C. Turner), p. 128.

97. Quoted by the Honorable Chancellor of the Judiciary, Mr. Justice Bishop. In *The State v Evelyn Dick and Alwyn Dodson Evelyn.* Criminal Appeals Nos. 42 and 43 of 1983, pp. 59, 60.

98. Per the Honorable Chancellor, Mr. Justice Bishop. In *The State v Evelyn Dick et al.,* p. 60. (Bracketed words are mine).

99. Ibid., pp. 57–59.

100. Several instances of police homicides in respect of misdemeanants are discussed in Chapter 6.

101. The Model Penal Code guidelines were drafted by the American Law Institute to guide states wanting to modify their criminal statutes. With regard to the use of deadly force to arrest, the Model Penal Code prohibits the use of deadly force to arrest for non-violent felonies and provides that (1) the crime in respect of which the arrest is being made involved the use or threatened use of deadly force; and (2) there must be substantial risk that the suspect will cause death or serious bodily harm if his apprehension is delayed.

102. Smith and Hogan, *Criminal Law.*

103. *The National Security (Miscellaneous Provisions) Act, 1966,* Sections 4, 5. Laws of Guyana.

104. Ibid., Section 17

105. Ibid., Section 15.

106. Ibid., Section 24.

107. Ibid., Section 32.

108. Ibid., Section 33.

6

Contemporary Police Violence in Guyana

This chapter analyzes empirical data collected on police violence, in particular the use of deadly force, during the period 1980 to 1994. The purpose of this analysis is to investigate the relationship between community violence and police violence in Guyana in order to determine to what extent, if any, police violence may be a response to the level of violence in the community and the everyday dangers of police work. Additionally, the proximate situation in which police violence occurs will be examined. Complete records in respect of a convenience sample of the total number of police homicides counted during this period will be subjected to interpretive analysis under the "alternative credible version technique" to determine to what extent these police homicides can be properly classified as justifiable homicide under the existing law regarding the circumstances under which the police may use deadly force. The findings of this analysis of causal explanations for police homicide will then be compared to the insights that emerge from examination of the data on the relationship between community violence and police violence.

The level of community violence has long been considered to be a causal factor in the explanation of the use of deadly force by the police.[1] The rationale for this conclusion is based on the expectation that the police would only use deadly force if necessary—in self-defense arising out of dangerous situations in which they find themselves. This explanation of police homicide, called the "community violence hypothesis," states that the level of police violence in a given society is dependent upon the level of community violence. Where the level of community violence is high, the police have to protect themselves in the course of performing their duties by using equal or greater force than that with which they are confronted, and therefore police violence will also be high, and vice versa.

One of the earliest studies on the subject of police homicide found that in each of the thirty-two cases examined during the eleven-year period 1950 to 1960 in Philadelphia, the officers were acting within a life-threatening situation, and the decedents were generally responsible for their own deaths.[2] Sherman and Langworthy used data from the National Center for Health Statistics and police-generated police homicide rates for selected years (1974–1976) and cities to analyze several variables related to community characteristics. They found that the violent crime index rate and the homicide rate exhibited strong and positive correlations with the police homicide rate. The authors rationalized that the violent index rate and the homicide rate could increase the level of perception of danger that police experience in their work and thus result in a propensity to use violence "as a possible preemption of attacks on them."[3] Similarly, James Fyfe, in a study of firearms discharges by the New York City Police in twenty command zones in New York City, found that total shooting rates were strongly correlated with arrest rates for violent crime as well as general homicide rates.[4] Binder and Fridell concluded that in two-thirds to three-fourths of the incidents studied where civilians were killed, they had precipitated their own deaths by the use or threatened use of weapons against the police.[5] Kenneth Matulia in conducting research for the International Association of Chiefs of Police (IACP) on justifiable homicide by police in the nation's fifty-seven largest cities during the period 1970 to 1983 found a robust and positive correlation between the rate of justifiable homicide by the police and variables operationalizing community violence, such as civilian homicide, rape, robbery, and aggravated assault.[6]

Similar conclusions were reached by Kania and Mackey when the FBI Crime Index of all reported offenses, and violent crime in particular, for the year 1970 was found to be significantly correlated with police homicide in thirty-nine of the fifty states. The authors, however, found that the correlation between property crime and police homicide for the same period was not significant.[7] The authors concluded that police violence is a function of community violence. Using the same data as Kania and Mackey, Jacobs and Britt created a *violent* crime index (using the mean of 1960 and 1962 statistics on violent crimes known to the police, and the number of riots in cities between 1960 and 1969) and found a statistically significant relationship between violent crime and police-caused homicide. Their conclusions concerning the significance of this finding, however, was much more subdued than those of Kania and Mackey, since Jacobs and Britt also found that, even after controlling for violent crime, economic inequality remained a significant predictor of police homicide. Sorenson and others, who conducted analysis on 169 U.S. cities with a population of more than 100,000, found that although the violent crime rate was predictive of police killings across cities, it tended to act as an intervening variable when the effect of other structural variables, such as economic inequality and the proportion of minorities in the population, are taken into account. Liska and Yu, in attempting to explain the effect of race threat (threatening people and threatening acts) on police use of deadly force in forty-five U.S. cities, found that a statistical relationship with police homicide was supported in the case of the general homicide rate.[8]

These studies all confirm a relationship between the violence in the community and police violence. Whether involving the analysis of aggregate data as in the studies conducted by Kania and Mackey (1977), Jacobs and Britt (1979), Sherman and Langworthy (1979), Fyfe (1980), Matulia (1985), Liska and Yu (1992), and Sorenson and others (1993), or the facts of cases of justifiable homicide by police as in the studies conducted by Robin (1963), and Binder and Fridell (1984), the explanation of police violence is directly related to police efforts to control crime and bring offenders to justice.

It is not possible to conduct similar research with regard to Guyana, and therefore the generalizablility of such findings to Guyana is severely limited. With regard to the studies that were based on the analyses of aggregate data, similar data are nonexistent in the case of Guyana, where there is no comparable system of official crime reporting, and no official reporting of police-caused homicide or justifiable homicide. Basic raw data on the incidence of crimes in the country are included in the *Guyana Police Force Annual Report*, which is presented to parliament each year for its approval. Police reports and records on cases of justifiable homicide are similarly not available for public scrutiny to investigate the extent to which the victim contributed to his own victimization, as was done in the studies conducted by Robin (1963) and Fridell (1984). For the purposes of this study, therefore, the researcher was confined to the use of analytical procedures that were amenable to the type of data and information that were available for scrutiny, which will now be discussed.

The analysis of the effect of community violence on police homicide rates in Guyana includes separate statistical analyses of the *Guyana Police Force Annual Report* of crimes and offenses reported to the police during the years 1980 to 1992. The crimes analyzed in this study include thirty-three separate criminal offenses, which have been classified under the headings of *civilian homicide* (murder, infanticide, manslaughter, and causing death by dangerous driving); *violent crimes* (attempted murder, rape, attempted rape, robbery with violence, robbery with aggravation, robbery and assault with intent to rob, larceny from the person, throwing corrosive fluid, felonious wounding and wounding with intent, assault causing and inflicting grievous bodily harm, assault causing and inflicting actual bodily harm, carnal knowledge of a girl between 12 and 13 years of age, indecent assault, buggery, abductions, incest, and common assault); *crimes involving the use of firearms* (robbery under arms, discharging loaded firearm with intent and unlawful possession of arms and ammunition); *property crimes* (burglary, house-breaking and larceny, shop and store breaking and entering with intent, breaking and entering dwelling house with intent, possession of house-breaking implements, attempt to break and enter dwelling house with intent, arson, attempted arson, and malicious damage to property); and *crimes against the police* (assaulting a peace officer).[9] The rationale for the choice of these crimes was discussed in chapter 2 and will be further elaborated later in this chapter. The significance of the size of the police force during this period will also be investigated because (1) it is theoretically related to the level of crime control, and (2) the police officer-to-population ratio, or police per capita, has been positively correlated with the number of homicides committed by police.[10] Before proceeding to the analysis, however, the results of field research conducted in Guyana, with regard to the frequency of the use of deadly force by the Guyana Police Force, will be outlined.

THE FREQUENCY OF POLICE-CAUSED HOMICIDE IN GUYANA

With reference to the Guyana Police, the analyses here examine the use of excessive and deadly force against civilians, which, when it ends in death is referred to as police-caused homicide.[11] This would include all cases where the use of such force ends in death and is not restricted to fatalities caused by firearms only. This is important because in several of the incidences involving the use of deadly force, serious injuries and death resulted allegedly from the use by the police of weapons other than the firearm that also can cause life-threatening injuries and/or precipitate the death of the victim.

The only independent source of record-keeping with regard to the frequent use of excessive and deadly force by police against civilians is the Guyana Human Rights Association (GHRA), a civic, nongovernmental organization incorporated in 1979. One of the objectives of this organization is to monitor events in Guyana pertaining to human rights. In pursuance of this objective, the GHRA publishes an *Annual Report* on human rights observances in Guyana. Included in this document are tallies of the total numbers of fatal and nonfatal shootings of civilians by police, deaths of civilians in police custody, and details of beatings and other forms of torture committed by the police.[12] The information provided by the GHRA is compiled from cases that are brought to its attention by victims, or relatives of victims, and other members of the public. Documentary sources are also utilized that include the press, correspondence from various parts of the country, official statements and publications, and releases from political parties. The limitations of this type of data have been discussed earlier,[13] and in addition, the GHRA is careful to point out that since 1983 the state-owned press has significantly reduced coverage of police shootings, and the list compiled by the organization is therefore partial and limited for the most part to Georgetown. The actual number of deaths, therefore, caused by police is unknown. The data relating to the number of cases of police-caused homicide for the period 1980 to 1986 were collected mainly from this source and therefore represents only an estimate of the number of deaths caused by police. After 1986, the format of the *Guyana Human Rights Report* was modified to accommodate changes in structure, length, and content. As a result of these changes in format, subsequent *Reports* no longer provide accounts of cases of police homicide with the degree of specificity and detail that are required for the purposes of this study.

The Guyana Police Force provided information on police-caused homicide for the period 1991 to 1994 from their internal records. No reliable source of data could be found for the intervening period (1987–1990). As explained earlier, there is no other official source of information on police-caused homicide in Guyana, and mortality data is not a feasible source of this information in the case of Guyana.[14] With regard to the data provided by the police, researchers have found that police departments are sometimes reluctant to make this information available, and even when it is made available, counts of police homicide sometimes tend to be lower than figures obtained from other sources for a variety of reasons.[15] Albert Meehan has also pointed out that police record-keeping practices inevitably reflect sensitivity to their own personal achievements as well as to the organizational concerns of their department.[16] In the case of such a controversial subject as police-caused homicide, police records are not a reliable source for measurement, and it is important to utilize other sources of data, if available, for the purpose of verification and corroboration. Wherever possible, newspaper reports have also been utilized for the purpose of corroboration, but in the case of Guyana, several years of media censorship of reports of police killings during the period under review[17] render this exercise to be of very limited value. The result is that the figures presented in this study concerning police-caused homicide only represent those cases of police-caused homicide in Guyana that have been verified with some degree of certainty.

Based on these sources, a total of 150 police-caused homicides were available for analysis in this study, covering the period 1980 to 1986 and 1991 to 1994. In order to provide an understanding of the magnitude of the problem of police homicide that this very conservative figure represents for a small country such as Guyana, a police homicide rate was calculated for the period 1980 to 1984 as follows:

$$\frac{\text{Police Homicide}}{\text{Total Population}} \times 100{,}000$$

With an estimated population of approximately 800,000 persons during this period,[18] a police homicide rate of 2.2 per 100,000 was calculated, and a comparison of this rate with the rates of other countries, both developed and underdeveloped, is presented in Table 6.1.

As can be readily seen, Guyana has an inordinately high rate of police homicide (2.2) when compared with other countries in Latin America (Costa Rica 0.70, Venezuela 0.85), the United States (0.18/1.14), and Canada (0.07) during the same time period. In fact, the police homicide rate for Guyana is second only to Brazil (4.06), a country that languished under military rule for over two decades (ending in 1986) with infamous death squads and a dismal human rights record.[19] Argentina is a close third, with a police homicide rate of 2.03 per 100,000.

Table 6.1
Rates of Civilians Killed by Police in Guyana, Latin America, the United States, and Canada per 100,000 Inhabitants

Country	Year	Rate per 100,000	Source
Guyana	1980–84	2.2	Current Study
Argentina*	1984	2.03	Chevigny (1991) p. 206
Brazil**	1982	4.06	Chevigny (1991) p. 209
Costa Rica	1982	0.70	Carranza et al. (1990) pp. 35–37
Venezuela	1981	0.85	Amnesty Int'l (1988) p. 7
Canada	1978	0.07	Chappel & Graham (1985)
United States	1979	0.18	Blumberg (1989) p. 453
	1975–79***	1.14	Liska & Yu (1992) p. 59

Note: The rate for Guyana was compiled from the *Guyana Human Rights Reports*, 1980–1984.
*Rate for Buenos Aires Metropolitan Area
**Rate for Sao Paulo Metropolitan Area
***Mean rate for 45 cities in the United States

Source: This table was adopted from Luis Gerardo Gabaldon. 1993. "Police Violence and Uncertainty in Latin America: Linking the Macro- and Micro-Levels of Analysis." *International Criminal Justice Review* 3:44–59, p. 45.

With reference to homicidal violence occurring in the general population, Guyana's rates are also high, and in this case, closer to rates occurring in the United States in the early years of its crime wave. In 1979 for example, the United States experienced 21,456 homicides (murder and nonnegligent manslaughter),[20] and with an estimated population of 200 million, the homicide rate per 100,000 was 10.7 persons. Meanwhile, Guyana experienced 94 nonnegligent homicides (murder, manslaughter, and infanticide) for that year,[21] and with a population of about 800,000 the homicide rate turned out to be 11.7 per 100,000 persons.

The line graph presented in Figure 6.1 shows how the incidence of police-caused homicide, as far as we are able to determine, varied during the period covered by this study (1980–1994). As can be seen, the number of police killings of civilians peaked around 1981 and then fluctuated around a relatively high average until around 1986, after which it has failed to approach the high levels observable in the early years of the period under review. As was pointed out in the previous chapter, during the first half of the 1980s there was much political repression in the society, and the activities of the police were directed primarily toward internal surveillance under the authoritarian rule of the Executive President Forbes Burnham and the PNC.

Another way of assessing the magnitude of police violence in society is by the creation of "disproportionate violence ratios," a technique used by Paul Chevigny in studies he conducted on police use of deadly force in Jamaica, Argentina, and

Figure 6.1
Variations in Police-caused Homicide, 1980 to 1994

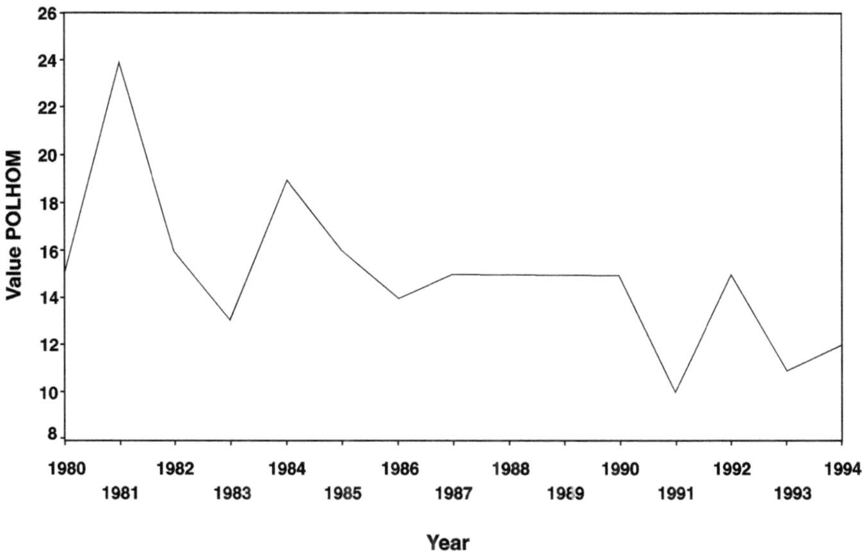

Note: POLHOM = Police-caused Homicide

Source: Data for the years 1980–1986 were collected from the Guyana Human Rights Association. Data for the years 1991–1994 were collected from the Guyana Police Force. Missing data for the years 1980, and 1987–1990, were assigned mean value.

Brazil.[22] Through the use of these ratios, an assessment of the seriousness of police violence can be made by comparing the levels of homicidal violence with the relative severity of the force that is being used. Chevigny created three sets of relationships comparing police homicide with civilian homicide and posited that if the ratios are disproportionately weighted with reference to the police, then it suggests a "pattern of violence" on the part of the police that warrants further investigation as to whether excessive force is being used for the purpose of social control. These relationships were as follows: (1) the relation between the number of homicides by police and the overall homicide rate; (2) the relation between killings of police and killings by police; and, (3) the relation between the number of shootings and the number of deaths caused by police.

Police Homicide as a Percentage of the Total Homicide Rate

If police homicide comprises a large percent of the total homicide rate, then according to Chevigny this is possibly an indication of the excessive use of violence by the police. Table 6.2 compares police homicide and civilian homicide during the years 1980 to 1994 and expresses police homicide as a percentage of the total homicide for each year. It will be seen that police homicide accounted for between 18.2 percent in 1981, its highest, to as low as 4.4 percent of the total number of homicides in 1992. The steep rise in civilian homicide that occurred in 1991 is the result of the more than doubling of the instances of murder (from 90 in 1990 to 192 in 1991), but as can be seen the numbers leveled off in subsequent years. It is noteworthy that in 1991, the police reported that there was a marked increase in crime generally by 101 percent over the figures for the previous year (1990).[23] In 1992 the police reported that there was again a marked increase in crime over the 1991 figures, although it was reflected in the less serious, summary offenses rather than the indictable offenses such as murder, manslaughter, and other forms of criminal homicide.[24] Guyana's ratio of police-caused homicide in relation to civilian homicide (ranging between 18.2 and 4.4 percent during the study period) seems to be rather large. This amounts to prima facie evidence at the least, that police in Guyana may be abusing their power to use deadly force.

Table 6.2
Homicide Statistics for Guyana, 1980 to 1994

Year	Civilian Homicide*	Police Homicide	Total Homicide	% Police Homicide
1980	118	—	—	—
1981	108	24	132	18.2
1982	121	16	137	11.7
1983	143	13	156	8.3
1984	123	19	142	13.4
1985	138	16	154	10.4
1986	83	14	97	14.4
1987	103	—	—	—
1988	99	—	—	—
1989	106	—	—	—
1990	114	—	—	—
1991	217	10	227	4.4
1992	125	15	140	10.7
1993	132	11	143	7.6
1994	111	12	123	9.7
Total	1,871	150	1,451**	10

Note: *Civilian homicide includes only murder, manslaughter, and infanticide reported to the police.
**Does not include years with missing data for police homicide.

Source: Civilian homicide was compiled from the *Guyana Police Force Annual Reports*, 1980–1994. Police Homicides for 1981–1986 are estimates provided by the Guyana Human Rights Association. Some of the deaths for 1981 may have occurred in 1980. Police Homicides for 1990–1994 were provided by the Guyana Police Force. Total homicide includes only murder, manslaughter, infanticide, and police homicide.

Killings of Police and Killings by Police

In this instance, if far more civilians are killed by police than police by civilians, then this would be an indication that the police may not really be facing a serious threat from the offenders they encounter in the course of the lawful performance of their duties. In the case of Guyana, the police reported that only one of their number was killed by a civilian during the entire study period (1980–1994). This creates a disproportionate ratio when compared to the 150 police-caused homicides investigated in this study and suggests that the risk faced by police of receiving fatal force from the offenders they encounter is much less than that faced by the offenders themselves. If the police are not facing a serious threat from the offenders they encounter in the performance of their duties, and are still responsible for causing the deaths of at least 150 persons during the study period, then the situation warrants further investigation into the causes of police violence.

Fatal and Nonfatal Police Shootings

If the majority of shootings by police end in deaths (the police are killing more people than they wound), then according to Chevigny, these figures themselves are suggestive of the possibility that police may be using excessive violence against civilians. Table 6.3 shows the results of a comparison of the fatal and nonfatal police shootings of civilians during the years 1981 to 1986. As can be seen, in every year examined, the majority of police shootings resulted in deaths. The figures range from the estimated "perfect" score of 100 percent in 1985, meaning that all the shootings that were counted resulted in deaths, to 76.5 percent, the lowest, in 1983, when 13 out of 17 shootings of civilians by police resulted in deaths. These percentages suggest that the majority of shootings are intended to cause death or serious bodily harm that may result in death, or that the police are shooting to kill most of the time when they discharge their firearms.[25]

Table 6.3
Relationship between Police Shootings and Deaths, 1981 to 1986

Year	Police Shootings	Fatal	Nonfatal	% Fatal
1981	28	24	4	85.7
1982	19	16	3	84.2
1983	17	13	4	76.5
1984	22	19	3	86.4
1985	16	16	—	100
1986	18	14	4	77.8

Source: The data were provided by the Guyana Human Rights Association.
Some of the deaths for 1981 may have occurred in 1980.

When all these relationships are taken together, the total picture seems to suggest that the use of deadly force by the Guyana Police Force warrants further investigation. The severity of the force that is being applied and the frequency of the use of deadly force establish a prima facie case of the abuse of police power to use fatal force. The picture that emerges from relationships discussed does not provide an explanation for the use of excessive force but only that prima facie, at least, it seems to be occurring. In order to verify that such abuses are indeed taking place, the situation in Guyana must be investigated further, since it is arguable that in each of the 150 cases police-caused homicide was justified and the police were acting in accordance with the law when the loss of human life occurred. Two ways of investigating the situation will be utilized in this study. First the efficacy of the explanation offered by the community violence hypothesis will be assessed with reference to Guyana, and then a closer look will be taken at the proximate situation relating to a convenience sample of 24 of the 150 cases for which sufficient material was available for scrutiny.

TESTING THE COMMUNITY VIOLENCE HYPOTHESIS

The community violence hypothesis is grounded in the assumption that police violence is committed in the course of the lawful performance of officers' duties of crime prevention and the apprehension of offenders against the criminal law. According to this hypothesis, where the level of crime and violence in the community is high, the police are more likely to use fatal force to protect themselves from the danger they face in the everyday performance of their duties.[26] Violence is measured not only by homicidal violence in the community, but generally by crimes that involve the use of violence and are likely to necessitate a violent response from law enforcement in order to apprehend suspects. The discussion of the community violence hypothesis with respect to Guyana includes (1) a discussion of the reasons why the empirical indicators of community violence were chosen, (2) a discussion of the techniques used to analyze the relationship between these indicators of community violence and police-caused homicide, and (3) the presentation of the results.

The data assembled on Guyana during the fifteen-year period with reference to police-caused homicide (1980–1994) were matched with data relating to crimes and offenses reported to the police during the period 1980 to 1992. The *Guyana Police Force Annual Reports* is the only source of crime statistics in Guyana and is subject to all the disabilities of official crime statistics, such as the FBI's *Uniform Crime Reports,* the validity of which is often called into question.[27] In the case of Guyana, two major issues are of concern for this study regarding the inaccurate measurement of crime. Many crimes such as burglary, robbery, and larceny from the person popularly called in Guyana "choke and rob" offenses, are not reported to police because people feel that the police will not be able to solve the crime or that they will be subject to reprisals. In a small country such as Guyana, in some cases the identity of the suspect is sometimes known to the victim.[28] With reference to sex crimes, there is general underreporting worldwide, especially in cases of rape, incest, and the sexual abuse of children by family members. In the United States, it is believed that fewer than half of the criminal acts that occur are reported to the police.[29] The situation is likely to be similar in Guyana.

Second, administrative practices can also result in the deliberate shaping of official crime statistics to reflect policy and performance directives, and this can result in the inaccurate measurement of crime. Several researchers have found that police record-keeping practices can reflect not only sensitivity to the personal achievements of individual police officers, but also the organizational concerns of the department and an anxiety to implement political directives.[30] Police authorities may be eager to present results that show they are effective in reducing crime in order to attract resources for the department. The fact that the Guyana Police Force has been subjected to major political influences during this period is of significance in this regard. Nevertheless, the data provided by the *Guyana Police Force Annual Reports*, like the *Uniform Crime Reports*,[31] are still considered to be a reliable indicator of serious crime.

The Validity of the Empirical Indicators of Community Violence

Composite variables that would adequately measure the presence of violence in the community were constructed based on thirty-three serious crimes listed in the *Guyana Police Force Annual Reports*. As stated earlier, these crimes then were classified under the headings of civilian homicide, violent crime, crimes involving the use of firearms, property crimes, and crimes against the police. With regard to crimes involving the use of firearms, however, it must be noted that although firearms may be used in the commission of all the thirty-three offenses that these categories represent, the use or possession of a firearm is an essential ingredient of the *actus reus* of the three offenses listed under this category, and it was therefore decided that it would be useful to treat these offenses as a separate category.[32]

The choice of variables to measure community violence was guided by existing studies that investigated the relationship between community violence and police-caused homicide and the subjective understanding of the level of violence indicated by the actus reus of the offenses specified. In one case all index offenses reported by the FBI were used, but separate analyses were conducted in respect of offenses representing violent crime and property crime.[33] Other studies were more innovative in arriving at measures of community violence. Jacobs and Britt created a violence index consisting of a crime rate component and a riot component.[34] The crime rate component was derived from the mean of 1960 and 1962 statistics on violent crimes known to the police, whereas the riot component was based on the number of riots in cities between 1960 and 1969. Sorenson and others used the violent crime rate to operationalize community violence that was calculated from a yearly average per 100,000 residents during 1980 to 1984 taken from the UCR.[35] Fyfe correlated police shooting rates with arrest rates for violent crime as well as general homicide rates.[36]

Crimes and offenses listed in the *Guyana Police Force Annual Reports* were grouped into the categories mentioned, which represent clusters of offenses that are fairly serious and involve the potential or actual use of violence. An attempt was made to be as inclusive as possible, covering all the crimes that would potentially involve violent contact between persons and the infliction of varying degrees of harm, including death. With regard to *civilian homicide*, the question has been raised as to its validity as a measure of community violence, since murder is considered to be more often than not a crime of passion between intimates and the police are usually called to the scene after the event has occurred. Even in the case of homicide between strangers, police are rarely in a position to apprehend the perpetrator at the crime scene. A similar argument can be made with regard to the offense of "causing death by dangerous driving," which is another offense that comprises civilian homicide. The argument may be persuasively advanced that these offenses do not necessarily place the perpetrators in a dangerous position vis-à-vis the police so as to precipitate police homicide in pursuance of an arrest. It must be noted, however, that although the likelihood of police involvement is lessened at the time the offense is being committed, the seriousness of these crimes increases the need for the apprehension of suspects who may be at large and justifies the use of the highest degree of force in order to effect an arrest.

The variety of offenses classified as *violent crime* all involve varying degrees of trespass against the person of another, and are undisputed indicators of community violence. All of the studies referred to earlier, as specifically stated, included violent crimes in their operationalization of community violence. The variety of crimes included in this category all represent violent acts that, under the laws of Guyana, would call forth the use of official force for the purpose of prevention, intervention, or apprehension after the fact.

Apart from the fact that the separate category *crimes involving the use of firearms* (also referred to in the study as *firearms crime*) represents offenses for which the use or possession of a firearm is a part of the actus reus, this category is also justified because gun density has been empirically associated with police homicide.[37] Guns are instruments of serious crime, and it was felt that in the absence of direct data on gun density in Guyana, it is important to investigate the relationship of offenses involving the use of firearms to police homicide both as a component of the underlying concept of community violence and as a separate factor precipitating the use of deadly force by the police.

As was stated previously, *property crime* has been used as an empirical indicator of community violence in the study conducted by Kania and Mackey, although the relationship to police-caused homicide was found to be insignificant. With reference to Guyana, perusal of the cluster of offenses included in this category reveals that in several cases the possibility of violence with regard to property damage and violence to persons present is real. House-breaking and arson, for example, may take place at night when occupants are asleep in the dwelling. Additionally, as pointed out in chapter 5, the criminal law of Guyana permits the use of deadly force to apprehend persons suspected of committing property offenses, thus justifying the inclusion of these offenses as a component of community violence.

No other crime is more relevant for inclusion in the concept of community violence for the purposes of this study than *crimes against the police* because this is the only one of the thirty-three crimes listed previously where an essential ingredient of the actus reus is physical contact between civilians and the police. The fact that only one police officer (a constable) was killed by a civilian during the entire period under review resulted in only one offense being listed under this heading, that is, "assault peace officer." Most police homicides arise out of confrontational situations between civilians and the police. Although, as will be discussed later, several instances of police killings in Guyana occurred *after* persons were allegedly taken into custody, this is an unusual state of affairs. The likelihood of persons who are assaulting police officers being fatally injured is great and the effect of this crime will be assessed collectively as a part of the underlying concept of community violence as well as singularly as a factor that may precipitate police homicide.

Techniques Used and Results of the Analyses

The five composite variables that were designated to be indicators of community violence—*civilian homicide, violent crime, property crime, firearms crime,* and *crimes against the police*—were then treated as items comprising a scale, and reliability analysis was conducted to determine the consistency with which each item measured the underlying concept of community violence across time and across random samples.[38] (The results of the reliability analysis are presented in Table 6.4. The item-total correlations indicated how well the individual *z* scores calculated for each item during the thirteen-year period (1980–1992) measure the underlying concept of community violence.) The first discouraging sign was a rather high computed score on scale variance of 8.5, thereby indicating that the variability of the scores on the various items around the mean of the group is fairly high. This could be a direct result of the small size of the data set and the limited number of cases represented by years.[39] Second, the standard deviation of scores from the mean of 2.9 indicated that the distribution is not very close to normal, whereby about 68 percent of the observations are to be found within the area covered between a distance of one standard deviation below the mean to one standard deviation above the mean.[40] The internal consistency of these items as measures of community violence individually or collectively was not expected to be strong.

It will be seen that property crime leads the list with an item-total correlation of .46, closely followed by crimes involving the use of firearms with an item-total correlation of .45. Civilian homicide very modestly measures the underlying concept with an item-total correlation of .27. Meanwhile, violent crimes and crimes against the police display very weak item-total correlations of .16 and .11, thereby indicating that, taken separately, they would not be very effective in consistently measuring community violence across random samples. However, when all the items are taken together, they produce an alpha of .52, which means that although the items possess some degree of internal consistency, they are rather weak measures of community violence statistically across random samples. Results obtained as a result of the investigation of the relationship between these variables and police-caused homicide must therefore be assessed in the light of this information and qualified accordingly. For the purposes of this study, this would mean that the results of statistical analysis should be corroborated by other analyses before reliance could be placed on the validity of the findings.

The nature of the analyses is also limited by the adequacy of the data that were collected for this study. The Guyana Police Force is a centralized organization, and there is therefore no scope for comparisons across cities as there is in the United States. Although police homicide data were collected over a fifteen-year period, figures for several years for which there were missing data had to be estimated. Official crime statistics were only available for a thirteen-year period (1980–1992) and therefore the data set is very small. It was not possible to conduct sophisticated statistical analyses, such as multiple regression analysis, that would allow the prediction of police homicide rates and significance testing. Instead, this study explored several alternate ways of identifying associations between variables and trends in police use of deadly force in Guyana over time.

Table 6.4
Reliability Analysis for Community Violence Scale

Item-total Statistics*

	Scale Mean if Item Deleted	Scale Variance if Item Deleted	Corrected Item-total Correlation	Alpha if Item Deleted
ZAPOLICE	.0000	6.9440	.1158	.5653
ZCIVHOM	.0000	6.1939	.2733	.4723
ZFIRECRI	.0000	5.4282	.4563	.3508
ZPROPCRI	.0000	5.4089	.4612	.3473
ZVIOCRIM	.0000	6.6876	.1676	.5358

Reliability Coefficients

N of Cases = 13.0 *N* of Item = 5 Alpha = .5194

*ZAPOLICE = *z* score for assault peace officer
ZCIVHOM = *z* score for civilian homicide
ZFIRECRI = *z* score for firearms crime
ZPROPCRI = *z* score for property crime
ZVIOCRIM = *z* score for violent crime

Analysis to Determine Relationship: Pearson's r *Correlation Coefficient*

Correlation analysis was done by calculating the Pearson *r* coefficients to measure the relationship between the variables comprising the concept of community violence and police homicide during the study period. The question of the reliability of such analysis is immediately raised by the imperfections of the data outlined previously, the smallness of sample size, missing data, and the possibility of existence of bias and inaccuracies in the data being relied upon both with regard to police-caused homicide and to the data on the crimes comprising community violence. The problems connected with the reliability of statistics, which were computed from the *Guyana Police Force Annual Reports* as well as the *Guyana Human Rights Reports*, have already been discussed.

The size of the data set is important if sufficient statistical control is to be maintained to ensure reliability of the results. Although each individual observation can be expected to differ somewhat from each other, the pattern of deviation from the limiting mean should be relatively stable if statistical treatment of the data is to be meaningful.[41] The larger the number of observations, the more likely that the data would be distributed normally around a central value. Here, the data consist of observations over a thirteen-year period, with cases represented by year, and therefore it must be noted that with the number of observations being less than thirty, the possibility of error is greater than it would be if more observations were available for analysis.[42]

Correlation analysis is used to measure the relationship between two variables. The correlation coefficient indicates the strength of the relationship. The coefficient lies between +1.00 and –1.00. A positive 1.00 denotes a perfect positive association, which means that if there is an increase or decrease in one variable there will be a corresponding increase or decrease in the other variable. A negative 1.00 indicates a perfect negative correlation, which means that if there is an increase in one there is a corresponding decrease in the other. A coefficient of zero would indicate that there is no relationship between the variables. Correlation analysis assumes linearity in the data.[43] The results of the analyses are presented in Table 6.5.

As can be observed from the correlation matrix presented in Table 6.5, civilian homicide (–.17), crimes involving the use of firearms (–.28), property crime (–.50), and violent crime (–.07) are all negatively correlated with police homicide. This means that when the level of these crimes are high, police homicide is low and vice versa. It should also be noted that most of the coefficients are relatively weak, being under at least –.30, except in the case of property crime. The only measure of community violence that is positively associated with police homicide is "crimes against the police" (.39) and it is quite moderate in strength. This makes perfect sense as the offense included in this category, "assault peace officer," is likely to elicit a violent response from the police. In the context of Guyana, however, and with reference to police homicide, it must be remembered that this crime is not referable to victims of police homicide but rather to civilians who

Table 6.5
Intercorrelation among Study Variables

	Correlation Coefficients* ** ***					
	APOLICE	*CIVHOM*	*FIRECRIM*	*POLHOM*	*PROPCRIM*	*STRENGTH*
APOLICE	1.0000 (13) *p* = .					
CIVHOM	.4058 (13) *p* = .169	1.0000 (13) *p* = .				
FIRECRIM	–.1625 (13) *p* = .596	.0644 (13) *p* = .834	1,0000 (13) *p* = .			
POLHOM	.3942 (13) *p* = .183	–.1799 (13) *p* = .557	–.2802 (13) *p* = .354	1.0000 (15) *p* = .		
PROPCRIM	.1248 (13) *p* = .684	.4752 (13) *p* = .101	.4360 (13) *p* = .136	–.5073 (13) *p* = .077	1.0000 (13) *p* = .	
STRENGTH	.3079 (13) *p* = .306	.4562 (13) *p* = .117	–.4712 (13) *p* = .104	.3534 (13) *p* = .236	–.4702 (13) *p* = .105	1.0000 (13) *p* = .
VIOCRIM	–.0631 (13) *p* = .838	–.2653 (13) *p* = .381	.7251 (13) *p* = .005	–.0752 (13) *p* = .807	.0366 (13) *p* = .906	–.2499 (13) *p* = .410

* Coefficient/(Cases)/2-tailed Significance
** "." is printed if a coefficient cannot be computed
*** APOLICE = Assault peace officer
CIVHOM = Civilian homicide
FIRECRIM = Firearms crime
POLHOM = Police-caused homicide
PROPCRIM = Property crime
STRENGTH = Police strength/size
VIOCRIM = Violent crime

survived their physical encounters with police. However, this offense is the only one that addresses direct encounters between police and civilians and it is not surprising that it is the only one of the measures of community violence that is positively associated with police homicide.

As can be seen, an additional variable called "strength," representing the size of the police force was also included in the correlation analysis. The ratio of police to the general population or police per capita has been found to be positively associated with police homicide in several of the studies cited previously.[44] Sherman and Langworthy (1979), Jacobs and Britt (1979), Matulia (1985) and Sorenson and others (1993), all found empirical support for this relationship. Not only do high crime rates result in the hiring of more police, but the presence of more police in the community or a high police-to-citizen ratio also results in the probability of higher arrest rates and a corresponding increase in the exposure of citizens to police and the use of deadly force by police. As Table 6.5 shows, the variable "strength" displays a positive coefficient of .35 with police homicide, thereby indicating that when the number of police in the community is high, the incidence of police-caused homicide is also expected to be high.

Analysis to Describe Trends: The Utility of Time Sequence Analysis

The relative smallness of this data set may significantly reduce the stability of the relationships revealed from correlation analysis and in such cases, triangulation is very useful. An alternative way of analyzing the data, time sequence analysis, was therefore conducted by preparing line graphs to plot the variations in the incidence of each of the variables representing community violence and in police-caused homicide. Measures of community violence and police-caused homicide represent the years 1980 to 1992. Figure 6.2 represents variations in the strength or size of the police force during the study period. Figures 6.3 through 6.7 represent variations in the actual composite raw scores of all the offenses representing community violence over time: "assault peace officer," civilian homicide, property crime, firearms crime, and violent crime, respectively. Figure 6.8 represents the total variations in community violence over the years as the line graph depicts the variable called "total crime," which was computed by adding all the composite variables representing community violence: violent crime, property crime, firearms crime, civilian homicide, and "assault peace officer." These figures give an indication of the how the frequency of the offenses reported varied over the years during the study period, separately as well as together. They also give a picture of the magnitude of the violence in the society, represented by the actual raw scores (number of offenses reported) displayed on the axis.

If these line graphs are compared with Figure 6.1, which depicts variations in the incidence of police homicide during the study period, it will be observed that the variables that are negatively associated with police homicide in the correlation analysis—civilian homicide, violent crime, property crime, and firearms crime, as well as all the community violence variables together, referred to as "total crime"—all experienced lower levels in the earlier years between 1980 to 1986 and sharp rises in the number of offenses from around 1991. The pattern is reversed with regard to the variables that are positively associated with police homicide—"assault peace officer" (Figure 6.3) and police strength or size (Figure 6.2). Like police homicide (Figure 6.1), the values are higher in the earlier years

(text continued on p. 151)

Figure 6.2
Variations in Police Strength/Size, 1980 to 1992

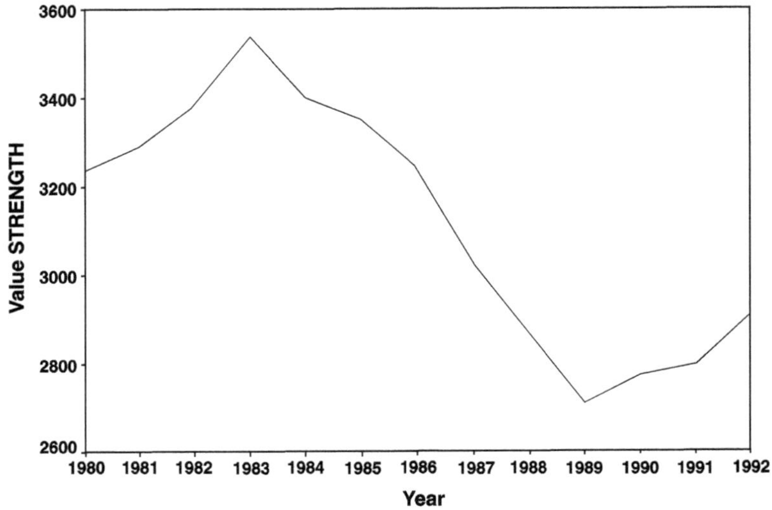

Note: STRENGTH = Police Strength/Size

Source: The *Guyana Police Force Annual Reports*, 1980–1992

Figure 6.3
Variations in "Assault Peace Officer," 1980 to 1992

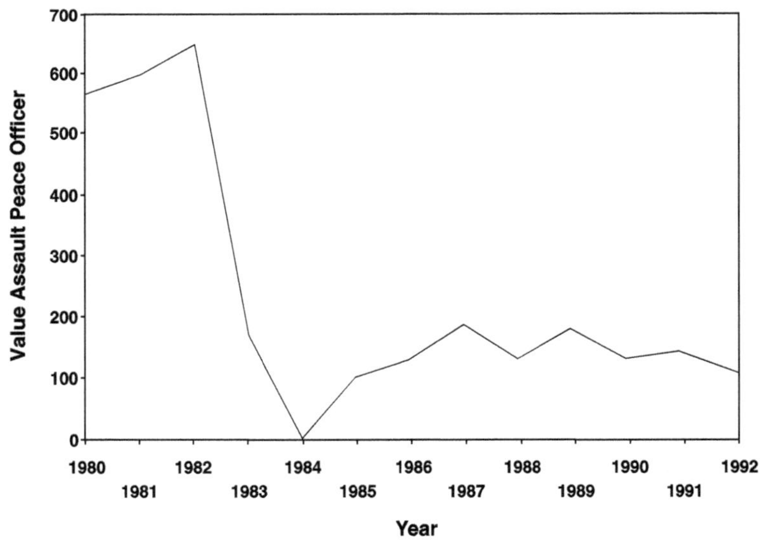

Source: The *Guyana Police Force Annual Reports*, 1980–1992

Figure 6.4
Variations in Civilian Homicide, 1980 to 1992

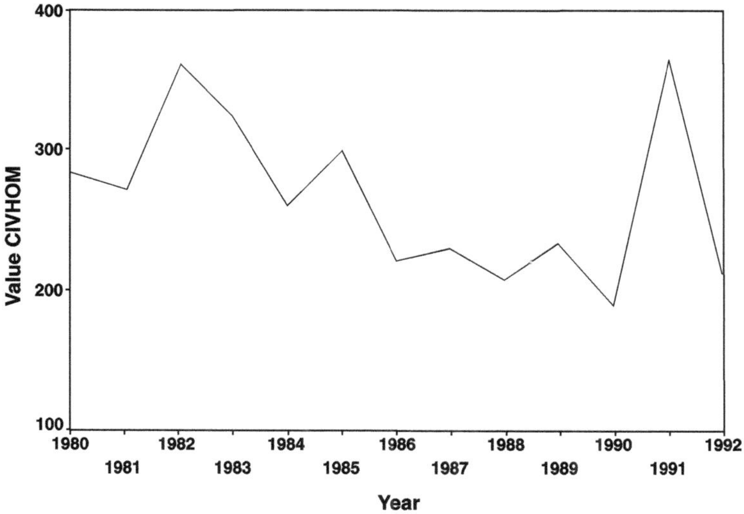

Note: CIVHOM = Civilian Homicide

Source: The *Guyana Police Force Annual Reports*, 1980–1992

Figure 6.5
Variations in Property Crime, 1980 to 1992

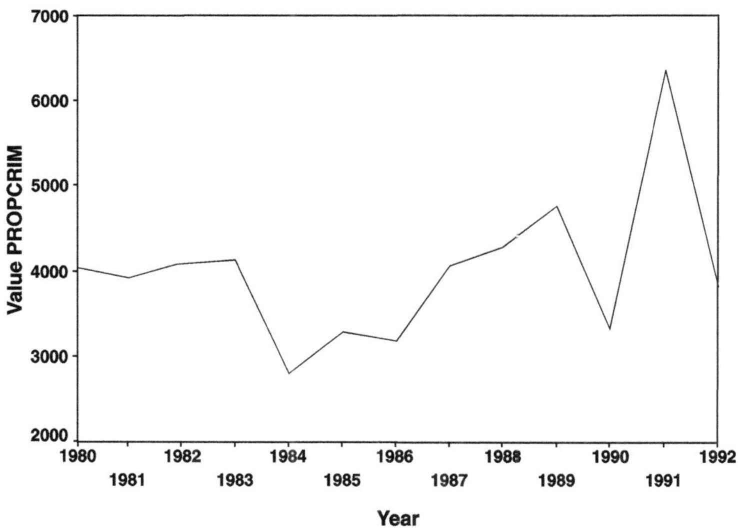

Note: PROPCRIM = Property Crime

Source: The *Guyana Police Force Annual Reports*, 1980–1992

Figure 6.6
Variations in Firearms Crime, 1980 to 1992

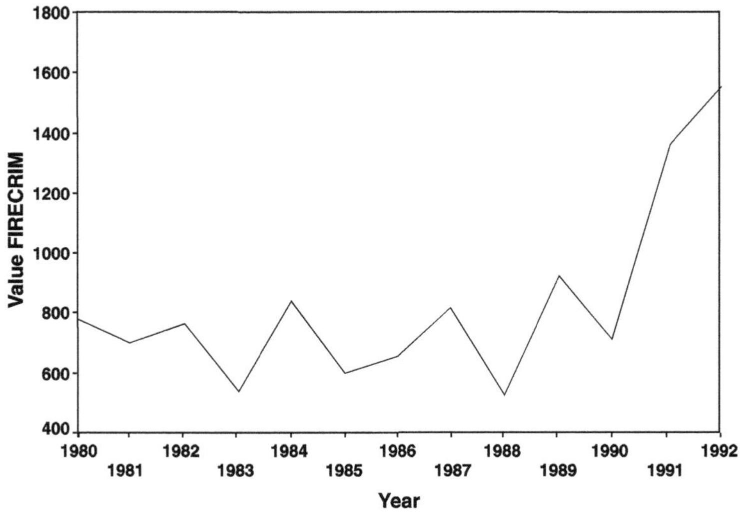

Note: FIRECRIM = Firearms Crime

Source: The *Guyana Police Force Annual Reports*, 1980–1992

Figure 6.7
Variations in Violent Crime, 1980 to 1992

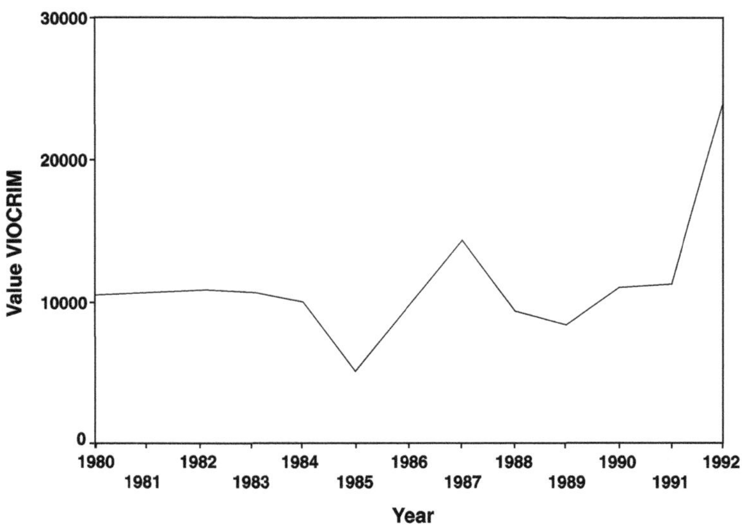

Note: VIOCRIM = Violent Crime

Source: The *Guyana Police Force Annual Reports*, 1980–1992

Figure 6.8
Variations in Total Crime, 1980 to 1992

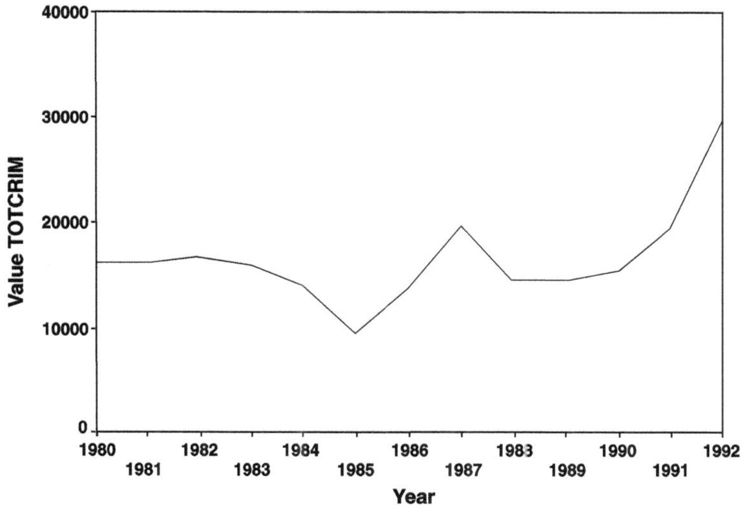

Note: TOTCRIM = Total Crime

Source: The *Guyana Police Force Annual Reports*, 1980–1992

(1980–85), peaking around 1980 to 1982, and then experiencing general decline over time. The existing social and political conditions in society during the early 1980s indicates, as discussed in the previous chapter, that the society was heavily policed and under the grip of a violent, authoritarian political dictatorship that began to be tempered after the death of President Burnham in 1985. The patterns revealed by these graphs support the associations between the variables and police homicide shown in Table 6.5.

Finally, in order to facilitate a more meaningful comparison of the variations in the variables comprising community violence, police size, and police homicide, over time, all the values for the variables were standardized by computing *z* scores. This was necessitated by the fact that police homicide is a relatively rare event, and great disparities in the values (raw scores) for each variable as well as for police homicide prevents comparison unless it is done with reference to the extent to which each variable deviates from its own average over time. After converting the values for each variable to *z* scores, line graphs were generated depicting the extent to which each variable deviated from its own mean compared to the extent to which police homicide similarly deviated from its own average, either by increasing or decreasing over time. This time sequence analysis graphically clarified the relationship between the variables that had been obtained from correlation analysis. The results are presented here, in Figures 6.9 through 6.15. The similarity in the variations between the variables positively associated with police homicide—police

Figure 6.9
Variations in Police Strength and Police-caused Homicide, 1980 to 1992

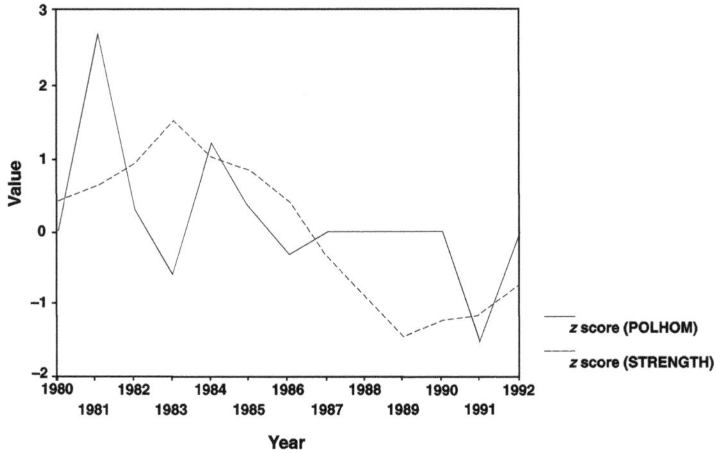

Note: POLHOM = Police-caused Homicide
STRENGTH = Police Size/Strength

Source: The *Guyana Police Force Annual Reports*, 1980–1992. The Guyana Human Rights Association and the Guyana Police Force supplied data on police-caused homicide. Missing data for years 1987 to 1990, were assigned mean value.

Figure 6.10
Variations in "Assault Peace Officer" and Police-caused Homicide, 1980 to 1992

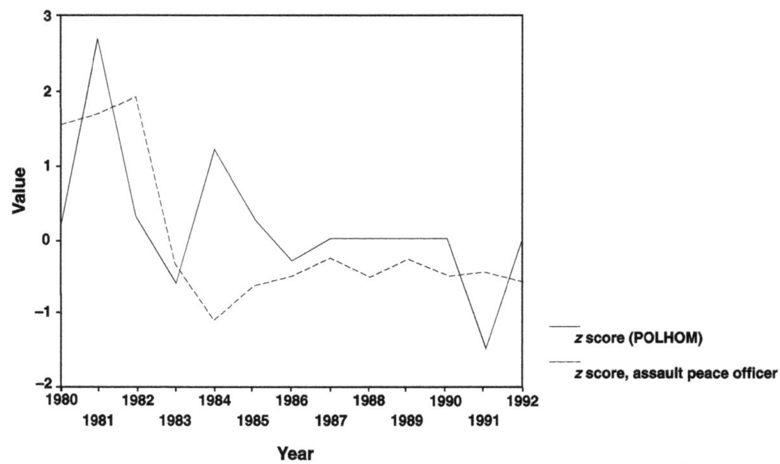

Note: POLHOM = Police-caused Homicide

Source: The *Guyana Police Force Annual Reports*, 1980–1992. The Guyana Human Rights Association and the Guyana Police Force supplied data on police-caused homicide. Missing data for years 1987 to 1990, were assigned mean value.

Figure 6.11
Variations in Total Crime and Police-caused Homicide, 1980 to 1992

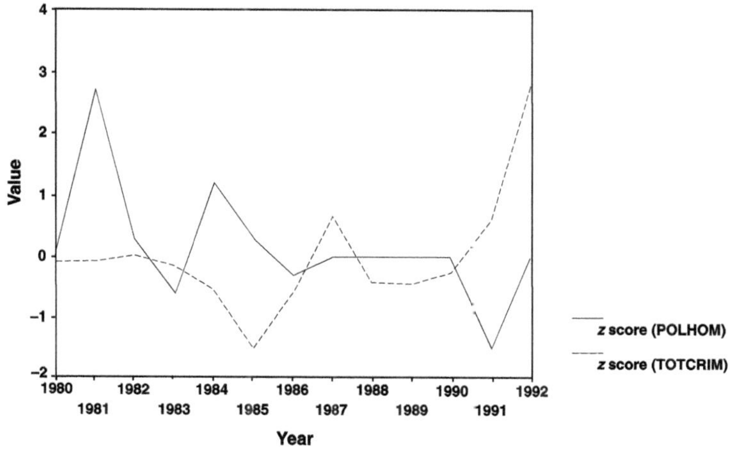

Note: POLHOM = Police-caused Homicide
TOTCRIM = Total Crime

Source: The *Guyana Police Force Annual Reports*, 1980–1992. The Guyana Human Rights Association and the Guyana Police Force supplied data on police-caused homicide. Missing data for years 1987 to 1990, were assigned mean value.

Figure 6.12
Variations in Firearms Crime and Police-caused Homicide, 1980 to 1992

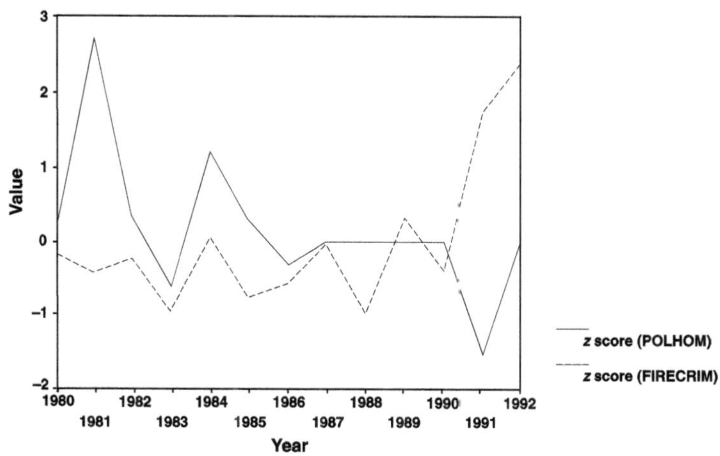

Note: POLHOM = Police-caused Homicide
FIRECRIM = Firearms Crime

Source: The *Guyana Police Force Annual Reports*, 1980–1992. The Guyana Human Rights Association and the Guyana Police Force supplied data on police-caused homicide. Missing data for years 1987 to 1990, were assigned mean value.

Figure 6.13
Variations in Property Crime and Police-caused Homicide, 1980 to 1992

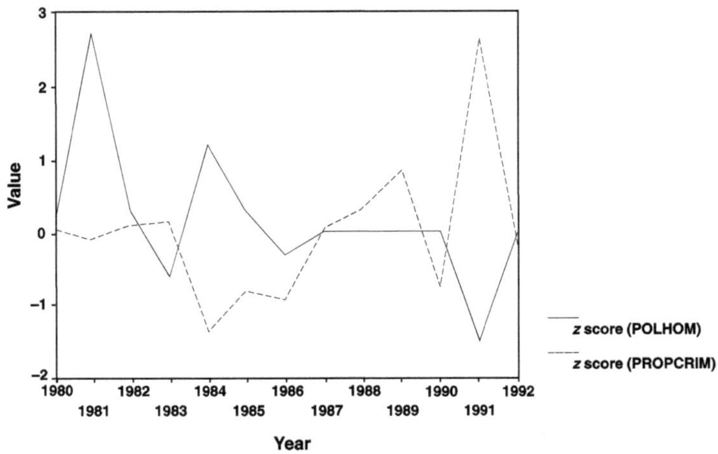

Note: POLHOM = Police-caused Homicide
PROPCRIM = Property Crime

Source: The *Guyana Police Force Annual Reports,* 1980–1992. The Guyana Human Rights Association and the Guyana Police Force supplied data on police-caused homicide. Missing data for years 1987 to 1990, were assigned mean value.

Figure 6.14
Variations in Civilian Homicide and Police-caused Homicide, 1980 to 1992

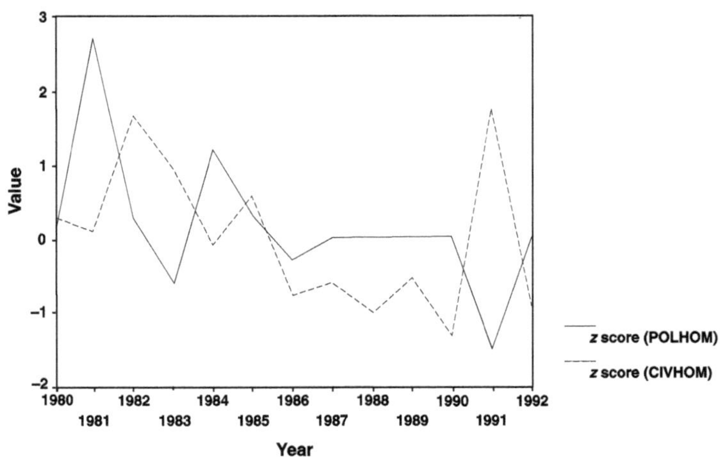

Note: POLHOM = Police-caused Homicide
CIVHOM = Civilian Homicide

Source: The *Guyana Police Force Annual Reports,* 1980–1992. The Guyana Human Rights Association and the Guyana Police Force supplied data on police-caused homicide. Missing data for years 1987 to 1990, were assigned mean value.

Figure 6.15
Variations in Violent Crime and Police-caused Homicide, 1980 to 1992

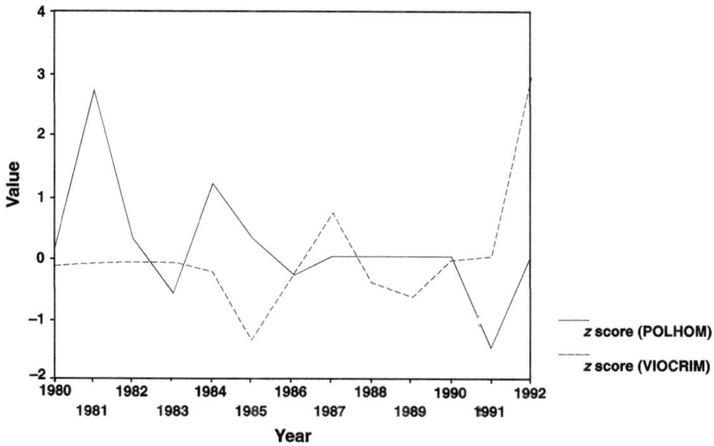

Note: POLHOM = Police-caused Homicide
VIOCRIM = Violent Crime

Source: The *Guyana Police Force Annual Reports*, 1980–1992. The Guyana Human Rights Association and the Guyana Police Force supplied data on police-caused homicide. Missing data for years 1987 to 1990, were assigned mean value.

strength or size (Figure 6.9)—and "assault peace officer" (Figure 6.10) and police homicide are graphically validated. They tend to rise and fall together, or deviate from their own average in similar fashion. On the other hand, the other variables negatively associated with police homicide—total crime (Figure 6.11), firearms crime (Figure 6.12), property crime (Figure 6.13), civilian homicide (Figure 6.14), and violent crime (Figure 6.15)—all tend to vary in different directions from police homicide, especially during the 1980 to 1983 period, when the country experienced its highest levels of police homicide, and after 1990, when a steep rise in crime was evident in direct contradiction to a sharp decline in police homicide.

Police Violence as a Function of Community Violence

The data on community violence have been looked at in three ways in the context of the police use of deadly force in Guyana. First, the relationship between the variables that measure community violence and police homicide have been investigated through the use of Pearson's r correlation analysis. Second, time sequence charts were prepared representing the actual values (raw scores) of the variables over time, and these were compared with the incidence of police homicide over time. Finally, the values of all the variables as well as police homicide were standardized by converting them to *z* scores, then time sequence analysis was done through the preparation of line charts showing how the variation in each variable compared with the variation in police homicide over time. Reliability analysis that was conducted on the variables chosen to represent community violence showed that when taken together they possess some degree of internal consistency (though rather weak) and will measure the underlying concept of community violence to a limited extent across random samples over time.

The results of these analyses consistently show that except for the case of the crime of "assault peace officer," the offenses that adequately measure the underlying concept of community violence are inversely related to police homicide. This means that an increase in any one of these variables will result in a corresponding decrease in police homicide and vice versa. This relationship is further clarified by the time sequence analyses, which show that fluctuations in raw scores of the variables representing community violence, as well as variations from their averages over time, do not follow the same pattern as in the case of police homicide. The sharp increase in the early years (1980–1983) that is evident in the case of police homicide, with a general decline over time, is reversed in the case of the variables under review, all of which experienced a sharp increase at the end of the study period (1990–1992), when police homicide was declining.

With regard to "assault peace officer" there is both a positive association, represented by a positive correlation of .39, with police homicide as well as similar variations over time as evidenced by the time sequence analysis. This variable is distinguishable from the others as it is the only one for which physical contact with the police is a certainty. The others, by definition, do not necessarily imply police intervention. "Assault peace officer," on the other hand, requires physical contact between police and civilians, and such contacts theoretically create the scenario where police homicide may result.

Similarly, the positive relationship of police homicide with police strength or police force size is not surprising. The greater the police-to-population ratio, the greater the risk of the exposure of citizens to police and the use of deadly force by police. The sharp increases in the early years and gradual decline that is evidenced by the time sequence analysis is similar to the pattern displayed by police homicide and is to be expected.

It is significant that the analysis shows that there was no sharp increase in community violence during the early years (1980–1985) of the period. Figure 6.11 shows that community violence represented by "total" crime was relatively stable and then experienced a sharp decline around 1985, only beginning to rise again significantly from around 1987, and peaking in 1992. Only "assault peace officer," when taken separately as an indicator of community violence, manifests a sequence in variance with this over the study period, rising sharply in the early years as does police homicide and then leveling off in the later period (Figure 6.10). As was discussed in the previous chapter, Guyana experienced severe political repression during the early years of the 1980s, when the society was heavily policed. Public demonstrations, meetings, and protests were frequently held by opposition political parties, especially the WPA. The usual scenario for these public meetings or mass protests was that the police would converge on the crowd in large numbers and brutally attack and beat those present in order to break up the meeting. Then, as many persons as possible would be arrested and taken into custody and charged with a variety of offenses, which invariably included "assault peace officer." The following quotation from a WPA press release dated Friday September 18, 1981, is representative of the usual scenario:

PNC UNLEASHES SAVAGERY ON PEACEFUL PICKET AND
PEOPLE'S MARCH: 28 ARRESTED, SOME HOSPITALISED
Crowds were fired upon, women and children beaten, WPA members hospitalised and arrested as Burnham's police and thugs smashed a peaceful picket and demonstration sponsored by the Working People's Alliance in Georgetown. In the early evening of Thursday 17 September 1981, police and other street enforcers of the PNC brutally attacked a peaceful picket and march by citizens in Georgetown . . .

Members of the Working People's Alliance were singled out for the most brutal assaults by police wielding hockey sticks, over-sized batons and other weapons. In one instance, a member of the public armed with a camera was fired upon and pursued by police with guns drawn. He gave himself up into custody, thereby avoiding the tragic fate of Father Bernard Darke, another photographer on another occasion. Also taken into custody were 26 members and supporters of the WPA. . . . Immediately following the beatings and arrests, 27 armed men, some of them police officers, executed a search under the National Security Act on the home and premises of Rupert Roopnarine. Nothing was found. The police however arrested lawyer Moses Bhagwan who was present.[45]

The variations in the variable "assault peace officer" is perfectly understandable if the social context is taken into account. After President Burnham died in 1985, the incidence of these kinds of scenarios were greatly reduced, and Figure 6.10 shows a corresponding leveling off of the incidences of this crime from around 1985.

Taken as a whole, the community violence hypothesis is not supported in the case of Guyana. The effect of community violence as a causal factor in the production of police violence is marginal. This finding contradicts the studies mentioned earlier, such as those done by Kania and Mackey (1979), Sherman and Langworthy (1979), and Matulia (1985), but builds on the conclusions of other studies that, though finding some support for indicators of community violence, concluded that other factors, based on the conflict theory perspective exhibit stronger causal connections with police homicide.

It will be remembered that after finding strong empirical support for a causal explanation based on the conflict perspective (economic inequality) while controlling, inter alia, for the effect of community violence, Jacobs and Britt concluded that structural inequality was the major predictor of police homicide. Sorenson and others also found empirical support for a relationship between community violence and police homicide, but suggested that the latter operated like an intervening variable mediating the relationship between predictors based on the conflict perspective (economic inequality) and police homicide. Chevigny, although not empirically testing the validity of the community violence hypothesis, discounted it as being "misleading" and searched for other explanations of police violence in the societies he studied (Jamaica, Argentina, and Brazil).[46]

The impact of police departmental policy in the reduction of police homicide in the United States, despite a concurrently rising violent crime rate during the material time,[47] has been well documented. The New York City Police Firearms Discharge Review Board stated in its 1985 *Report* that, as a result of the implementation of new policy guidelines with regard to police use of deadly force, police homicide had been significantly reduced. Sherman and Cohen found a decline of about 50 percent in police homicide in the United States from the early 1970s, when police departments began to respond to public pressure to reduce the police homicide rate, up to 1984, the last year covered by their study. As a result of the implementation of a more restrictive firearms policy in almost all police departments serving large communities, the numbers killed had declined from 353 in 1971 to 172 in 1984.[48] Fyfe and Blumberg have also made similar observations.[49] Apart from improved training, disciplinary procedures, and the proliferation of civil suits by relatives of victims, researchers have also credited the effect of the Supreme Court decision in the case of *Tennessee v Garner*, 471 US 1 (1985), (outlawing the use of deadly force against nondangerous, *unarmed* fleeing felons) with a reduction in the incidence of police homicides in the United States.[50] Regardless of the reason for the declining rate of police-caused homicide in the United States, until 1994 the country had experienced a consistently rising *violent crime rate*,[51] and that fact greatly diminished the explanatory potential of the community violence hypothesis. The findings with reference to Guyana are therefore not completely at variance with current research findings on the utility of the community violence hypothesis.

This analysis explored the relationship between police homicide and community violence and found the latter to be inversely related to the former, except for the single crime directly concerning the police, "assault peace officer," for which a contextual explanation has been offered. The search for a causal explanation for police violence in Guyana will now be shifted from the analysis of the level of general crime in the community to the situations in which force was used. Here the actual circumstances of the homicide by police is investigated to determine whether the level of threat the officer was facing justified the use of fatal force.

THE PROXIMATE SITUATION

The purpose of this analysis of the proximate situation in which police homicide occurs is that it is the only means by which we can assess what *actually* happens during a violent encounter between police and civilians and why deadly and/or excessive force is used. In a sense, this is indeed the *best* explanation that one can find for police use of deadly force, but it is also the most elusive, as police homicide does not often take place in the presence of impartial and independent witnesses. The police tend to consider all killings as justifiable, and police cover-ups are considered to be part of their occupational subculture, which fosters a "cult of secrecy."[52]

The analysis of the proximate situation is based on a convenience sample of 24 out of a total of 150 cases of police-caused homicide for which verifiable information was obtained for the purpose of this study. Sampling of these cases was dictated by the availability of complete accounts of the circumstances under which the homicide took place from which both the police version and alternative credible version could be pieced together. The use of the "alternative credible version" technique in order to arrive at an independent determination of the circumstances under which the homicide took place and whether it was justifiable under the existing law relating to police use of deadly force (discussed in chapter 2) requires that exhaustive accounts of the incident be available for scrutiny. Only those cases for which verifiable records exist, such as records of coroners' inquests and court proceedings, statements of independent witnesses, statements given by police either under oath or to their attorneys, independent accounts given by victims before death, reports of the coroner's pathologist based on an autopsy, and the reports of the medical examiner concerning the internal and external condition of the body and the cause of death, could be used for the purpose of arriving at a reliable reconstruction of the circumstances surrounding these homicides.

The analytical technique, as outlined by Richard Harding and Richard Fahey,[53] requires that all the versions of the incident be examined. It is different from the technique used in other studies, which looked at the facts of individual cases, because it is intended to determine independently and subjectively whether the incident was one of justifiable homicide or of criminal homicide based on cases for which a wide variety of independent sources of information are available. The classification is done not on the basis of the police evaluation of the incident but on the subjective interpretation of the extent to which the facts of the case justified the use of deadly force under the existing law. The analysis is both legal and sociological. The version of the incident derived from the alternative source (other than the police) becomes more credible in direct proportion as the police version becomes less believable. If the police version lacks corroboration, then the alternative version increases in credibility. It may also be added that the alternative version would increase in credibility to the extent that it accords with the injuries displayed on the body of the deceased victim, and in this regard reports of the pathologist or medical examiner who performed the post-mortem examination are of great value. The most credible version is then considered on the basis of the existing law relating to justifiable homicide. It is not the apparent injustice of the killing that is of significance, but rather the legality of it. Many cases of police homicide, as, for example, the shooting of a fleeing felon in the back of the head, are morally repugnant but yet perfectly legal and justifiable in Guyana and must be classified as such under this analytical method. The result of using the alternative credible version technique to make a subjective determination of whether police-caused homicide was justified in the twenty-four cases analyzed is presented in Table 6.6. Factual details of the cases are included in Appendix B.

Justifiable homicide is determined by prima facie evidence of factors that would make the homicide justifiable according to existing law. This is a separate question than the one asked earlier as to whether the state has violated the rule of law by passing unjust laws that erode the fundamental rights and freedoms of the individual. The laws are applied in this analysis as they currently exist, the only question being whether the police acted in accordance with the law. The types of situations that would result in the homicide being justifiable according to law in the case of the prevention of a serious criminal offense, referred to as a felony, or the apprehension of a person suspected of having committed or about to commit a serious criminal offense, are classified under the headings of *fleeing felon* and *confrontation*. Under the "fleeing felon rule" as it applies in Guyana, situations are categorized to reflect the scenarios where the decedent was fleeing and armed with a firearm, fleeing and armed with a knife, fleeing and armed with a cutlass or galvanized pipe, and fleeing and unarmed. In all these cases, homicide by police would be justifiable under the existing law even where the felony in respect of which the decedent was fleeing was property crime. As discussed in the previous chapter, the exception under the English common law fleeing felon rule in the case of property crime does not apply to Guyana. Under the heading of "confrontation," situations include the victim armed with a firearm, armed with a knife, or armed with a cutlass or galvanized pipe and threatening the police officer who committed the homicide. In all these instances, homicide by police would be justifiable under the laws of Guyana. The final scenario, where an unarmed victim is involved in a confrontation with police, would result in criminal homicide if deadly force is used by the officer.

With regard to the prevention of a less serious offense, referred to as a misdemeanor, or the apprehension of a person suspected of committing or being about to commit a misdemeanor, the categories used are *fleeing misdemeanant* and *confrontation.* Under the heading of "fleeing misdemeanant," situations are defined to include scenarios where the misdemeanant was fleeing and armed with a knife, fleeing and armed with a stick, and fleeing and unarmed. In all these cases, it is submitted that based on the English common law fleeing felon rule, the use of deadly force by the officer to apprehend a misdemeanant will be unjustifiable. Under the heading of "confrontation" in the first scenario—armed with a knife—homicide by police would be justifiable. In the case of the second scenario—armed with a stick—the principles laid down by the Guyana Court of Appeal of the Supreme Court in the case of *The State v Evelyn Dick and Alwyn Dodson Evelyn,* discussed in the previous chapter, would be used to determine whether there was substantial disproportion between the actual threatened danger and the lethal retaliation. In the third instance—unarmed—the use of deadly force by police would amount to criminal homicide.

A third category, *other persons,* is included to account for situations where the circumstances indicated that the victim was not connected with criminal activity

Table 6.6
Justification for Police Use of Deadly Force

Type of Situation	Prima Facie Legal Implications of such a Situation	Number According to Credible Police Versions of the Facts	Number According to Alternative Versions of the Facts
Fleeing Felon			
(a) Armed with firearm	Justifiable under Art. 138 of Const. & Fleeing Felon Rule		
(b) Armed with knife	Justifiable under Art. 138 of Const. & Fleeing Felon Rule		
(c) Armed with cutlass/ galvanized pipe	Justifiable under Art. 138 of Const. & Fleeing Felon Rule		
(d) Unarmed	Justifiable under Art. 138 of Const. & Fleeing Felon Rule	1	
Confrontation			
(a) Armed with firearm	Justifiable under Art. 138 of Const. & Defense of Life Rules	1	
(b) Armed with knife	Justifiable under Art. 138 of Const. & Defense of Life Rules	3	
(c) Armed with cutlass/ galvanized pipe	Justifiable under Art. 138 of Const. & Defense of Life Rules	2	
(d) Unarmed	Not justifiable under existing law		3
Fleeing Misdemeanant			
(a) Armed with knife	Not justifiable under existing law		
(b) Armed with stick	Not justifiable under existing law		
(c) Unarmed	Not justifiable under existing law		2

(continued)

Table 6.6
Justification for Police Use of Deadly Force (*continued*)

Type of Situation	Prima Facie Legal Implications of such a Situation	Number According to Credible Police Versions of the Facts	Number According to Alternative Versions of the Facts
Confrontation			
(a) Armed with knife	Justifiable under Art. 138 of Const. & Defense of Life Rules		
(b) Armed with stick	Not justifiable unless circumstances indicate no substantial disproportion between the actual danger and the lethal retaliation		2
(c) Unarmed	Not justifiable under existing law		3
Other Persons			
No connection with criminal activity & unarmed	Not justifiable under existing law		7
Total		7	17

Source: Adapted from Richard W. Harding and Richard P. Fahey. 1973. "Killings by Chicago Police, 1969–70: An Empirical Study." *Southern California Law Review* 46:292–93. This table was prepared from information on police homicide supplied by the Guyana Human Rights Association, court records, medical records, sworn and unsworn statements of witnesses, press reports, etc.

and was unarmed. As Table 6.6 shows, in a total of seventeen cases the scenarios that were reconstructed, based on alternative credible versions of the incident and the medical evidence where available, indicate that the deaths amounted to criminal homicide under the law. In seven of the cases examined, no connection to criminal activity could be conclusively established either before or during the encounter that led to homicide by police, and the decedents were all unarmed. In three cases the decedents were unarmed suspected felons when they engaged in a confrontation with police and were fatally shot. In seven cases the incident involved misdemeanants or suspected misdemeanants, five of whom were unarmed when either fleeing or engaging in a confrontation with the police. In all these cases except two (where the misdemeanants were armed with a stick while engaging in a confrontation with the police), the capital offense of murder is indicated by the circumstances. In three of the seventeen cases, although the police officers' versions of the incidents completely exonerated them, they were subsequently charged, as a result of public outrage over the incidents. One officer was charged for murder, which carries the singular penalty of death and the others for manslaughter, which carries penalties involving varying terms of imprisonment, the highest being imprisonment for life. In both of the cases where the officers were charged for manslaughter, they were acquitted, and in the third case where the officer was charged for murder, the charge was subsequently reduced to manslaughter and the very light penalty of four years' imprisonment was imposed by a judge. In the seven cases where it was determined that police homicide was justifiable based on the alternative credible version technique, one of the suspected felons was unarmed and fleeing. In the six cases where the evidence supports the finding of a confrontation with police, the decedents were more than likely armed with weapons that would allow the police to retaliate with deadly force.

Seventeen of the twenty-four cases analyzed, 70.8 percent, reveal that death more than likely did not take place in accordance with the law of justifiable homicide. Yet, the State only saw fit to institute criminal proceedings in three of these twenty-four cases. The circumstances surrounding the death of the victims not previously connected with criminal activity are mysterious. Four of the victims died allegedly after they were already in police custody. These cases are grouped under *other persons*, and the activities that precipitated their deaths involve the alleged use of torture. Civil actions are currently pending in court with respect to three of these cases, and the police have denied all the allegations that are being made against them. In the other case, which occurred in 1984, one policeman was indicted for manslaughter but acquitted by a High Court jury.

The Guyana Police Force routinely releases statements after police killings, setting out justifiable cause for homicide committed by the police. The allegation is usually made that the police were attacked with a knife, galvanized pipe, or other weapon and had to defend themselves. In response to an item requesting information on the forty-eight cases of police homicide confirmed by the police for the period 1991 to 1994, the police stated that *all* the homicides had occurred within departmental guidelines and were justifiable homicides.[54] Notwithstanding, the press reported in 1993 that police officers, who fatally shot two citizens, were decorated by the Force with respect to the incident two days after the shooting.[55] The two officers involved were presented with Certificates of High Commendation and monetary awards of $5,000 and $10,000, respectively. One of the victims was a key witness in a court case against the police regarding a person who had died in police custody. He had also given evidence in a civil action seeking damages for wrongful death against the police and was shot in execution style, by a bullet in the mouth.[56] The civil action, in which this victim was to have appeared as a witness, was abandoned after his death. The police claimed that the victims were engaged in the commission of a robbery and had attacked the officers who were attempting to arrest them. The unseemly haste to reward officers for the use of fatal force in the alleged execution of their duties is disturbing. In December, 1993, Amnesty International wrote to the Minister of Home Affairs requesting that a "full and impartial investigation" into the shootings be carried out,[57] but this has not yet been done.

Based on the findings resulting from the alternative credible version technique and presented in Table 6.6, it may be concluded that it is more than likely that many of the instances of police homicide in Guyana during this study period are really instances of criminal homicide, and that in many cases, the police did not exercise their power to use deadly force in accordance with the laws of Guyana.

Police internal regulations require them only to use that degree of force that is "essential to deal with the immediate situation."[58] They may fire in defense of self or others or to prevent crime and protect property. They are also required to fire when given orders by a superior rank.[59] The internal guidelines can be said to be generally consistent with the requirements of the law, but when police are confronted with the actual situation where a decision has to be made concerning the use of the firearm or other weapon, these guidelines may be of little value in preventing the use of excessive force.

CONCLUSION

This chapter addressed the question of finding an explanation for police violence in Guyana. First, the nature of police violence was discussed and data were presented, based on field research conducted in Guyana in 1995, to assess the prevalence of police homicide in Guyana. Comparisons with the police homicide rate and violence rate measured by civilian homicide in other countries were used to show that Guyana had an alarmingly high rate of police homicide per 100,000 persons in the population (2.2) during several years of the study period. The "disproportionate violence ratio" method used by Chevigny to establish the "pattern of violence" in the society was also applied in the case of Guyana, and it was concluded that the situation clearly indicated a prima facie case of the abuse of police power to use deadly force and that the situation required further investigation.

The quantitative data that were collected in the field in Guyana, as far as possible, were subjected to analyses to investigate the relationship that has been established in the technical literature, between police violence and community violence. Several prior studies have found a positive relationship between indicators of community violence (such as the violent crime index) and police violence. In the absence of data that would allow statistical techniques such as multiple regression analyses to be performed, three ways of examining this relationship were utilized.

First, a scale of items representing criminal offenses that would consistently measure community violence was subjected to reliability analysis to determine their internal consistency and the ability to measure community violence over time. All the items revealed positive but modest-to-weak item-to-total correlations with community violence. An alpha of .52 was obtained when the items were combined together; this means that the items possess a limited degree of internal consistency as measures of community violence. The items comprising the scale consisted of criminal offenses representing five categories of crime: violent crime, firearms crime, crimes against the police, property crime, and civilian homicide. These variables were then correlated with police homicide using Pearson's *r* coefficient to determine whether and to what extent they were empirically associated. It was found that all the variables except "assault peace officer" were negatively associated with police homicide, meaning that when the incidence of these crimes are low, the incidence of police-caused homicide tends to be high, and vice versa. A contextual explanation was offered for the positive relationship between the variable "assault peace officer" and community violence. In addition, the crime of "assault peace officer" is the only one of all the thirty-three crimes included in the underlying concept of community violence that involves direct physical contact between police and civilians. The relationship of police homicide to the size of the police force was also investigated and a positive association was found, indicating that when the presence of police in the community is high, the levels of police homicide may be correspondingly high.

Second, time sequence analysis was conducted by preparing line graphs to chart the variations in the incidence of the empirical indicators of community violence separately and collectively, and to compare these with the corresponding time sequence data relating to police homicide during the study period. It was found that the variables that were negatively associated with police homicide, violent crime, property crime, firearms crime, and civilian homicide exhibited a contradictory pattern of variation over time than that exhibited by police violence. Whereas police violence rose sharply in the early years and consistently declined over time, these variables exhibited low levels for the most part during the early years and sharp increases from around 1990. Police size showed a corresponding pattern in the early years when police homicide was high but to a lesser extent in the years following 1986, when the size of the police force declined dramatically.

Third, in order to facilitate comparisons in the variations over time between the individual variables that displayed great disparities in raw numbers, the values were standardized, by computing *z* scores, to a mean of zero and a standard deviation of one, which allowed comparisons between variations in police homicide and the indicators of community violence separately and collectively over time. The results of these analyses were presented using line graphs to depict variations from the mean.

The divergences that were apparent from the charts, which plotted the raw scores on the variables, were removed in the charts displaying the *z* scores, and it was possible to more readily compare the effect of the pattern discussed in the previous paragraph. The variables negatively associated with police homicide were seen to be deviating markedly from the mean at different times and in different directions from the variations observed in the incidence of police homicide over time. Essentially, only the variable "assault peace officer" behaved in a way that was compatible with the observable trend in the variation of police homicide—a sharp rise in the early years, peaking around 1981 and then a gradual and consistent decline, including some variation in the decline after 1989.

Separate consideration was given to the effect of police force size or strength. This variable had been included in the correlation matrix that was generated because it has been empirically associated with the increased risk of police violence in society. Police force strength or size was also found to be positively associated with police homicide in Guyana, exhibiting a moderate correlation coefficient of .35. This factor is also an important item in the discussion because of the increases in the strength of the police force that took place during the Burnham years. The similarity in the behavior of police force size and police homicide over the years can be observed from inspecting the line graph that depicts changes in the raw scores representing the strength of the police force over time (Figure 6.2), as well as the chart depicting the relationship between police force strength and police homicide over time (Figure 6.9).

The results of the above analyses showed, to the degree that the data allow conclusions, that the community violence hypothesis was not supported in the case of Guyana. The importance of community violence has also been tempered by several researchers as the primary factor in explaining police violence. The declining police homicide rate in the United States during the period when violent crime was rising (the 1970s and 1980s) also weakens this hypothesis considerably.

Finally, the "alternative credible version" analytical technique was used to investigate the factual circumstances surrounding a convenience sample of cases of police-caused homicide. Analysis of the proximate situation in which the killings occurred revealed that in seventeen of the twenty-four cases analyzed, the use of deadly force by police amounted to criminal rather than justifiable homicide. The findings in this chapter seem to suggest that the explanation for police violence in Guyana, while taking into account the possible effects of violence in the community, should also include the effect of other factors that could precipitate the excessive use of violence in police work. Foremost among these factors is the significance of the contextual framework, which may create the underlying conditions for violence to become part of the occupational subculture of policing.

NOTES

1. See Richard R. E. Kania and Wade C. Mackey. 1977. "Police Violence as a Function of Community Characteristics." *Criminology* 15:27–48; Kenneth J. Matulia. 1985. *A Balance of Forces. Model Deadly Force Policies and Procedure.* 2nd ed. Gaithersburg, Md.: International Association of Chiefs of Police, p. 88.

2. Gerald D. Robin. 1963. "Justifiable Homicide by Police Officers." *Journal of Criminal Law, Criminology and Police Science* 54:225–31.

3. Lawrence W. Sherman and Robert H. Langworthy. 1979. "Measuring Homicide by Police Officers." *The Journal of Criminal Law and Criminology* 70:546–80.

4. James J. Fyfe. 1978. *Shots Fired. An Examination of New York City Police Firearm Discharges.* Unpublished Ph.D. Dissertation. State University of New York at Albany.

5. A. Binder and L. A. Fridell. 1984. "Lethal Force as a Police Response." *Criminal Justice Abstracts* 16:250–80.

6. Matulia, *A Balance of Forces*, p. 8.

7. Richard R. E. Kania and Wade C. Mackey. 1977. "Police Violence as a Function of Community Characteristics." *Criminology* 15:27–48, pp. 34–39.

8. Allen E. Liska (ed.). 1992. *Social Threat and Social Control.* Albany, NY: State University of New York Press, pp. 62–63.

9. These crimes were taken from the *Guyana Police Force Annual Reports, 1980–1992.*

10. See David Jacobs and David Britt. 1979. "Inequality and Police Use of Deadly Force. An Empirical Assessment of a Conflict Hypothesis." *Social Problems* 26:403–12; Sherman and Langworthy, *Measuring Homicide by Police Officers*; Matulia, *A Balance of Forces*; Allen E. Liska and Jiang Yu. 1992. "Specifying and Testing the Threat Hypothesis: Police Use of Deadly Force." In *Social Threat and Social Control,* Allen E. Liska, ed., pp. 53–68. Albany, NY: State University of New York Press; Jonathan R. Sorenson, James W. Marquart, and Deon E. Brock. 1993. "Factors Related to Killings of Felons by Police Officers: A Test of the Community Violence and Conflict Hypotheses." *Justice Quarterly* 10:417–40. Note also, that Liska and Yu found that police force size tended to decrease the level of police homicide.

11. See Chapter 1, where the meaning of "police violence" is defined.

12. For a full discussion of issues of reliability and validity of this source of data, please see Chapter 2.

13. See Chapter 2.

14. Ibid.

15. Fyfe, *Shots Fired: A Typological Examination of New York City Police Firearms Discharges;* Sherman and Langworthy, "Measuring Homicide by Police Officers," p. 550.

16. Albert J. Meehan. 1986. "Record-Keeping Practices in the Policing of Juveniles." *Urban Life* 15:70–102.

17. See *Guyana Human Rights Association Members Annual Reports* 1980–1986 generally, and especially the section regarding freedom of expression.

18. *Guyana Police Annual Report* for 1980 and 1981, p. 4, respectively. By 1994 the World Health Organization estimated Guyana's population to be approximately 825,000 persons. See *World Health Statistics Annual, 1994.* Geneva: World Health Organization, p. A-4.

19. *Amnesty International Report, 1986.* London: Amnesty International Publications, pp. 129–32. See also Jose deSouza Martins. 1991. "Lynchings—Life by a Thread: Street Justice in Brazil, 1979–1988." In *Vigilantism and the State in Modern Latin America, Essays on Extralegal Violence,* Martha K. Huggins, ed. New York: Praeger Publishers, pp. 21–32.

20. Federal Bureau of Investigation, U.S. Department of Justice. 1980. *Crime in the United States, 1979: Uniform Crime Reports.* Washington, D.C.: U.S. Government Printing Office.

21. *Guyana Police Force Annual Reports, 1979.*

22. Paul Chevigny. 1990. "Police Deadly Force as Social Control: Jamaica, Argentina, and Brazil." *Criminal Law Forum* 1:389–426.

23. *Guyana Police Force Annual Report,* 1991, p. 4.

24. *Guyana Police Force Annual Report,* 1992, p. 4.

25. In subsequent years, beyond the study period, the trend has continued with eleven out of sixteen police shootings resulting in death in 1995, sixteen out of twenty in 1996, and twenty-seven out of forty-seven in 1997. In 1997, however, the large number of nonfatal

shootings included eleven persons allegedly injured when police fired upon demonstrators who were protesting the results of national elections outside the Elections Commission in Georgetown. See Guyana Human Rights Association, *Overview of Police Conduct, Police Lock-ups, Deportees, Prison Conditions.* September 1999, p. 8.

26. See for example, James J. Fyfe. 1980. "Geographic Correlates of Police Shootings: A Microanalysis." *Journal of Research in Crime and Delinquency* 17:101–13.

27. Lawrence Sherman and Barry Glick. 1984. "The Quality of Arrest Statistics." *Police Foundation Reports* 2:1–8; Walter Gove, Michael Hughes, and Michael Geerken. 1985. "Are Uniform Crime Reports a Valid Indicator of the Index Crimes? An Affirmative Answer with Minor Qualifications." *Criminology* 23: 451–501.

28. See Chapter 2 on Research Design and Methods.

29. Joseph J. Senna and Larry J. Siegel. 1993. *Introduction to Criminal Justice.* St. Paul, Minn.: West Publishing Co., p. 65.

30. See David Seidman and Michael Couzens. 1974. "Getting the Crime Rate Down: Political Pressure and Crime Reporting." *Law and Society Review* 8:457; Albert Meehan. 1986. "Record-Keeping Practices in the Policing of Juveniles." *Urban Life* 15: 70–102.

31. Walter Gove, Michael Hughes, and Michael Geerken. 1985. "Are Uniform Crime Reports a Valid Indicator of the Index Crimes? An Affirmative Answer with Minor Qualifications." *Criminology* 23:451–501.

32. See *Guyana Police Force Annual Reports.*

33. Kania and Mackey, "Police Violence as a Function of Community Characteristics," pp. 34–40.

34. Jacobs and Britt, *Inequality and Police Use of Deadly Force*, p. 406.

35. Sorenson, Marquart, and Brock, "Factors Related to Killings of Felons by Police Officers," at pp. 427–28.

36. Fyfe, *Shots Fired. An Examination of New York City Police Firearm Discharges.*

37. Both Sherman and Langworthy, "Measuring Homicide by Police Officers," and Matulia, *A Balance of Forces,* found gun density to be highly correlated with police homicide.

38. Anthony Walsh. 1990. *Statistics for the Social Sciences.* New York: Harper & Row, pp. 7, 336–37; Mordecai Ezekiel and Karl A. Fox. 1963. *Methods of Correlation and Regression Analysis.* New York: John Wiley & Sons, Inc., pp. 293–95.

39. Ezekiel and Fox, *Methods of Correlation and Regression Analysis*, pp. 24–29.

40. Morris Hamburg. 1985. *Basic Statistics, a Modern Approach.* 3rd ed. Orlando, Fla.: Harcourt Brace Jovanovich, pp. 135–65; Also, Ezekiel and Fox, *Methods of Correlation and Regression Analysis,* pp. 6–13.

41. John Keenan Taylor. 1990. *Statistical Techniques for Data Analysis.* Chelsea, Mich.: Lewis Publishers, Inc., p. 23.

42. Ezekiel and Fox, *Methods of Correlation and Regression Analysis,* p. 30.

43. Leonard J. Tashman and Kathleen R. Lamborn. 1979. *The Ways and Means of Statistics.* New York: Harcourt Brace Jovanovich, Inc., pp. 139–60.

44. See Sherman and Langworthy, "Measuring Homicide by Police Officers"; Jacobs and Britt, "Inequality and Police Use of Deadly Force"; Matulia, *A Balance of Forces*; and Sorenson and others, "Factors Related to Killings of Felons by Police Officers."

45. Working People's Alliance Press Release, dated Friday, September, 1981.

46. Paul Chevigny. 1990. "Police Deadly Force as Social Control: Jamaica, Argentina, and Brazil," *Criminal Law Forum* 1:389–425.

47. See the *Uniform Crime Reports.*

48. Lawrence Sherman and E. Cohen. 1986. *Citizens Killed by Big City Police, 1970–1984.* Washington, D.C.: Crime Control Institute.

49. Fyfe, *Shots Fired. An Examination of New York City Police Firearm Discharges*, and "Police Use of Deadly Force: Research and Reform." *Justice Quarterly* 5:165–205; Mark Blumberg. 1994. "Police Use of Deadly Force: Exploring Some Key Issues," in *Police Deviance.* 3rd ed., Thomas Barker and David L. Carter, eds. Cincinnati, Ohio: Anderson Publishing, pp. 201–25.

50. Abraham N. Tennenbaum. 1994. "The Influence of the Garner Decision on Police Use of Deadly Force." *Journal of Criminal Law & Criminology* 85:241–60.

51. According to the *Uniform Crime Reports*, the number of violent crimes reported to the police increased more than 30 percent between 1981 and 1994, while the violence rate increased by 25 percent.

52. Discussed in chapter 2. See also William A Westley. 1970. *Violence and the Police: A Sociological Study of Law, Custom and Morality.* Cambridge, Mass.: MIT Press.

53. Discussed in detail in Chapter 2. See also Richard W. Harding and Richard P. Fahey. 1973. "Killings by Chicago Police, 1969–70: An Empirical Study." *Southern California Law Review* 46:284–315.

54. Police response to item no. 14 on Police Survey instrument.

55. *The Stabroek News*, dated September 9, 1993.

56. Guyana Human Rights Association Press Release, October, 1993, *GHRA Calls for Action From DPP (Director of Public Prosecutions) in Police Killings.*

57. *Amnesty International Report*, 1994, pp. 148–49.

58. *Guyana Police Force Special Order*, April 23, 1963.

59. Ibid.

7

Discussion and Conclusions: The Contextual Approach

The problem of the excessive use of deadly force by police is by no means limited to Guyana. It tarnishes the practice of policing in modern society all over the world and has engaged the attention of criminal justice researchers for decades.[1] This study adds to the existing literature on the police in Guyana,[2] by examining the persistent problem of the use of deadly violence in police work. Notwithstanding that police-caused homicide is a relatively rare event, the sacredness of human life, whether that of a saint or sinner, requires that the police use fatal force only when it is absolutely necessary, and only in the performance of a lawful duty.

This study expanded the explanatory framework of police violence to include the historical, social, political, and legal context in which it is embedded. The search for a causal explanation was conducted with reference to two broad periods. The first, referred to as the colonial/pre-independence period, began in the early seventeenth century when the territory now known as Guyana was first settled by the Dutch, until independence from the United Kingdom was achieved in1966. The second period, referred to as the post-independence/modern period, covered the remaining years to 1994. Detailed investigation of the context in which police violence occurred during these periods was conducted in this study from the conflict theoretical perspective, using primarily qualitative research techniques.

Investigation of the historical context revealed that the requirements of the colonial system dictated the type of policing that developed in Guyana and the role that was defined for the police. As distinct from the situation in the metropolitan country of the colonial rulers (the United Kingdom), policing in Guyana, as in the case of the majority of dependencies of the United Kingdom, was cast within a military role, and the police force was trained and equipped to operate like an occupying army, capable of unleashing deadly violence for the purpose of population control. The divide-and-rule policies of the colonial state authority, coupled with the deliberate measures to promote ethnic and class differentiation, exacerbated the lack of social cohesion in the plural society, which was ruled by coercion, force, and the threat of force. From the year 1891, when the British Guiana Police Force was transformed from a civilian into a semi-military force, throughout the entire colonial period, policing was characterized by violence.

Upon the attainment of independence from the United Kingdom in 1966, the chance to redefine the role and function of the Guyana Police Force was forever lost as the local state authority drafted the security forces, including the police, into a master plan for the maintenance of political power and the reordering of a potentially conflictful society toward the attainment of socialist goals. Measures adopted to strengthen the police for political purposes included internal surveillance, political indoctrination, the expansion of police powers under the law, and increased militarization. Counter-insurgency training, the acquisition of weapons of war, and significant increases in the ratio of police to the general population, also increased the political potency of the police as the principal expression of authoritarian state rule. The semi-military role of the police as a hostile force vis-à-vis the general population was strengthened as police power was used as a weapon against political opponents, and the police became instruments of public intimidation and repression. This state of affairs endured until the early 1990s, when free and fair elections resulted in a change in the political leadership of the country.

The extent to which the socio-political and legal environment created the underlying conditions for the excessive use of violence in police work during the post-independence/modern period was given special attention in this study. Within the conflict theoretical framework adopted, it was pertinent to consider whether socio-economic and political conditions fostered social conflict and the perception of social threat that could elicit a repressive governmental response. It was concluded that rather than economic stagnation, politically engineered class and inter-ethnic conflict resulted in a continuing perception of social threat that was ultimately transformed into a political threat by the successors to state power after independence. The doctrine of "Paramountcy of the Party," coupled with the politicization of policing, produced a force that became a weapon in the hands of an authoritarian and unpopular government that had to rely on coercion in order to maintain political power and social control. Weak legal controls on the power of the police to use fatal force, and permissive constitutional provisions, augmented by the passing of the National Security Act, enabled the police to violate the rights of citizens without due regard for accountability and restraint. Taken together, these conditions created the environment for the excessive use of violence in police work.

The technique of triangulation was applied to investigate the use of deadly force by the police during the post-independence/modern period. Statistical data on crime and police-caused homicide were analyzed in several different ways in order to develop an explanation for variations in the use of deadly force by police over time. The analyses revealed that during the study period (1980–1994), Guyana experienced an inordinately high rate of police-caused homicide when compared to other developing and developed countries. Relationships between police homicide and the total number of homicides, killings of police and killings by police, and fatal and nonfatal police shootings all supported a conclusion that the use of fatal force by police warranted further investigation regarding the possibility that police violence was occurring.

Investigation of the community violence hypothesis revealed that police-caused homicide was inversely related to violent crime, crimes involving the use of firearms, civilian homicide, and property crime. Time sequence charts showed that during the first half of the decade of the 1980s police homicide peaked around 1981, then declined in 1983, only to rise again in 1984. Meanwhile, community violence remained for the most part, at a constant level, slightly increased, or declined significantly during the same period. These measures of community violence all experienced a sharp increase around 1991, whereas police homicide decreased significantly, although it has begun to reverse this trend since 1992. Only the crime known as "assault peace officer" was positively related to police-caused homicide, and the scenarios under which citizens were being charged for this offense shows that the relationship may be misleading. The majority of these offenses represented the early period of the 1980s, when the repression of opposition political parties was very extreme and peaceful public demonstrations and meetings were violently disrupted by police. Demonstrators were routinely arrested and charged for a number of offenses, including "assault peace officer." The prevalence of the offense is therefore more indicative of police violence rather than community violence. As the political repression in the society declined after 1985, so did the incidence of this offense, and the presence of high rates of crime in the community exerted little influence on the causal chain.

The ratio of police to population, measured by the increase in the size of the police force over time, was positively correlated with police-caused homicide. As the number of police increased, so did the incidences of police killings. This finding supports the view that the increase of numbers in the police force increases the risk that citizens will come into contact with the police and be subjected to police violence. Analyses of the proximate situation in which police use of deadly force occurred was conducted on a convenience sample of twenty-four actual cases of police-caused homicide to determine if the circumstances support the classification of these cases as justifiable homicide, that is homicide excused under the existing law. The analysis revealed that seventeen of the twenty-four cases more than likely involved the excessive use of force, amounting to criminal homicide rather than justifiable homicide. In only three of these cases had the officers responsible been prosecuted, and only one officer was convicted, after having the charge of murder reduced to manslaughter. The officer was given the extremely light sentence of four years' imprisonment for the crime. This analysis reveals the weakness of legal controls on the use of excessive force by police, and the need for effective mechanisms of public accountability for members of the Guyana Police Force. It also supports the conclusion that the police are not adhering to their responsibility to use force only when it is absolutely necessary for the performance of their lawful duties.

Meaningful interpretation of these findings requires an understanding of the social and political influences that were brought to bear on the police during the post-independence period, when police power was openly utilized as a means of maintaining political power. In addition to contemporary social conditions, the context should also be expanded to include historical factors that shaped the role of police in society, and the occupational subculture of policing. In the case of Guyana, there is compelling historical evidence that the role of police has always been one of coercion rather than service, backed up by the legitimization of violence in police work.

The enduring influence of colonial rule remained a cogent factor in terms of understanding what appears to be a police occupational subculture of violence. After having crafted the police force as a quasi-military arm of the state for the suppression of internal disturbances, violence was encouraged and rewarded by the colonial authorities. After independence, the culture of violence in police work was further strengthened and legitimized as the state assumed a more active role in the production of police violence. Both during and after the colonial period, police violence was at its highest when coercive state rule, state repression, and population control were most pervasive. This study also revealed that notwithstanding the level of violence in the community, the frequency of the use of fatal force by police has remained inordinately high. Policing in Guyana still follows the colonial model of a quasi-military function designed to enforce social control by coercion and the use of force. The law still empowers the police to perform military duties when called upon to do so. In the exercise of the power to use deadly force, the police in Guyana currently still fail to meet the required standards of professionalism that are expected of an organized system of public safety and protection as exemplified by the Sir Robert Peel model.

The generalizability of the findings of this study lies in its potential for supporting the expansion of the explanatory framework in which the examination of police violence should be conducted. Implicit in the findings of this study is the argument that the controversy that surrounds the validity of the community violence hypothesis could be resolved by expanding the analysis to include the impact of contextual factors in each case. This study also holds special relevance for comparative analyses of the experiences of colonial policing, especially in the anglophone Caribbean. The pervasive impact of colonial, military-style policing, based on the predominant function of internal security, tends to prevent the development of policing as a public service, and allows police forces to emerge after independence ideally fitted for use in the furtherance of political tyranny when, as in the case of Guyana, violence becomes identified with police work, it tends to take on a life of its own.

Policing in Guyana is in urgent need of review and reform. Even after the return to democratic rule under the People's Progessive Party in 1992, the apparent abuse of the power to use deadly force remains a distinguishing feature of what is arguably an unpopular, semi-military police undertaking. In a recent public opinion survey, seventy-five percent of those interviewed said that they did not trust the police.[3] Meanwhile, there has been an escalation of police killings of civilians under allegedly suspicious circumstances. During the period January 1995 to September 1999, the Guyana Human Rights Association reported seventy-four cases of deaths caused by police,[4] and a recent update added an additional thirty-one cases, thereby bringing the grand total for the period 1995 to 2001 to 105 police-caused homicides.[5] Apart from the apparent continuing abuse of fatal force, the reemergence of the Quick Reaction Squad, and allegations of public, summary executions of crime suspects, some of whom were allegedly unarmed and had already surrendered to police,[6] all support the need for immediate implementation of effective measures for police accountability.

In 1989, a Police Complaints Authority (PCA) was established by virtue of the Police Complaints Authority Act (No. 9 of 1989), but it functions mainly as an advisory body, rather than as a mechanism of accountability. Under the PCA Act, the Authority is empowered to receive and inquire into allegations of misconduct by members of the police force, including "using any unnecessary violence to any prisoner, or other person with whom he may be brought into contact in the execution of his duty" (section 7). The Authority may direct the police to record and investigate such complaints in accordance with the Police (discipline) Act, but can only provide "comments" on the decisions taken under police internal disciplinary procedures. The authority may also receive complaints of unlawful killings by police (section 12), and supervise the investigation of such complaints by the police force (section 14), but has no role in the enforcement function other than to submit a statement to the Director of Public Prosecutions regarding the conduct of the investigation (section 15). The PCA is also required to submit annual reports on its activities to the Minister of Home Affairs, the Director of Public Prosecutions, and the Commissioner of Police (section 23).

The Guyana Human Rights Association has recently called for the creation of a National Police Oversight Committee to promote professionalism and reduce the abuse of force by police.[7] There is no doubt that the entire spectrum of police operations needs to be reviewed in order to facilitate a return to civilian, service-oriented policing in Guyana. However, the continuing crisis in the frequent use of deadly force by police seems to require immediate interventions that could be speedily implemented to save lives. The enforcement of clearly defined limits on the exercise of police discretion to use deadly force should be given urgent attention. Written policies and rules regarding the handling of the variety of situations in which deadly force may be used will remove uncertainty and confine the circumstances to those justified under existing law. Compliance with such rules could be enhanced by a requirement for written reports to be filed for review by supervisors. Officers who violate polices should be turned over to the Director of Public Prosecutions. The current situation clearly requires the intervention of the Ministries of Home Affairs and Legal Affairs, as well as the institutional will and the commitment of the police administration.

In this regard, it has long been established that restrictive administrative policies and procedures concerning the use of force can have a positive effect on the reduction of police shootings.[8] Police departmental policy has had a significant impact on the reduction of police homicide in the United States during the past three decades. In 1979, Fyfe found that the introduction of stringent administrative guidelines and review procedures concerning police shooting discretion in the New York City Police Department in 1972 resulted in significant reductions in "police use of force" incidents, both fatal and nonfatal, despite increases in arrests for violent crime during the study period.[9] Sherman and Cohen reported a fifty-percent decline in police-caused homicide in the United States (from 353 in 1971 to 172 in 1984) as a result of the implementation of more restrictive firearms policies in almost all police departments serving large communities.[10] A review of the impact of these measures on the departments found no evidence that officer safety had been compromised thereby.[11] It is also interesting to note that internal mechanisms of accountability have been more successful than external mechanisms and legal remedies in producing lasting changes in police behavior.[12]

Current directives involving the use of force by the Guyana police are not only vague but also outdated, having been implemented by Special Order No. 7 of 1963, dated April 23, 1963. Under the general principles outlined, the Order expresses the concept of "minimum force only" but permits the use of "offensive weapons," when, in "the honest opinion of the police present . . . less extreme measures will not suffice" (section (a)(i)). The Order prohibits the use of excessive or unnecessary force, or the use of force for the purpose of deterrence or punishment (section (a)(ii)–(vii)). The Order also refers, in general terms, to six circumstances whereby the firearm may be used, including the protection of property, and in obedience to an order given by a superior rank (section (b)(i)–(vi)).

The need for law reform and the removal of military influences from police operations are clearly evident and have been discussed in this study. In the short term, however, the above directives need to be expanded into standard operating procedures for the use of force, clearly specifying the areas in which no discretion will be permitted, and the rules to be followed for every encounter that could result in the use of force. The effectiveness of such policies will depend on the commitment of the police to strict enforcement, and their willingness to bring an end to the current crisis. There is urgent need for the Guyana Police Force to be guided by those "two well-known principles of policing a free society" identified by Lord Scarman in his Report on the Brixton Disorders as "consent and balance" and independence and accountability."[13]

NOTES

1. See the numerous studies mentioned in the earlier chapters of this work.

2. See W. A. Orrett. 1951. *The History of the British Guiana Police.* Georgetown, Guyana: The Daily Chronicle Ltd., Printers and Publishers; George K. Danns. 1982. *Domination and Power in Guyana, A Study of the Police in a Third World Context.* New Brunswick, N.J.: Transaction, Inc.; John Campbell. 1987. *History of Policing in Guyana.* Georgetown, Guyana: Guyana Police Force.

3. See results of public opinion survey conducted by the St. Augustine Research Associates (SARA) in *Hopes and Aspirations: Political Attitudes and Party Choices in Contemporary Guyana.* St. Augustine, Trinidad: Institute of Social and Economic Research, August–September 2000.

4. Guyana Human Rights Association. 1999. *Overview of Police Conduct, Police Lock-ups, Deportees, Prison Conditions.* Georgetown, Guyana: Guyana Human Rights Association.

5. Guyana Human Rights Association. 2001. *Ambivalent About Violence: A Report on Fatal Shootings by the Police in Guyana, 1980–2001.* Georgetown, Guyana: Guyana Human Rights Association.

6. See chapter on Guyana in U.S. Department of State. 2000. *Country Report on Human Rights Practices.* Washington, D.C.: U.S. Government Printing Office; the following press releases from the Guyana Human Rights Association Executive Committee: *Violence Begets Violence,* dated July 28, 2001; *Police Excesses Do Not Justify Contempt for the Law,* dated February 21, 2000; *Police Encourage Shootings,* dated February 3, 1994; *GHRA Calls for Action from DPP in Police Killings,* dated October 1, 1993.

7. Guyana Human Rights Association. 2001. *Ambivalent About Violence: A Report on Fatal Shootings by the Police in Guyana, 1980–2001.*

8. Gerald F. Uelman. 1973. "Varieties of Public Policy: A Study of Policy Regarding the Use of Deadly Force in Los Angeles County." *University of Loyola at Los Angeles Law Review,* Vol. 6, pp. 1–65.

9. James J. Fyfe. 1979. "Administrative Interventions on Police Shooting Discretion: An Empirical Examination." *Journal of Criminal Justice,* Vol. 7, pp. 309–23.

10. Lawrence N. Sherman and E. Cohen, with P. Garten, E. Hamilton, and D. Rogan. 1986. *Citizens Killed by Big City Police: 1970–1984.* Washington, D.C.: Crime Control Institute.

11. Mark Blumberg. 1994. "Police Use of Deadly Force: Exploring Some Key Issues." In Thomas Barker and David Carter (eds.) *Police Deviance,* 3rd ed. Cincinnati, Ohio: Anderson Publishing Co.

12. Samuel Walker. 1999. *The Police in America: An Introduction.* 3rd ed. Boston, Mass.: McGraw Hill.

13. *Report of an Inquiry into the Brixton Disorders, Cmnd. 8427* (1981), para 4.55, cited by Laurence Lustgarten. 1985. "Democratic Constitutionalism and Police Governance." In *Law, Legitimacy and the Constitution, Essays Marking the Centenary of Dicey's Law of the Constitution,* edited by Patrick McAuslan and John F. McEldowney. London: Sweet and Maxwell, pp. 128–50 (144); also Robert Reiner. 1985. *The Politics of the Police.* New York, N.Y.: St. Martin's Press, Inc., p. 200.

Appendix A

Geographical Map of Guyana

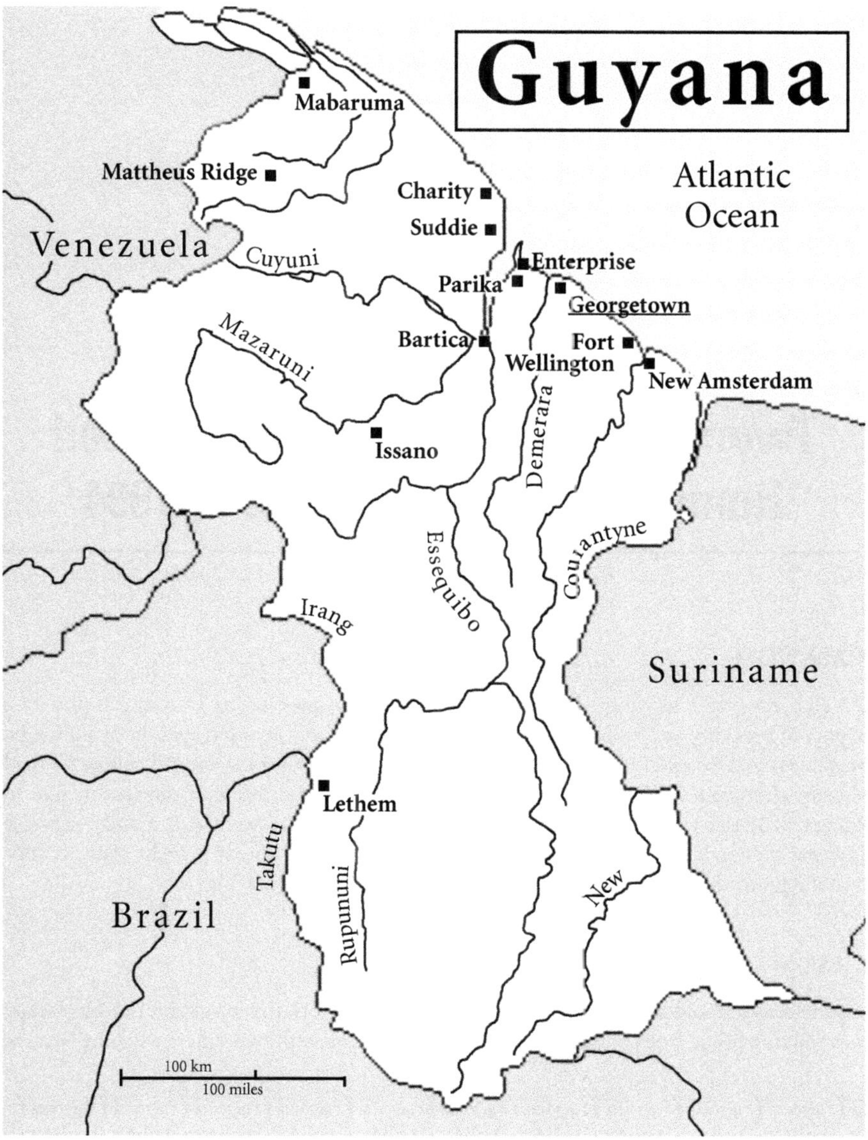

Appendix B

Twenty-four Cases of Police-caused Homicide in Guyana, 1980 to 1994

CASE NO. 1

An eighteen-year-old youth was taken into custody for questioning in connection with a report of breaking and entering and larceny. After five hours of interrogation by police, he was taken to a hospital in an unconscious state, bleeding from the mouth, where he died shortly afterward. The autopsy report listed the cause of death as asphyxiation due to edema of the larynx and vocal cords. The following injuries were also noted: extensive internal hemorrhage; multiple abrasions on forehead, right forearm, right clavicle, subcostal region, abdomen, and scapula; dislocation of left shoulder joint.

CASE NO. 2

A nineteen-year-old male, unarmed except for a dinner fork that was found in his pocket, was walking home from a public fairground in company with two others when he became

Disclaimer: The researcher disclaims liability for inaccuracies, inconsistencies, or errors in the reports on which the above information is based. Material information has been omitted to protect the privacy of the relatives of victims.

involved in an altercation with an officer, who allegedly shot him in the back of the head as he was walking away. He died instantly. The autopsy report listed the cause of death to be multiple systems failure due to brain damage by missile.

CASE NO. 3

A fourteen-year-old youth was playing in the street with five other children when police came on the scene and told them to "freeze." All the other children immediately ran away except the deceased, who received a bullet in the head allegedly while standing with his hands in the air begging not to be shot. The autopsy report listed the cause of death to be a fracture of the skull with laceration and hemorrhage of the brain from gunshot injury.

CASE NO. 4

A twenty-three-year-old male snatched a shopper's handbag containing money, driver's license, a check book, and other documents, and ran. He was chased and caught by police and then allegedly attacked police. He was shot, and died instantly.

CASE NO. 5

A twenty-five-year-old male ex-convict, recently released from prison, was wanted for questioning by police. A group of officers encircled residence where the deceased was celebrating his birthday. In full view of dozens of curious onlockers who had gathered on the street, he was shot repeatedly as he emerged from the house, allegedly with a knife in his hand. He died instantly.

CASE NO. 6

A twenty-six-year-old male was taken into custody by police for questioning. The next day, his family was notified by police that he had died. The autopsy report listed the cause of death as pneumonia of left lung and pleurisy of left lung. Other injuries reported include left and right eyes swollen, with subconjunctival hemorrhage present; punctured wounds on right eye lid upper; abrasions on forehead, eyes, neck, earlobes, right and left shoulder, forearm, elbows, ankle, knee upper limbs, instep; body greenish discoloration, grass and sand on genitals, mud on buttocks; hematoma present on scrotal sacs; bleeding from both nostrils.

CASES NOS. 7 AND 8

Two young male adults (ages unknown) were shot several times while allegedly attempting to break into and enter a building. Both are alleged to have attacked police. They both died as a result of their injuries.

CASE NO. 9

A twenty-one-year-old male was taken into custody by police for questioning. Two days later, his family was notified that he had died. The body of the deceased was allegedly observed to be badly bruised, swollen, and discolored. The medical report listed the cause of death to be acute pulmonary edema.

CASE NO. 10

A twenty-one-year-old male allegedly broke into and entered a church and allegedly stole glass fixtures. He allegedly attacked police when they arrived on the scene, and gave chase. He died as a result of gunshot wounds he received when police opened fire.

CASE NO. 11

A sixty-year-old male civilian police employee was shot allegedly by a police officer while at work. The medical report gave the cause of death as hemorrhage and shock as a result of gunshot injuries. Also noted was a perforation of the right lung and perforation of the aorta.

CASE NO. 12

A male youth (age unknown) was shot while allegedly resisting arrest by police in connection with the investigation of a report of larceny.

CASE NO. 13

A forty-seven-year-old male of unsound mind allegedly escaped from police lock-ups and attacked police. He was shot by the police and died subsequently of his injuries. The autopsy report listed the cause of death to be laceration of the kidney, liver, and right lung due to gunshot injury.

CASE NO. 14

A twenty-four-year-old man was allegedly overheard planning a robbery. He was shot behind the left ear by police after allegedly attacking them.

CASE NO. 15

A twenty-three-year-old male was taken into custody by police for questioning. Although he allegedly submitted to the arrest, he was shot in the leg while entering the police vehicle. He allegedly resisted arrest while in the vehicle and was shot at least twice. He was taken to a hospital where he died of his injuries.

CASE NO. 16

A twenty-six-year-old ex-convict was allegedly observed running with a bulky bag and resisted arrest by police, when he was shot. He was taken to a hospital, where he died shortly afterward.

CASE NO. 17

A thirty-one-year-old male allegedly discharged a firearm in the direction of a police officer who was attempting to arrest him. The officer discharged four rounds in the direction of the deceased, who died instantly.

CASE NO. 18

A twenty-four-year-old male was wanted by the police for questioning. He ran and hid in a structure located in the yard of a house. The police allegedly pursued him and he was shot. He died instantly.

CASE NO. 19

A twenty-eight-year-old male was wanted by police for questioning and was allegedly riding home when a policeman called out to him to stop. He allegedly failed to do so and was fatally shot.

CASE NO. 20

A party of policemen went to a home to carry out a search. A male of unknown age who was wanted for questioning by police was hiding in the home. He was found and shot at close range. He died of his injuries shortly afterward.

CASE NO. 21

A twenty-five-year-old male was shot in the head in his yard after an altercation with police. He had allegedly refused to give police his name.

CASE NO. 22

A male of unknown age was taken into police custody in connection with a report of malicious damage to property. Two days later he was taken to a hospital where he was pronounced dead on arrival.

CASE NO. 23

A twenty-year-old male was arrested at his home and taken into custody by police. He was taken to a hospital the next day nursing a gunshot wound in the groin. He was allegedly taken to a seaside location and tortured before being shot. He gave deathbed accounts of his ordeal before dying of his injuries.

CASE NO. 24

An eighteen-year-old female was shot and killed near her home by armed police. She had allegedly insisted on taking food for a wanted man.

Selected Bibliography

Abel, Richard L. 1990. "Capitalism and the Rule of Law: Precondition or Contradiction?" *Law & Social Inquiry* 15: 685–97.

Ake, Claude. 1974. "Modernization and Political Instability: A Theoretical Exploration." *World Politics* XXVI: 353.

Alavi, Hamza. 1979. "The State in Post-Colonial Societies: Pakistan and Bangladesh." Pp. 38–69 at pp. 43–44 in *Politics and State in the Third World*, edited by Harry Goulbourne. London: Macmillan.

Alpert, Geoffrey P., and William C. Smith. 1994. "How Reasonable Is the Reasonable Man?: Police and Excessive Force." *The Journal of Criminal Law & Criminology* 85: 481–501.

Amnesty International. 1985–1995. *Amnesty International Report*. London, United Kingdom: Amnesty International Publications.

Anderson, David M., and David Killingray, eds. 1991. *Policing the Empire, Government, Authority and Control, 1830–1940*. Manchester, U.K.: Manchester University Press.

———. 1992. *Policing and Decolonisation, Politics, Nationalism and the Police, 1917–1965*. Manchester, U.K.: Manchester University Press.

Anderson, Sir Norman. 1978. *Law, Liberty and Justice (The Hamlyn Lectures, 30th Series)*. London: Stevens & Sons.

Arkes, Hadley. 1990. *Beyond the Constitution*. Princeton, N.J.: Princeton University Press.

Bayley, David H., and Harold Mendelsohn. 1969. *Minorities and the Police*. New York: The Free Press.

Binder, A., and L. A. Fridell. 1984. "Lethal Force as a Police Response." *Criminal Justice Abstracts* 16: 250–80.

Blalock, Hubert M. 1967. *Toward a Theory of Minority-group Relations*. New York: John Wiley.

Blumberg, Mark. 1985. "Research on Police Use of Deadly Force: The State of the Art." Pp. 340–50 in *The Ambivalent Force: Perspectives on the Police*, 3rd ed., edited by

Abraham S. Blumberg and Elaine Niederhoffer. New York: Holt, Rinehart and Winston, Inc.

———. 1989. "Controlling Police Use of Deadly Force: Assessing Two Decades of Progress." Pp. 442–64 in *Critical Issues in Policing,* edited by R. G. Dunham and G. P. Alpert. Prospect Heights, Ill.: Waveland Press.

———. 1994. "Police Use of Deadly Force: Exploring Some Key Issues." Pp. 201–15 in *Police Deviance*, 3rd ed., edited by Thomas Barker and David L. Carter, Cincinnati, Ohio: Anderson Publishing Co.

Braithwaite, Lloyd. 1953. "Social Stratification in Trinidad." *Social and Economic Studies* 22: 111–20.

British Parliamentary Papers, 1847–48, xxiii, p. 199 in Madan N. Gopal. 1992. *Politics, Race and Youth in Guyana.* New York: Edwin Mellen Press, p. 35.

Brooks, J. Michael, Russell R. Dynes, and E. L. Quarantelli. 1972. "Police Department Planning for Civil Disturbances: Organization Factors Involved in Changes." P. 81 in *Politics, Crime and the International Scene: An Inter-American Focus,* edited by Freda Adler and G. O. W. Mueller. San Juan, Puerto Rico: North-South Center Press.

Buckley, Roger Norman. 1979. *Slaves in Red Coats: The British West India Regiments, 1795–1815.* New Haven, Conn.: Yale University Press.

Burnham, Forbes. 1975. *Toward the Socialist Revolution.* Georgetown, Guyana: People's National Congress.

Campbell, John. 1987. *History of Policing in Guyana.* Georgetown, Guyana: Guyana Police Force.

Candler, A., ed. 1910. *The Colonial Records of the State of Georgia,* Vol. 18. Atlanta: Chas. P. Byrd, State Printer.

Caribbean Conference of Churches. 1993. *Who's Included? A Survey of Poverty in Guyana.* Bridgetown, Barbados: Caribbean Conference of Churches.

Carranza, E., H. I. El Khoury, and M. R. Leon. 1990. *Sistema penal y derechos humanos en Costa Rica.* San Jose, Costa Rica: Educa.

Chambliss, William J., and Robert B. Seidman. 1971. *Law, Order and Power.* Reading, Mass.: Addison-Wesley.

Chappell, D., and L. P. Graham. 1985. *Police Use of Deadly Force: Canadian Perspectives.* Toronto, Canada: Centre of Criminology, University of Toronto.

Chase, Ashton. 1964. *A History of Trade Unionism in Guyana: 1900–1961.* Georgetown, Guyana: New Guyana Company Ltd.

Chevigny, Paul. 1990. "Police Deadly Force as Social Control: Jamaica, Argentina, and Brazil." *Criminal Law Forum* 1: 389–426.

———. 1995. *Edge of the Knife, Police Violence in the Americas.* New York: The Free Press.

Clementi, Sir Cecil. 1937. *A Constitutional History of British Guiana.* London: Macmillan.

Collection of Papers: Movement against Oppression. Unpublished document.

Conklin, John E. *Criminology.* 5th ed. Boston, Mass.: Allyn & Bacon.

Constitution of Guyana, 1980.

Constitution of the Cooperative Republic of Guyana. 1980. Georgetown, Guyana: Guyana National Lithographic Co. Ltd.

Coser, Lewis. 1966. "Prospects for the New Nations: Totalitarianism, Authoritarianism or Democracy?" in *Political Sociology*, edited by Lewis Coser. New York: Harper and Row.

Covert Action Information Bulletin: Destabilization in the Caribbean. 1980. No. 10, August–September. Washington, D.C.: Covert Action Publications.

Dahrendorf, Ralf. 1958. "Out of Utopia: Toward a Reorientation of Sociological Analysis." *American Journal of Sociology* 64: 115–27.

———. 1968. *Class and Class Conflict in Industrial Society*. Stanford, Calif.: Stanford University Press.

Danns, George K. 1982. *Domination and Power in Guyana: A Study of the Police in a Third World Context*. New Brunswick, New Jersey: Transaction, Inc.

Despres, Leo A. 1964. "The Implications of Nationalist Politics in British Guiana for the Development of Cultural Theory." *American Anthropologist* 66: 1051–77.

———. 1967. *Cultural Pluralism and Nationalist Politics in British Guiana*. Chicago: Rand McNally & Co.

Duff, Ernest A., and John F. McCamant. 1976. *Violence and Repression in Latin America*. New York: The Free Press.

Economic and Social Progress in Latin America. 1995 Report. Special Report. *Overcoming Volatility*. Washington, D.C.: Johns Hopkins University Press.

Economic Commission for Latin America and the Caribbean. 1994. *Statistical Yearbook for Latin America and the Caribbean, 1994*. New York: United Nations.

Eisenstadt, S. N. 1966. *Modernization, Protest and Change*. Englewood Cliffs, N.J.: Prentice Hall.

Engels, Frederick. 1977. *Marx and Engels: Selected Works*. New York: International Publishers.

Enloe, Cynthia H. 1980. *Police, Military and Ethnicity: Foundations of State Power*. New Brunswick, N.J.: Transaction, Inc.

Ezekiel, Mordecai, and Karl A. Fox. 1963. *Methods of Correlation and Regression Analysis*. New York: John Wiley & Sons, Inc.

Federal Bureau of Investigation, U.S. Department of Justice. 1980. *Crime in the United States, 1979: Uniform Crime Reports*. Washington, D.C.: U.S. Government Printing Office.

Foner, P. S. 1975. *History of Black Americans: From Africa to the Emergence of the Cotton Kingdom*. Westport, Conn.: Greenwood Publishers.

Fraser, Peter D. 1981. "The Immigration Issue in British Guiana, 1903–1913: The Economic and Constitutional Origins of Racist Politics in Guyana." *Journal of Caribbean History* 14: 18–45.

Friedrich, J. Robert. 1980. "Police Use of Force: Individuals, Situations, and Organizations." *Annals of the American Academy of Political and Social Science* 452: 82–97.

Fuller, Lon. 1964. *The Morality of Law*. 2nd ed. New Haven, Conn.: Yale University Press.

Furnival, J. S. 1948. *Colonial Policy and Practice: A Comparative Study of Burma and Netherlands India*. London: Cambridge University Press.

Fyfe, James J. 1978. *Shots Fired. An Examination of New York City Police Firearms Discharges*. Unpublished Ph.D. Dissertation. State University of New York at Albany.

———. 1979. "Administrative Interventions on Police Shooting Discretion: An Empirical Examination." *Journal of Criminal Justice* 7: 309–23.

———. 1980. "Geographic Correlates of Police Shootings: A Microanalysis." *Journal of Research in Crime and Delinquency* 17: 101–13.

———. 1988. "Police Use of Deadly Force: Research and Reform." *Justice Quarterly* 5: 165–205.

———. 1989. "The Split-Second Syndrome and Other Determinants of Police Violence." P. 493 in *Critical Issues in Policing: Contemporary Readings*, edited by Roger G. Dunham and Geoffrey P. Alpert. Prospect Heights, Ill.: Waveland Press.

Gabaldon, Luis Gerardo. 1993. "Police Violence and Uncertainty in Latin America: Linking the Macro- and Micro-Levels of Analysis." *International Criminal Justice Review* 3: 44–59.

Galliher, John F. 1985. "Explanations of Police Behavior: A Critical Review and Analysis." Pp. 56–63 in *The Ambivalent Force: Perspectives on the Police*, 3rd ed., edited by Abraham S. Blumberg and Elaine Niederhoffer. New York: Holt, Rinehart and Winston, Inc.

Gittens, Thomas. 1982. "The Post-Colonial State, Class Formation and Social Transformation: A Return to Theory." *Transition* 5: 21–41.

Glaser, Barney, and Anselm Strauss. 1967. *The Discovery of Grounded Theory*. Chicago, Ill.: Aldine.

Gouveia, Elsa. 1971. "Change and Stability in West Indian Slave Society." Pp. 21–29 in *Readings in Government and Politics of the West Indies*, edited by Trevor Munroe and Rupert Lewis. Kingston, Jamaica: Department of Government, University of the West Indies.

Gove, Walter, Michael Hughes, and Michael Geerden. 1985. "Are Uniform Crime Reports a Valid Indicator of the Index Crimes?: An Affirmative Answer with Minor Qualifications." *Criminology* 23: 451–501.

Green, Edward. 1971. "The 1968 General Elections in Guyana and the Introduction of Proportional Representation." Pp. 134–36 in *Readings in Government and Politics of the West Indies*, edited by Trevor Munroe and Rupert Lewis. Kingston, Jamaica: University of the West Indies.

Green, William A., Jr. 1969. "The Apprenticeship in British Guiana, 1834–1838." *Caribbean Studies* 9: 44–66.

Griffith, Ivelaw. 1990. *The Quest for Security in the Caribbean*. Unpublished Ph.D. Dissertation, City University of New York.

———. 1991. "The Military and the Politics of Change in Guyana." *Journal of Interamerican Studies and World Affairs* 33: 141–73.

Gurr, Ted Robert. 1976. *Rogues, Rebels and Reformers: A Political History of Urban Crime and Conflict*. London: Sage Publications Ltd.

Guyana Human Rights Association. 1988. *Brief on Police Violence*. Georgetown, Guyana: Guyana Human Rights Association.

———. 1999. *Overview of Police Conduct, Police Lock-ups, Deportees, Prison Conditions*. Georgetown, Guyana: Guyana Human Rights Association.

———. 2001. *Ambivalent about Vioilence: A Report on Fatal Shootings by the Police in Guyana, 1980–2001*. Georgetown, Guyana: Guyana Human Rights Association.

———. 1980–2000. *Guyana Human Rights Association Members Annual Report*. Georgetown, Guyana: Guyana Human Rights Association.

Guyana Independence Act, May 12, 1966. Laws of Guyana.

Guyana Police Force. 1980–1992. *Guyana Police Force Annual Report*. Georgetown, Guyana: Guyana Police Force.

Guyana Police Special Order, April 23rd 1963, Nov. 7/63. Guyana Police Force.

Hall, Jerome. 1961. *General Principles of Criminal Law*. Charlottesville, Va.: Michie.

Hamburg, Morris. 1985. *Basic Statistics, A Modern Approach*. 3rd ed. Orlando, Fla.: Harcourt Brace Jovanovich, Inc.

Hammersley, Martyn, and Paul Atkinson. 1991. *Ethnography: Principles in Practice*. London: Tavistock Publications.

Harding, Richard W., and Richard P. Fahey. 1973. "Killings by Chicago Police, 1969–70: An Empirical Study." *Southern California Law Review* 46: 284–315.

Huntington, Samuel P. 1964. "Political Development and Political Decay." *World Politics* 3: 386.

———. 1968. *Political Order in Changing Societies.* New Haven, Conn.: Yale University Press.

———. 1977. "Remarks on the Meanings of Stability in the Modern Era." Pp. 269–82 in *Radicalism in the Contemporary Age, Vol 3: Strategies and Impact of Contemporary Radicalism,* edited by Seweryn Bialer and Sophia Sluzar. Boulder, Colo.: Westview Press.

Inter-American Development Bank. 1995. *Economic and Social Progress in Latin America.* Washington, D.C.: Author.

Jackson, Pamela I. 1989. *Minority Group Threat, Crime, and Policing: Social Context and Social Control.* New York: Praeger.

Jacobs, David. 1979. "Inequality and Police Strength: Conflict Theory and Coercive Control in Metropolitan Areas." *American Sociological Review* 44: 913–25.

Jacobs, David, and David Britt. 1979. "Inequality and Police Use of Deadly Force. An Empirical Assessment of a Conflict Hypothesis." *Social Problems* 26: 403–12.

Jagan, Cheddi. 1972. *The West on Trial.* Berlin: Seven Seas Publishers.

Jayawardena, Chandra. 1971. "East Indians and the Plantation System in Guyana." Pp. 31–33 in *Readings in Government and Politics of the West Indies*, edited by Trevor Munroe and Rupert Lewis. Kingston, Jamaica: Department of Government, University of the West Indies.

Jeffries, Sir Charles. 1952. *The Colonial Police.* London: Max Parrish & Co.

Johnson, Howard. 1986. "Social Control and the Colonial State: The Reorganization of the Police Force in the Bahamas 1888–1893." *Slavery and Abolition* 7: 46–58.

Kania, Richard R. E., and Wade C. Mackey. 1977. "Police Violence as a Function of Community Characteristics." *Criminology* 15(1): 27–48.

Kappeler, Victor E., Mark Blumberg, and Gary W. Potter. 1993. *The Mythology of Crime and Criminal Justice.* 2nd ed. Prospect Heights, Ill.: Waveland Press.

Kelling, George L., and Mark H. Moore. 1988. "The Evolving Strategy of Policing." *Perspectives on Policing,* No 4. Washington, D.C.: National Institute of Justice and Harvard University.

Kenny, C. S. 1965. *Outlines of Criminal Law*, 19th ed. J. W. C. Turner. Cambridge, U.K.: Cambridge University Press.

Kirk, Jerome, and Marc L. Miller. 1986. *Reliability and Validity in Qualitative Research.* Beverly Hills, Calif.: Sage Publications, Inc.

Klare, Michael T., and Cynthia Arson. 1981. *Supplying Repression: U.S. Support for Authoritarian Regimes Abroad.* Washington, D.C.: Institute for Policy Studies.

Kobler, Arthur L. 1975. "Police Homicide in a Democracy." *Journal of Social Issues* 31: 163–84.

Krygier, Martin. 1990. "Marxism and the Rule of Law: Reflections After the Collapse of Communism." *Law & Social Inquiry* 15: 633–63.

Liska, Allen E., ed. 1992. *Social Threat and Social Control.* Albany, N.Y.: State University of New York Press.

Liska, Allen E., and Jiang Yu. 1992. "Specifying and Testing the Threat Hypothesis: Police Use of Deadly Force." Pp. 3–68 in *Social Threat and Social Control*, edited by Allen E. Liska. Albany, N.Y.: State University of New York Press.

Liska, Allen E., Joseph J. Lawrence, and Michael Benson. 1981. "Perspectives on the Legal Order: The Capacity for Social Control." *American Journal of Sociology* 87: 412–26.

Lustgarten, Laurence. 1985. "Democratic Constitutionalism and Police Governance." Pp. 144 in *Law, Legitimacy and the Constitution, Essays Marking the Centenary of Dicey's Law of the Constitution*, edited by Patrick McAuslan and John F. McEldowney. London: Sweet and Maxwell.

Mars, Pairadeau. 1975. *Political Modernization and Stability in a Developing State: The Guyana Example.* Unpublished Ph.D. Thesis, Carleton University, Ontario.

Martins, Jose deSouza. 1991. "Lynchings—Life By a Thread: Street Justice in Brazil, 1979–1988." Pp. 21–32 in *Vigilantism and the State in Modern Latin America, Essays on Extralegal Violence,* edited by Martha K. Huggins. New York: Praeger Publishers.

Matulia, Kenneth J. 1985. *A Balance of Forces. Model Deadly Force Policies and Procedure.* 2nd ed. Gaithersburg, Md.: International Association of Chiefs of Police.

McAuslan, Patrick, and John F. McEldowney, eds. 1985. *Law, Legitimacy and the Constitution: Essays Marking the Centenary of Dicey's Law of the Constitution.* London: Sweet & Maxwell.

McCoy, Candace. 1986. "The Cop's World: Modern Policing and the Difficulty of Legitimizing the Use of Force." *Human Rights Quarterly* 8: 270–93.

McNamara, John H. 1967. "Uncertainties in Police Work: The Relevance of Police Recruits' Backgrounds and Training." Pp. 163–252 in *The Police*, edited by David J. Bordua. New York: John Wiley & Sons.

Meehan, Albert J. 1986. "Record-Keeping Practices in the Policing of Juveniles." *Urban Life* 15: 70–102.

Moore, Brian. 1987. *Race, Power and Social Segmentation in Colonial Society: Guyana after Slavery, 1838–1891.* Philadelphia, Pa.: Gordon and Breach Science Publishers.

NAACP Legal Defense and Educational Fund, Inc. 1993. *Death Row.* U.S.A., New York: Author.

Nascimento, C. A., and R. A. Burrowes, eds. 1970. *A Destiny to Mould: Selected Discourses by the Prime Minister of Guyana.* Trinidad and Jamaica: Longman Caribbean Ltd.

Netscher, P. M. 1888. *History of the Colonies Essequibo, Demerary and Berbice: From the Dutch Establishment to the Present Day*, translated by W. E. Roth. Gravenhage, Provincial Utrecht Society of Arts and Sciences.

Niederhoffer, Arthur. 1969. *Behind the Shield: The Police in Urban Society.* New York: Doubleday & Co.

Orrett, W. A. 1951. *The History of the British Guiana Police.* Georgetown, Guyana: The Daily Chronicle Ltd., Printers and Publishers.

Palmer, Stanley H. 1988. *Police and Protest in England and Ireland, 1780–1850.* Cambridge, U.K.: Cambridge University Press.

Parks, Evelyn. 1970. "From Constabulary to Police Society." *Catalyst* 5: 76–97.

Pearce, Jenny. 1981. *Under the Eagle.* Boston, Mass.: South End Press.

Premdas, Ralph R. 1972. "Voluntary Associations and Political Parties in a Racially Fragmented State: The Case of Guyana." *University of Guyana: Occasional Papers.* No. 2, Feb. 1972.

———. 1975. "The Rise of the First Mass-Based Multi-Racial Party in Guyana." *Caribbean Quarterly* 20: 5–20.

Pye, Lucian. 1966. *Aspects of Political Development.* Boston, Mass.: Little, Brown and Co.

Pye, Lucian, and Sidney Verba, eds. 1965. *Political Culture and Political Development.* Princeton, N.J.: Princeton University Press.

Quinney, Richard. 1977. *Class, State and Crime.* New York: Mckay.

———. 1979. *Criminology.* Boston, Mass.: Little, Brown and Co.

Reichel, P. L. 1988. "Southern Slave Patrols as a Traditional Police Type." *American Journal of Policing* 7: 51–77.

Reidel, M. 1990. "Nationwide Homicide Data Sets: An Evaluation of the Uniform Crime Reports and the National Center for Health Statistics Data." Pp. 175–205 in *Measuring Crime: Large Scale, Long-Range Efforts*, edited by D. Mackenzie Layton, P. J. Baunach, and R. R. Roberg. Albany: State University of New York Press.

Reiner, Robert. 1985. *The Politics of the Police*. New York: St. Martin's Press, Inc.

Report of the British Guiana Commission of Inquiry: Racial Problems in the Public Service. 1965. Geneva, Switzerland: International Commission of Jurists.

Report of the Enmore Enquiry Commission. 1948. Georgetown, Demerara: British Guiana Legislative Council No. 10/1948.

Reubens, Edwin P., and Beatrice G. Reubens. 1962. *The Sugar Industry of British Guiana.* Kingston, Jamaica: Institute of Social and Economic Research.

Roberts, G. W. 1948. "Some Observations on the Population of British Guiana." *Population Studies* 2: 185–218.

Robin, Gerald D. 1963. "Justifiable Homicide by Police Officers." *Journal of Criminal Law, Criminology and Police Science* 54: 225–31.

Rodney, Walter. 1981. *A History of the Guyanese Working People, 1881–1905.* Baltimore, Md.: Johns Hopkins University Press.

Rodway, James A. 1891. *A History of British Guiana from the Year 1668 to the Present Time (3 vols.)* Georgetown, Guyana: J. Thompson.

Ross, Jeffrey Ian. 1994. "The Future of Municipal Police Violence in Advanced Industrialized Democracies: Towards a Structural Causal Model." *Police Studies XVII* (2): 1–27.

Rubin, Vera, ed. 1960. *Social and Cultural Pluralism in the Caribbean.* New York: Annals of the New York Academy of Sciences.

Schuler, Monica. 1988. "Plantation Labourers, the London Missionary Society and Emancipation in West Demerara, Guyana." *The Journal of Caribbean History* 22: 88–115.

Seidman, David, and Michael Couzens. 1974. "Getting the Crime Rate Down: Political Pressure and Crime Reporting." *Law and Society Review* 8: 457.

Selsam, Howard, David Goldway, and Harry Martel, eds. 1970. *Dynamics of Social Change: A Reader in Marxist Social Science.* New York: International Publishers Co., Inc.

Senna, Joseph J., and Larry J. Siegel. 1993. *Introduction to Criminal Justice.* St. Paul, Minn.: West Publishing Co.

———. 1996. *Introduction to Criminal Justice.* 7th ed. New York: West Publishing Co.

Shahabuddeen, M. 1973. *The Legal System of Guyana.* Georgetown, Guyana: Guyana Printers Ltd.

———. 1978. *Constitutional Development in Guyana: 1621–1978.* Georgetown, Guyana: Guyana Printers Ltd.

Shapiro, Ian, ed. 1994. *The Rule of Law.* New York: New York University Press.

Sherman, Lawrence N., and E. Cohen, with P. Garten, E. Hamilton, and D. Rogan. 1986. *Citizens Killed by Big City Police—1970–1984.* Washington, D.C.: Crime Control Institute.

Sherman, Lawrence W., and Barry Glick. 1984. "The Quality of Arrest Statistics." *Police Foundation Reports* 2: 1–8.

Sherman, Lawrence W., and Robert H. Langworthy. 1979. "Measuring Homicide by Police Officers." *The Journal of Criminal Law & Criminology* 70: 546–80.

———. 1980. "Causes of Police Behavior. The Current State of Quantitative Research." *Journal of Research in Crime and Delinquency* 17: 69–100.

Silver, Allan. 1966. "The Demand for Order in Civil Society. A Review of Some Themes in the History of Urban Crime, Police and Riot," in *The Police: Six Sociological Essays*, edited by David Bordua. New York: John Wiley.

Singham, Archie. 1968. *The Hero and the Crowd.* New Haven, Conn.: Yale University Press.

Skapska, Grazyna. 1990. "The Rule of Law from the East Central European Perspective." *Law & Social Inquiry* 15: 699–706.

Skolnick, Jerome H. 1975. *Justice without Trial.* 2nd ed. New York: John Wiley & Sons.

———. 1969. *The Politics of Protest.* New York: Simon and Schuster.

Smelser, Neil J. 1962. *Theory of Collective Behavior.* New York: The Free Press.

Smith, J. C., and Brian Hogan. 1965. *Criminal Law.* 1st ed. London: Butterworths.

Smith, M. G. 1960. "Social and Cultural Pluralism," in *Social and Cultural Pluralism in the Caribbean*, edited by Vera Rubin. *Annals of the New York Academy of Science.* 83: 1–15.

———. 1960. "Discussion: Multiracialism and the Plural Society." *Annals of the New York Academy of Sciences* 83: 912–14.

———. 1965. *The Plural Society in the British West Indies.* Berkeley, Calif.: University of California Press.

Smith, R. T. 1964. "Ethnic Difference and Peasant Economy in British Guiana," in *Capital, Saving and Credit in Peasant Societies*, edited by Raymond Firth and B. S. Yamey. London: Allen & Unwin.

———. 1980. *British Guiana.* Westport, Conn.: Greenwood Press.

———. 1988. *Kinship and Class in the West Indies.* Cambridge, U.K.: Cambridge University Press.

Sorenson, Jonathan R., James W. Marquart, and Deon E. Brock. 1993. "Factors Related to Killings of Felons by Police Officers: A Test of the Community Violence and Conflict Hypotheses." *Justice Quarterly* 10: 417–40.

Spinner, Thomas J., Jr. 1984. *A Political and Social History of Guyana. 1945–1983.* Boulder, Colo.: Westview Press.

Stinchcombe, Arthur. 1994. "Freedom and Oppression of Slaves in the Eighteenth-Century Caribbean." *American Sociological Review* 59: 911–29.

Stone, Carl. 1978. *Decolonization and the Caribbean State System—The Case of Jamaica.* Paper presented to Conference on the Caribbean sponsored by the Center for Inter-American Relations, New York.

Strauss, Anselm, and Juliet Corbin. 1990. *Basics of Qualitative Research: Grounded Theory Procedures and Techniques.* Newbury Park, Calif.: Sage Publications.

Summers, Robert S. 1984. *Lon L. Fuller (Jurists: Profiles in Legal Theory).* Stanford, Calif.: Stanford University Press.

Takagi, Paul. 1979. "Death by Police Intervention." Pp. 31–38 in *A Community Concern: Police Use of Deadly Force,* edited by Robert N. Brenner and Marjorie Kravits. Washington, D.C.: U.S. Department of Justice.

Tashman, Leonard J., and Kathleen R. Lamborn. 1979. *The Ways and Means of Statistics.* New York: Harcourt Brace Jovanovich, Inc.

Taylor, John Keenan. 1990. *Statistical Techniques for Data Analysis.* Chelsea, Mich.: Lewis Publishers, Inc.

Tennenbaum, Abraham N. 1993. "The Supplemental Homicide Report: A Neglected but Valuable Source for Homicide Research." Pp. 77–88 in *Questions and Answers in Lethal and Non-Lethal Violence: Proceedings of the Second Annual Workshop of the*

Homicide Research Working Group, edited by Carolyn Rebecca Block and Richard L. Block. Washington, D.C.: National Institute of Justice.

———. 1994. "The Influence of the Garner Decision on Police Use of Deadly Force." *Journal of Criminal Law & Criminology* 85: 241–60.

The Daily Chronicle, 1905. Georgetown, Demerara: Estate of C. K. Jardine, Decd., Printers, Publishers and Bookbinders.

The National Security (Miscellaneous Provisions) Act, 1966. Laws of Guyana.

The Police Act, 1957. Laws of Guyana.

Thomas, Clive Y. 1984. *The Rise of the Authoritarian State.* New York: Monthly Review Press.

———. 1984. *Plantations, Peasants and State (A Study of the Modes of Sugar Production in Guyana).* Institute of Development Studies, University of Guyana, Georgetown, Guyana/International Labour Office, Geneva, Switzerland: Jointly sponsored and published by Institute of Development Studies, University of Guyana and International Labour Office, Geneva, Switzerland.

Thompson, Alvin O. 1987. *Colonialism and Underdevelopment in Guyana, 1580–1803.* Bridgetown, Barbados: Carib Research and Publications, Inc.

Tilly, Charles. 1975. "Revolutions and Collective Violence," in *Handbook of Political Science.* Vol. III. Reading, Mass.: Addison-Wesley, Inc.

Tolnay, Stewart E., and E. M. Beck. 1992. "Toward a Threat Model of Southern Black Lynchings." Pp. 33–52 in *Social Threat and Social Control*, edited by Allen E. Liska. Albany, N.Y.: State University of New York Press.

Turk, Austin. 1969. *Criminology and the Legal Order*. Chicago, Ill.: Rand McNally.

———. 1982. *Political Criminality, the Defiance and Defense of Authority*. Beverly Hills, Calif.: Sage Publications, Inc.

Uelman, Gerald F. 1973. "Varieties of Public Policy: A Study of Policy Regarding the Use of Deadly Force in Los Angeles County." *University of Loyola at Los Angeles Law Review* 6: 1–65.

United Nations Department for Economic and Social Information and Policy Analysis. 1995. *World Statistics in Brief.* Series V, No. 16. New York: United Nations.

U.S. Department of Justice Federal Bureau of Investigation. 1984. *Uniform Crime Report Handbook*, Washington, D.C.: Author.

U.S. Department of State. 1994. 2000. *Country Reports on Human Rights Practices*. Washington, D.C.: U.S. Government Printing Office.

Viotti da Costa, Emilia. 1994. *Crowns of Glory, Tears of Blood, The Demerara Slave Rebellion of 1823.* New York: Oxford University Press.

Walker, Samuel. 1977. *A Critical History of Police Reform: The Emergence of Professionalism.* Lexington, Mass.: Lexington Books.

———. 1999. *The Police in America: An Introduction*, 3rd ed. Boston, Mass.: McGraw-Hill.

Walsh, Anthony. 1990. *Statistics for the Social Sciences*. New York: Harper & Row.

Weber, Max. 1947. *The Theory of Social and Economic Organization*. Translated by A. M. Henderson and Talcott Parsons. New York: Oxford University Press.

Westley, William A. 1951. *The Police: A Sociological Study of Law, Custom and Morality.* Unpublished Ph.D. Dissertation, University of Chicago, Department of Sociology.

———. 1970. *Violence and the Police: A Sociological Study of Law, Custom and Morality.* Cambridge, Mass.; MIT Press.

Williams, Alan. 1979. *The Police of Paris 1718–1789.* Baton Rouge, La.: Louisiana State University Press.

Williams, Hubert, and Patrick V. Murphy. January 1990. "The Evolving Strategy of Police: A Minority View." *Perspectives on Policing,* No 13. Washington, D.C.: National Institute of Justice and Harvard University.

Wood, B. 1984. *Slavery in Colonial Georgia.* Athens, Ga.: University of Georgia Press.

World Bank. 1992. Guyana: *From Economic Recovery to Sustained Growth.* Washington, D.C.: World Bank.

Young, Allan. 1958. *The Approaches to Local Self-Government in British Guiana.* London: Longman, Green and Co.

Index

ABOUT THE AUTHOR

Joan R. Mars is an Attorney-at-Law and Assistant Professor in the Department of Sociology, Anthropology, and Criminal Justice at the University of Michigan–Flint.

www.ingramcontent.com/pod-product-compliance
Ingram Content Group UK Ltd.
Pitfield, Milton Keynes, MK11 3LW, UK
UKHW020813290926
15470UKWH00003B/1135

9 780313 31104